# *the*
# writer's
## brief handbook

*second*
*Canadian*
*edition*

# THE QUICK REFERENCE GUIDE

## HOW TO USE THIS BOOK

When you need to find information, use one of these aids:

1. The **Quick Reference Guide** on the next page will lead you to the information you need. Notice that the tabs, chapter titles, and information in each horizontal row are keyed to the actual stacked tabs in this book. Suppose you wish to find out how to use a comma with the coordinating conjunction. Find PUNCT (for "punctuation") in the first row (second box across). Then move your finger across the row and down to the actual tab labelled PUNCT.
2. The **Tabbed Dividers** let you access the fourteen main subject areas of the text. On the reverse side of each tabbed divider is a detailed outline of the chapter with page numbers. Under "The comma" you will find the heading "Coordinating conjunctions" with the page number.
3. The **Detailed Contents** immediately follows the Preface and Acknowledgements.
4. The **Index**, an alphabetical listing of the contents, appears at the back of the book.
5. The **Correction Symbols** at the very end of the book are an alphabetical listing of marks teachers often use to identify errors in writing. Each mark is keyed to the section of the book that explains the error and how to correct it. For example, if you find the mark "cs" on your returned essay, find "cs" (comma splice) in the list of symbols, and turn to EDIT 6 to learn how to correct a comma splice.

# TO THE STUDENT ─────────────────

You can find what you are looking for in *The Writer's Brief Handbook, Second Canadian Edition,* by using the Quick Reference Guide at the front of the book. The Quick Reference Guide contains the general contents of the fourteen chapters of the text. Scan the Guide, find the subject you need, and locate the appropriate chapter tab. Flip to the chapter divider, turn it over, and you will see an outline for the chapter. Find the subject you want and turn to that page.

Let's suppose your question is about whether to use a singular or plural verb in your sentence. First locate the Editing for Grammar section in the Quick Reference Guide, flip to the EDIT tab, turn the divider page to the outline, and find Subject-verb Agreement (EDIT 1). Look under this heading until you find Identifying Subjects (EDIT 1a, page 127 reproduced on the next page). Until you are familiar with the contents of the various chapters, you may find it necessary to use either the Detailed Contents beginning on page xii or the Index at the end of the book to find the subjects and page numbers you need.

To get the most out of this handbook, you will find it helpful to review the "How to Use This Book" information on page ii.

**Page tab** indicates the chapter title (EDIT) and the number of the subsection (1a).

**Running head** on right-hand page indicates the subject discussed last on this page. (Would not actually appear on first page of chapter.)

**Section number and title.**

**Boldface key terms** are defined in text.

**Examples** illustrate the point of the section.

**Subsection headings** indicate the main rules or conventions.

**Cross-references** indicate where related information can be found.

**Part of speech/sentence labels** highlight featured words or word groups in sentences.

**Coloured** corrections show revisions and corrections.

**Bracketed explanations** provide reasons for changes.

---

# EDIT 1
## SUBJECT-VERB AGREEMENT

In grammar, **subject-verb agreement** refers to the relationship between a verb and its subject. Every verb in a clause or sentence must agree in *number* and *person* with its subject. That is, a verb must be singular if its subject is singular; a verb must be plural if its subject is plural. Also, a verb must agree in person (i.e., the doer of the action—first person, second person, third person) with its grammatical subject.

SINGULAR SUBJECT AND SINGULAR VERB

*Overcrowding causes* many of the discipline problems in our schools.

PLURAL SUBJECT AND PLURAL VERB

*Fires destroy* millions of dollars worth of property each year.

Normally, we do not think twice about subject-verb agreement. A few constructions, however, can be troublesome. In most cases, the problem results from not having correctly identified the subject of the sentence.

### EDIT 1a    To choose the correct verb form, identify the subject of the sentence.

Sometimes intervening word groups obscure the relationship between the subject (S) and the verb in a sentence. When this happens, the culprit is usually a prepositional phrase. Mentally eliminate all the prepositional phrases in a sentence, and see what is left. One of these leftover words must be the subject because a subject never appears in a prepositional phrase (see GRAM 3a).

The first three weeks of basic training is the worst.

[The plural subject *weeks* takes a plural verb.]

Another word group that can cause confusion about subject–verb agreement is the subordinate clause (see GRAM 4). Neither the subject nor the verb of a sentence will ever appear in a subordinate clause.

The use of mood-altering drugs, although they sometimes provide great medical benefits, are generally criticized by the public.

[The singular subject *use* takes a singular verb.]

*Alfred Rosa*
University of Vermont

*Paul Eschholz*
University of Vermont

*John Roberts*
Mohawk College

*the*

# writer's

## brief handbook

*second*
*Canadian*
*edition*

ALLYN AND BACON CANADA
SCARBOROUGH, ONTARIO

**Canadian Cataloguing in Publication Data**

Rosa, Alfred F.
    The writer's brief handbook

2nd Canadian ed.
Includes index.

ISBN 0-205-28153-2

1. English language—Grammar—Handbooks, manuals,
etc. 2. English language—Rhetoric—Handbooks,
manuals, etc. I. Eschholz, Paul A. II. Roberts,
John A., 1944–    . III. Title.

PE1408.R675  1999  808'.042  C99-930512-0

Allyn and Bacon, Inc., Needham Heights, MA
Prentice-Hall, Inc., Upper Saddle River, New Jersey
Prentice-Hall International (UK) Limited, London
Prentice-Hall of Australia, Pty. Limited, Sydney
Prentice-Hall Hispanoamericana, S.A., Mexico City
Prentice-Hall of India Private Limited, New Delhi
Prentice-Hall of Japan, Inc., Tokyo
Simon & Schuster Southeast Asia Private Limited, Singapore
Editora Prentice-Hall do Brasil, Ltda., Rio de Janeiro

Vice President, Editorial Director: Laura Pearson
Acquisitions Editor: Nicole Lukach
Developmental Editor: Lisa Berland
Production Editor: Avivah Wargon
Copy Editor: Marie Graham
Marketing Manager: Kathleen McGill
Production Coordinator: Wendy Moran
Permissions/Photo Research: Susan Wallace-Cox
Cover Design: Monica Kompter
Page Layout: B.J. Weckerle

Original English language edition published by Allyn and Bacon, Inc., Needham Heights,
MA. © 1999.

Credits appear on page xxvii, which constitutes a continuation of this copyright page.

1 2 3 4 5    03 02 01 00 99

Printed and bound in Canada.

Visit the Prentice Hall Canada web site! Send us your comments, browse our
catalogues, and more at **www.phcanada.com**. Or reach us through e-mail at
**phabinfo_pubcanada@prenhall.com**.

# PREFACE

*The Writer's Brief Handbook, Second Canadian Edition,* is a compact, easy-to-use guide to writing. It offers clear definitions of important terms and concepts, as well as helpful explanations of the rules and principles underlying effective written English. We believe *The Writer's Brief Handbook* is the best concise yet comprehensive reference available for today's diverse Canadian student population. Notice its important features:

**User-Friendly, Multi-Faceted Access System.** The more students consult *The Writer's Brief Handbook,* the more user-friendly they will find it. The Quick Reference Guide, keyed to the tabbed dividers with their complete chapter outlines, along with the Detailed Table of Contents and the Index, make it as easy as possible to locate information.

**Writing Process Orientation.** *The Writer's Brief Handbook* covers all stages of the writing process in depth: generating ideas, drafting, revising, editing, and proofreading. A sample student paper is presented with annotations and commentary.

**Clearly Stated Learning Objectives.** Students can find a list of what they should learn from each section of the *Handbook* on the tabbed divider page for that section.

**More Computer Tips.** This edition of the *Handbook* contains yet more "C-Tips," strategically positioned in shaded boxes throughout the text, to remind students of how they can take full advantage of the computer while writing.

**New Section on Oral Presentations.** A section on speaking skills prepares the student to make an effective oral presentation, and integrates the speaking and writing processes.

**New Tabbed Section on Argumentation and Writing About Literature.** Two new annotated student papers illustrate the advice given for writing argumentative essays or papers that analyze a literary text.

**Self-Contained ESL Section.** A comprehensive, easy-to-use chapter answers ESL questions without requiring students to search throughout the book. This chapter offers students for whom English is not their native language help with verb forms, nouns, adjectives and adverbs, prepositional phrases, parts of sentences, and word groups.

**More Advice on Avoiding Bias in Writing.** An extensive section on avoiding bias and sexism offers students strategies for eliminating racial, ethnic, and gender bias in their writing.

**Manuscript Format Chapter.** A tabbed section on manuscript formatting provides basic guidelines for academic manuscripts using either MLA or APA style, as well as such essential business documents as letters, résumés, and memos. Helpful advice on page design, improving readability, and creating visuals is presented.

**Enlarged Library Section on Using Electronic Resources.** *The Writer's Brief Handbook* is still the only brief handbook to offer a separate tabbed section on the use of the library. This section, which provides a sound introduction to the resources of the campus library, has been expanded to include electronic research. Students are instructed on what is available to them on the World Wide Web, how to use search engines and subject directories to locate worthwhile web sites, and how to download and print files. A list of web sites for improving writing and researching skills is provided.

**Expanded Instruction for Using Online Sources for Research Papers.** Numerous examples and illustrations show how students can use online sources to complement print sources in their research. Students are shown how to locate and evaluate online sources, compile a preliminary bibliography of these sources, and take notes online. A sample student research paper in the MLA style, with annotations and commentary, accompanies this chapter.

**Latest MLA, APA, and Chicago Documentation Guidelines.** Two separate documentation sections provide extensive models of correct citation format. New in-text directories in both sections help students quickly locate the particular type of source they are trying to document. Now included in the MLA DOCU section are the new MLA guidelines for electronic citations. New to the OTHER DOCU section are the guidelines for using the *Chicago Manual of Style* citation system. Also included in OTHER DOCU is a sample student research paper in APA style.

**More Help for Students.** A separate publication, *Exercise Book for The Writer's Brief Handbook*, is designed for those students who need extra practice with paragraphing, grammar, punctuation, mechanics, manuscript format, library resources, and research documentation styles. The exercises, keyed to the chapters of the *Handbook* so that students can consult the *Handbook* as they work, provide practice at both sentence and paragraph levels. An Answer Key to the *Exercise Book* is available to instructors.

# ACKNOWLEDGEMENTS ⎯⎯⎯⎯

During the writing and rewriting of the *Handbook*, we have bene-fited immensely from honest and wise advice from teachers of writing around the country. We are happy to acknowledge them here:

Judy Cummins, Lethbridge Community College
Frank Gavin, Centennial College
Philip Lanthier, Champlain Regional College
Judy O'Shea, Lethbridge Community College
Brian Patton, King's College
Jim Streeter, Seneca College

At Prentice Hall Allyn and Bacon Canada, we would like to thank David Stover, Acquisitions Editor; Lisa Berland, Developmental Editor; and Avivah Wargon and Rodney Rawlings, Production Editors. Thanks to Marie Graham for her admirable copyediting, and to proofreaders Pat Thorvaldson and Rebecca Vogan. Rebecca Vogan's thorough and excel-lent work on the first proofs of this book was a valuable contribution to this edition.

A.R.
P.E.
J.R.

# DETAILED CONTENTS _____

# ESL   ESL Basics

# EDIT   Editing for Grammar

# PUNCT    Punctuation _____

## MECH    Mechanics

## FORMAT   Essentials of Formatting

## ARGUE/LIT    Writing an Argumentative Essay and Writing About Literature _____

# MLA DOCU    MLA-Style Documentation

# OTHER DOCU    Other Systems of Documentation

# TABLE OF COMPUTER TIPS (C-TIPS) _____

# CREDITS

# COMP

## Composing

### *Learning Objectives*

After reading this section, you should

1. know how to plan a writing assignment, taking audience and purpose into account,
2. understand the back-and-forth nature of the writing process,
3. know the difference between revising, editing, and proofreading,
4. be able to conduct a student conference as part of revising your work,
5. be able to prepare and deliver an oral presentation.

# COMP

## Composing

A good prose composition, regardless of its length, is purposeful and well organized. In the following essay, H. Allen Smith perceives the humour in everyday life and captures this humour in his writing.

## Claude Fetridge's Infuriating Law

Fetridge's Law, in simple language, states that important things that are supposed to happen do not happen, especially when people are looking; or conversely, things that are supposed not to happen do happen, especially when people are looking. Thus a dog that will jump through a hoop a thousand times a day for his owner will not jump through a hoop when a neighbour is called to watch; and a baby that will say "Dada" in the presence of its proud parents will, when friends are summoned, either clam up or screech like a jaybird.

Fetridge's Law takes its name from a onetime radio engineer named Claude Fetridge. Back in 1936, Mr. Fetridge thought up the idea of broadcasting the flight of the famous swallows from San Juan de Capistrano mission in Southern California. As is well known, the swallows depart from the mission each year on St. John's Day, October 23, and return on March 19, St. Joseph's Day. Claude Fetridge conceived the idea of broadcasting the flutter of wings of the departing swallows on October 23. His company went to considerable expense to set up its equipment at the mission; then with all of North America waiting anxiously for the soul-stirring event, it was discovered that this year the swallows, out of sheer orneriness, had departed a day ahead of schedule. Thus did a flock of birds lend immortality to Claude Fetridge.

Television sets are, of course, often subject to the workings of Fetridge's Law. If a friend tells me he is going to appear on a television show and asks me to watch it, I groan inwardly, knowing this is going to cost me money. The moment this show comes on the air, my screen will snow up or acquire the look of an old school tie pattern. I turn it off and call the repair shop. The service technician travels miles to my house and turns the set on. The picture emerges bright and clear, the contrast exactly right, a better picture than I've ever had before. It's that way always and forever, days without end.

A woman neighbour of mine drives her husband to the railroad station every morning to catch the commuter train to Toronto. On rare occasion she has been late, and hasn't had time to get dressed. These times she has thrown a coat over her nightgown and, wearing bedroom slippers, headed for the road. Fetridge's Law always seems to give her trouble. Once she clashed fenders with another car on the highway and had to go to the police station in her night shift. Twice she has had motor trouble in the parking lot of the railway station, requiring that she get out of her car in robe and slippers. The last I heard, she was considering sleeping in her street clothes.

Fetridge's Law operates fiercely in the realm of dentistry. In my own case, I have often noted that whenever I develop a raging toothache it is a Sunday and the dentists are all on the golf course. Not long ago, my toothache hung on through the weekend, and Monday morning it was still throbbing and pulsating like a diesel locomotive. I called my dentist and proclaimed an emergency, and drove to his office. As I was going up the stairway, the ache suddenly vanished. By the time I got into his chair, I was confused and embarrassed and unable to tell him with certainty which tooth it was that had been killing me. The X-ray showed no shady spots, though it would have shown several if the dentist had been pointing the thing at my brain. Claude Fetridge's Law clearly has its good points; it can exasperate, but it can also cure toothaches.

From the title, which hints at the humorous aspects of the essay, to the use of topic sentences, which serve to control and focus the material in each of the essay's five paragraphs, Smith focuses every element of his essay on his purpose—to argue that there are forces in this life outside of our understanding and control, and that these forces often lead to humorous situations.

Writers like H. Allen Smith do not rely on luck or inspiration to produce an effective piece of writing. Good writers plan, write, revise, and edit. Keep in mind, however, that the writing process is rarely as simple and straightforward as this. Usually the process is recursive, moving back and forth among the four stages. Moreover, writing is very personal—no two people go about it in the same way. Still, it is possible to describe steps in the writing process and thereby have a reassuring and reliable method for undertaking a writing task and writing a good composition.

# COMP 1 _____

## WRITING WITH A COMPUTER

Throughout *The Writer's Brief Handbook*, but most frequently in COMP, you will find suggestions to help you make the most of writing with a computer. You do not need a computer to write, of course, but many students prefer to work on one. The computer tips are labelled **C-Tip** and are found in the shaded boxes in the text. The tips are not exhaustive, nor are they a substitute for the directions and advice offered by your computer manual; rather, the tips serve as a bridge between the instruction in writing and the many ways a computer can facilitate the composing process. Here, to begin with, are some general computer tips.

 C-Tip

## Saving files

The best tip anyone can give you about using a computer is this: *always* save your work as you compose. If you do not have an automatic save feature, make it a habit to press the save key periodically. By doing so you will not lose your work because of a general power failure or because your computer crashes.

## Backing up files

Almost as important as periodically saving your files is making a backup copy of your finished work. Preferably, do this on a diskette and not on your hard drive; if your hard drive fails, you can simply run the diskette on another computer.

## Saving drafts

Rather than revising the same draft over and over again, keep each draft intact. Copy your file and designate it filename 1, filename 2, filename 3, and so on. If you want to return to an earlier draft at a later stage, you will have it. An earlier organizational pattern or a particular phrasing may have been the best after all.

## Using school computers

If you plan to use your school's computer lab, check the hours it is open, and keep in mind that other students will want computer time, too. Leave enough time in your schedule to be flexible.

## Keeping supplies

Keep a supply of spare diskettes on hand to make backup copies. Change the ribbon or toner cartridge in your printer regularly. (It is a good idea to have a spare cartridge, too.)

# COMP 2 _____
## PLANNING

The planning stage of the writing process encompasses everything you do before you begin to write. In planning, you

a. analyze the writing task,
b. choose a subject,
c. focus on a topic,
d. generate ideas and collect information,
e. formulate a thesis statement,
f. determine your purpose,
g. analyze your audience, and
h. make an outline.

Each of these stages is discussed in detail in this section.

## COMP 2a    Analyze the writing task.

Much of your college writing will be in response to specific assignments: your physical science professor may ask you to write a paper presenting pro and con evidence of the greenhouse effect. With such a narrowed topic, you can move ahead to collecting information and formulating a thesis, a one- or two-sentence statement of your main idea. Sometimes your instructor may assign only a general subject and ask you to choose a particular aspect of it to write on. For example, your business teacher may assign a paper on retail merchandising, giving you the opportunity to choose a specific topic (say, the popularity of recreational vehicles), and develop your own thesis (how the sale of recreational vehicles is affected by the economy).

At other times your instructor will allow you to write on any subject that interests you. In such a case, you may already have an idea for a paper (why you feel that federal funding for post-secondary education should be increased, for instance). What happens, however, when you are free to choose your own subject and you cannot decide what to write about? If this happens, follow the advice set forth in the rest of this section. We give many approaches to selecting a suitable subject and topic; one will work for you.

## COMP 2b    Choose a subject.

A **subject** is a general field of knowledge; farming, clothing, business, ecology, and transportation are all subjects. You may know a great deal about the subject of your essay or you may simply be curious about a topic and wish to expand your knowledge of it.

If you are free to choose your own subject, begin by asking yourself these questions: "What do I really care about?" "What am I interested in?" "What do I know about?" "What do I want to learn about?" Your answers will provide you with potentially good subjects. Resist the temptation to seize the first subject that comes to mind. Take your time. Review the possibilities, and then pick the one subject that most appeals to you and best suits your audience (see COMP 2g).

## COMP 2c    Focus on a topic.

A **topic** is the specific aspect of a subject on which the writer focuses. Subjects such as literature, television, and sports are too broad to be dealt with adequately in a short composition. Even books focus on only aspects of these and other subject areas. The writer's task is to select a manageable topic within the chosen or assigned subject area. Thus, if your subject is sports, you might choose as your topic the growing popularity of soccer in Canada, violence in hockey, types of fan behaviour, the psychology of marathon runners, or the growth of sports medicine.

When moving from a subject to a particular topic, take into account any length or format constraints and the amount of time you have to write. These practical considerations affect the scope of your topic.

The following example, based on the essay by Andy Pellett "The Perils of Astroturf" (see COMP 6), illustrates how to limit a topic:

sports → professional sports → football and baseball → playing surfaces → artificial turf → advantages/disadvantages

Note that each successive topic is more limited than the previous one. Moving from general to specific, the topics become appropriate for essay-length work.

C-Tip

## *Scan for viruses*

Software can be infected by computer viruses: computer programs that attack other programs and cause the infected computer to malfunction in some way. Be sure to scan for viruses before you use a disk, or purchase antivirus software for your computer.

## COMP 2d    Generate ideas and collect information.

Ideas and information lie at the heart of good prose. Ideas grow from information; information (facts and details) supports ideas. To inform and intellectually stimulate your readers, gather as many ideas and as much specific information as you can about your topic. If you try to write before doing so, you run the risk of producing a shallow, boring draft. Good strategies for generating ideas and collecting information—and for beginning to make connections within the body of information you accumulate—include asking questions, brainstorming, clustering, keeping a journal, researching, rehearsing ideas, visualizing your topic, and always trying to think creatively.

### Asking questions

Ask questions about your topic to discover areas for exploration and development. The newspaper reporter's 5Ws and an H—*Who?*, *What?*, *Where?*, *When?*, *Why?*, and *How?*—are excellent questions to start with. Usually, too, questions give rise to yet more questions. Every set of questions will vary with the topic and with the person formulating them. Here is one sample set.

1. *Who* discovered it?
2. *What* does it look like?
3. *Where* was it discovered?
4. *When* was it discovered?
5. *Why* did it take so long to be discovered?
6. *How* can I get some of it?
   a. How much does it cost?
   b. Are there limitations on how much I can buy?
   c. Who sells it?

    d.  Where can I buy it?
    e.  Can I resell it?

 C-Tip

### *Saving key questions*

Develop a master file of key questions to ask yourself at various stages of the writing process: questions about your subject, your topic, various drafts you write, and so on. Leave several lines of space between the questions. This way you can copy (and rename) the file each time you begin an assignment, typing in answers and notes as you work and keeping the original for use again. Over time, you will find yourself revising your master file questions as you discover more about your personal writing style.

### Brainstorming

    If you already know something about your topic, you might begin collecting ideas by **brainstorming,** listing the things you know in no particular order. Freely associate one idea with another; let your mind take you in whatever direction it will. Try not to censor yourself or edit your brainstorming because you simply do not know what will emerge or how valuable it might be in the end. Write quickly. Do not worry about spelling or punctuation; abbreviate. Also, because all your ideas may not occur during one brainstorming session, keep your list over several days, adding new thoughts as they come to you. Here is a typical brainstorming list.

    When you complete your brainstorming list, number or colourcode the entries that closely relate to one another. This is *sorting,* the first step in thinking about possible organizational patterns and outlining.

> *Artificial Surfaces*
>
> *should be banned*
> *football and baseball examples*
> *high install. costs*
> *needs to be repaired freq.*
> *weather resistant*
> *fan satisfaction*
> *player injuries—turf burn, foot ailments*
> *unnatural element*
> *player perf. affected*
> *traditions changed*
> *resurfacing expensive*
> *team strategy changes*
> *players dislike*
> *monetary advan. overrated*

 C-Tip

## *Brainstorming*

Brainstorming on a computer stimulates your thinking because it allows you to keep up with your thoughts, especially if you are a fast typist. Moreover, because a computer is a different medium for capturing your thoughts, it may take you down more imaginative paths.

Try brainstorming with your screen switched off or turned down low. Because brainstorming relies on free-association (the presence of one idea suggesting another), some people find that looking at what they have written inhibits rather than stimulates their thinking. If you try this, turn on the screen momentarily every so often to make sure nothing has gone wrong technically and that you are actually capturing your thoughts. When you are done, turn on the screen to see what you have and print it out if you wish.

## Clustering

Another strategy for generating ideas and gathering information is **clustering**. Put your topic, or a key word or phrase about your topic, in the centre of a sheet of paper and draw a circle around it. (The example on the next page shows the topic *artificial turf* in the centre.) Draw four or five (or more) lines out from this circle, and jot down main ideas about your topic; draw circles around them. Repeat the process by drawing lines from the secondary circles and adding examples, details, and questions you may have. Or, you may find yourself pursuing one line of thought through many add-on circles before beginning a new cluster. Do whatever works for you. As with brainstorming, keep writing—do not stop to think about being neat or capitalizing correctly.

Clustering allows you to generate material and sort it into meaningful groups at the same time. Again, sorting is the first step to outlining.

 C-Tip

### *Clustering*

If your computer has graphics capability, try clustering on screen. Use balloons, boxes, tree diagrams, and lines to diagram and group your ideas. This can be fun as well as productive.

### Keeping a journal

Many people find their best ideas come when they are not actually working on a writing assignment, so they have learned to keep a **journal**. They carry a little notebook to record thoughts and observations, bits of overheard conversation, ironies, insights, and interesting facts and statistics from newspaper and magazine articles.

### Freewriting

Journals are also useful for doing **freewriting**. Freewriting is simply writing for a brief uninterrupted period of time, say five or ten minutes, on anything that comes into your mind. It is a way of getting your mind working and easing into the writing task. Start with a blank sheet of paper or computer screen and write as quickly as you can without stopping for any reason whatsoever. Don't worry about punctuation or

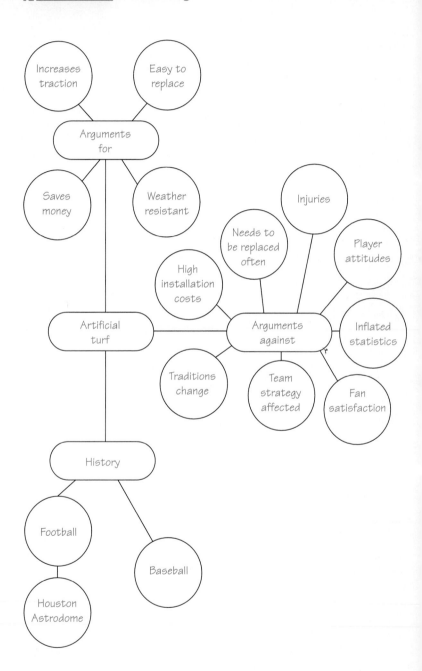

spelling. Write as if you were talking to your best friend. If you run dry, don't stop; repeat the last few things you wrote or write "I have nothing to write" over and over again, and you'll be surprised—writing with more content will begin to emerge. Once you have become comfortable with open-ended freewriting, you can move to more focused freewriting in which you write about specific aspects of your topic. By freewriting regularly, you will come to feel more natural and comfortable about writing.

## Researching

You may sometimes want to supplement what you know about your topic with **research**. This does not necessarily mean formal library work (see LIB). Firsthand observations and interviews with people knowledgeable about your topic are also forms of research and usually more up-to-date. Whatever your form of research, take careful notes (see RESCH 2c), so you can accurately paraphrase an author or quote interviewees.

## Rehearsing ideas

Some writers find it helpful to **rehearse** what they are going to write before committing their thoughts to paper. Rehearsal involves running ideas or phrasings through your mind until they are fairly well crafted and then transferring them to paper. The image of the writer at the keyboard, staring off into space, perhaps best captures the essence of this technique. Rehearsing may suit your personality and the way you work. Moreover, because it requires a lot of thought, rehearsing may help you generate ideas. Rehearsing may also be done orally. Try taking 10 or 15 minutes to talk your way through your paper with a roommate or friend.

## Visualizing your topic

Some experts believe that much of our thinking is visual—done through images. Tapping into those images can be a productive way of developing your ideas. For example, if you wish to describe a totem pole, **visualizing** one you once saw in British Columbia can make your task easier. Imagining that totem pole can also help you to visualize the lives of the traditional Haida people on the west coast.

## Thinking creatively

There are many definitions of creativity, but in one way or another, **creativity** involves moving beyond what is generally regarded as normal or expected. To push an idea one step further, to make a connection not recognized by others, to step to one side of your topic and see it in a new light, to ask a question no one else would, to arrive at a fresh insight, is to be creative. Creativity and inspired thinking are possible for most writers if they take the writing process seriously and work hard.

## COMP 2e    Formulate a thesis statement.

Having generated ideas and information, you are ready to begin organizing your thoughts. At this stage, you must commit to a controlling idea, a **thesis**. The thesis of a prose composition is its main idea, the point it is trying to make. The thesis is often expressed in one or two sentences called a **thesis statement**. Because everything you say in your composition must be logically related to your thesis statement, the thesis statement controls and directs the choices you make about the content of your essay (see PARA 1). That does not mean your thesis statement is a strait-jacket. As your essay develops, you may want to modify your thesis statement. This is not only acceptable, it is normal. Remember that writing is a recursive process; you move back and forth among the stages as you clarify your thoughts and try to communicate them to your readers.

Here are some examples of thesis statements.

> More than a quarter of a century after it was released, *Face Off* (1971) stands as the most exquisitely awful Canadian movie ever made.
> —G. Pevere and G. Dymond

> Late in the spring of last year, my fancy turned to thoughts of real estate and I joined the growing ranks of Canadians in their 20s who were looking for their first homes.                    —Evelyn Lau

These are good thesis statements because they lead naturally into the rest of the essay: we want to know more about the movie *Face Off*, and we want to know what Lau discovered when she began looking for her first home. Both thesis statements set up expectations in the reader's mind. For the writer, both thesis statements strike a level of generality that is not so broad as to be impossible to support in the space allotted or so focused as to require virtually no supporting evidence.

The thesis statement is usually set forth near the beginning of the composition, sometimes after a few sentences that establish a context. In the beginning of an essay on the harmful effects of disposable diapers, Lisa Denis builds a context for the last two sentences in which she presents her thesis statement:

Picture yourself having to change a child's diaper. I'll bet you don't see yourself using a cloth diaper and pins. The use of disposable diapers has become the norm in today's fast-paced society. But the fact is we have no idea of the damage they do. The time has come to put an end to their use. Disposable diapers are expensive, potentially harmful to babies, and environmentally unsound.
—Lisa Denis, student

On occasion you may want to delay presenting the thesis until the middle or end of a composition. If the thesis is controversial or needs extended background discussion, presenting it later may make it easier for readers to understand and accept it. Also, appearing near or at the end of an essay, a thesis gains prominence, and giving it such a position of importance may suit your purpose.

You may also have to adapt your thesis statement to the type of essay you are writing. The essay by Pevere and Dymond is based on *description*; it describes the movie and its faults. Lau's essay is a *narrative*; it tells a story. If your essay is based on argument or persuasion, you must state the thesis for your *argument* in the thesis statement:

Television has its time and place, and that's where it should be kept.

### Cause/effect

Tattoos are a source of pride and pleasure to those who wear them, but the havoc they cause the body is far from pleasant.

### Definition

To be a Canadian is to be someone who is neither a European nor an American.

### Comparison/contrast

Who is the greatest hockey player of all time, Gordie Howe or Wayne Gretzky?

### Division/classification

The word "kitchen" can mean different things to different people, depending on the gadgets available to the modern cook.

### Process analysis

No garden is complete without a compost heap.

Example

> We all deal with homework in our own way.

## COMP 2f  Determine your purpose for writing.

Implied in your thesis statement is your **purpose,** the answer you give to the question, "What am I trying to accomplish in this composition?" Being clear about your purpose helps you choose the best supporting details and arrange them in the most effective order (see PARA 3a). For example, it is clear that Pevere and Dymond's purpose is to describe the movie *Face Off* and give reasons why this is one of the worst Canadian movies ever made. Lau wants to tell the story of her search for her first home. Lisa Denis ends her paragraph with the thesis statement that it is time to stop using disposable diapers because they are harmful, especially to the environment, a statement she will try to prove in order to persuade her readers. At the editing stage, keeping your purpose in mind helps you use language with an awareness of the effect you want it to have on your readers (see COMP 4b and WORD 1).

Generally, nonfiction writing has one of three purposes: (1) to express the writer's thoughts and feelings about a life experience, (2) to inform readers by explaining something about the world around them, or (3) to persuade readers to some belief or action.

### Writing from experience

In writing from experience, or writing expressively, you put your thoughts and feelings before all other concerns. When you express yourself about what it felt like to turn 18, describe the relationship you have with your father, narrate a camping experience you had with a friend, or share an insight about the career you want to pursue, you are writing from experience. The first purpose of expressive writing is, therefore, to clarify life's experiences, and the second purpose is to communicate what you learn to someone else. That is not to say expressive writing is not immensely appealing to readers; the reflections of a thoughtful and sensitive writer illuminate the reader's experiences and clarify his or her own feelings and ideas. Here, for example, are the reflections of a writer on her ambitious nature.

> I've always liked ambitious people, and many of my closest friends have had grandiose dreams. I like such people, not because I am desperate to be buddies with a future secretary of state but because I find ambitious people entertaining, interesting to talk to, and fun to watch. And, of course, I like

such people because I am ambitious myself, and I would rather not feel apologetic about it. —Perri Klass, "Ambition"

## Writing to inform

Informative writing focuses on the world outside the writer—the events, people, places, things, and ideas in the *objective* or *real* world. In informative writing you report, explain, analyze, define, classify, compare, describe a process, or get at causes and effects (see PARA 2b). Informative writing is most often found in newspaper and magazine articles and nonfiction books. Informative writing encompasses everything from an article on better parenting, your chemistry textbook, and a news update on a railroad strike to a provincial government subcommittee report on housing, a travel guide, and a computer manual.

The following example of informative writing provides useful information about Canadian history:

> No study of Canadian history is intelligible without some understanding of Canada's geography. Indeed, geography has been (and still is) one of Canada's chief problems and has, therefore, been a vital factor in determining its history. —J.A. Lower, *Canada: An Outline in History*

## Writing to persuade

In writing to persuade you attempt to influence your reader's thinking and attitudes toward a subject or issue and sometimes move him or her to a particular course of action. Persuasive writing uses logical reasoning and authoritative evidence and testimony, and sometimes emotionally charged language and examples (see WORD 1b).

> There was a time when I travelled everywhere by train. The overnight trip from Toronto to Halifax aboard *The Ocean* or *The Scotian* used to be a delight and an adventure that most people today will never experience. But the government has decided to drastically reduce rail service, and Canada will be poorer for it. —Roger Mann, *The Reluctant Writer*

Most of the writing that you do in college or university will be informative and some will be persuasive in character; occasionally you may be asked to write from experience. Often you will use some combination of these types of writing in a single composition. For example, as an environmental science student you may find yourself informing your readers about the dangers of clear-cut logging, expressing your own beliefs about its effect, telling of an experience you had with an environmental group that has dealt with logging companies, and attempting to persuade your readers that changes are needed.

## COMP 2g   Analyze your audience.

Having arrived at a thesis statement and decided on your purpose for writing, it is time to consider your **audience** or intended readership. Pevere and Dymond's audience would be fairly general—readers who are interested in movies—whereas Evelyn Lau's audience would be more specific—people buying their first home. Lisa Denis's audience would be even more specific than Evelyn Lau's—those who use or could potentially use disposable diapers.

Students often mistakenly assume their instructor is their only audience. Though it is true that your teacher will read your composition, do not forget the other students in your class. They, after all, make up the writing community to which you belong.

Use the following list of questions to identify your audience so you can make appropriate decisions on content, sentence structure (see SENT 7), and word choice (see WORD 1 and 2).

### Checklist for Audience Questions

1. Who are my readers?
2. Is my audience specialized (my chemistry lab partners, other piano players) or general (literate adults)?
3. What do I know about my audience (age; sex; amount of education; religious, social, economic, and political attitudes)?
4. What does my audience know about my subject? What is their knowledge level—expert or novice?
5. What does my audience need to know that I can tell them?
6. Will my audience have misconceptions that I can clarify?
7. What is my relationship to my audience: Boss? Equal? Subordinate?
8. How will my audience respond to what I have to say (interested, open-minded, resistant, hostile)?
9. Is there any specialized language my audience needs or that I should avoid?
10. What do I want my audience to do? How can I help them?
11. How should I sound—formal or informal?

The best writers empathize with their readers. They try to see things as their readers might, recognize and understand their problems and address them, and appeal to their emotions, their rational faculties, and their humanity.

## COMP 2h  Make an outline.

Organize your material so as to present a logical sequence or flow of ideas and provide the strongest support for your thesis statement. Begin by making an informal outline. State your title, purpose, and thesis at the top. List the three parts of your essay—introduction, body, conclusion. Select those ideas from your brainstorming or clustering activities that are essential to your thesis; these will form the body of your essay.

**INFORMAL OUTLINE**

Title:  Signs of the Times: Bumper Stickers

Purpose:  Informative: to explain the purpose of bumper stickers

Thesis:  Bumper stickers express people's beliefs, interests, and attitudes.

1. Introduction

2. Body—types of bumper stickers arranged in order of increasing social and cultural significance

   a. Advertising on bumper stickers—examples

   b. Humorous bumper stickers—examples

   c. Ethnic and religious statements on bumper stickers—examples

   d. Environmental, political, and social issues on bumper stickers—examples

3. Conclusion

Following is the formal outline for the Annotated Student Essay in COMP 6. Andy Pellett, a university student, prepared this outline to submit with his essay.

**FORMAL OUTLINE**

Title:      The Perils of Astroturf

Purpose:  Persuasive: an argument for banning artificial turf and returning to natural turf as a playing surface for football and baseball

Thesis:    Artificial turf is a change for the worse.

I. Arguments for artificial turf
  A. Astroturf saves money.
    1. Counterargument: Installation costs are high.
    2. Counterargument: Artificial turf needs to be replaced more frequently, which further increases costs.
  B. Astroturf increases traction, especially during inclement weather.
    1. Counterargument: Football and baseball are meant to be played in all kinds of weather.
    2. Counterargument: Fans' satisfaction is increased by seeing their teams playing in inclement weather.
II. Arguments against artificial turf
  A. Artificial turf causes the ball to bounce unnaturally, affecting player statistics and game strategy.
  B. Artificial turf causes player injuries.
III. Conclusion: If we stick with real grass we cannot go wrong.

In writing a formal outline, follow these rules:

1. Include the title, a statement of purpose, and the thesis statement.
2. Write in complete sentences unless your meaning is immediately clear from a phrase.
3. Divide each category into at least two subcategories. The reason for this is simple: you cannot logically divide something into fewer than two parts.
4. Observe the traditional formal outline pattern. Notice how each new level of specificity is given a new letter or number designation.

   I.
    A.
    B.
     1.
     2.
      a.
      b.
       (1)
       (2)
        (a)
        (b)
   II.

C-Tip
### Outlining

Develop a master outline file that can be copied for use with each writing project. Fill it in on the screen. Having a master file assures correct outline form (Roman numerals, letters, and numerals), and using a computer makes it easy to revise your outline during the writing process—adding, deleting, and rearranging ideas as you develop your composition, all without the chore of retyping each time.

# COMP 3
## WRITING A DRAFT

Sometimes we are so eager to get on with the actual writing that we begin before we are ready, and the results are disappointing. Before beginning to write, therefore, ask yourself, "Am I ready to write?" If you have done a thorough job of gathering ideas and information, if you feel you can accomplish the purpose of your paper, and if you are comfortable with your organizational plan, your answer will be "yes."

If, however, you feel uneasy, review the steps in the planning stage to get at the cause of your uneasiness. Do you need to gather more information? Adjust your thesis? Rethink your purpose? Refine your organization? Now is the time to engage in critical thinking, to evaluate and clarify your writing plan. Time spent at this juncture is time well spent, and although it may not exactly feel as if you are making progress, you are making critical decisions that will affect the outcome of your composition.

## COMP 3a    Choose a good title.

When you write your title is a matter of preference. Some people like to write it first, using it as a banner to guide the rest of the writing. Others prefer to write it last, after they have seen the final development of their ideas. Either way, when you decide to write your title, instead of trying to create *the* best one, brainstorm about a half dozen so you can choose among them.

A good title announces your subject and prepares your readers for the approach you take. For example, "Why We Crave Horror Movies" by Stephen King is an essay that delivers what its title promises: it explains what for many people is a difficult phenomenon to understand. A good title also hooks your readers. It sets up a question that makes your readers want to read on for an answer. Some titles, such as "Cholesterol" or "The Campus Bookstore," are merely labels. They are not bad, but they do not grab the readers' interest the way these titles do: "Never Get Sick in July" (why is July worse than other months?); "When Television Is a School for Criminals" (do criminals get ideas by watching television?).

 C-Tip

## *Capturing titles*

As you work on your composition, titles will occur to you. Do not lose your good ideas. Designate an area at the beginning or end of your file and label it "Title Ideas," so that when a good idea comes along, you can quickly move to that area of the file and type it in. Then, when it comes time to decide on a title, you will have some possibilities and not have to start from scratch.

## COMP 3b    Write the body of your composition.

In writing a draft, your main concern is to get your ideas down on paper. To a certain extent, let the topic take you where it will. Keep writing and do not be overly concerned about the exact wording or whether you punctuate correctly; concentrate on producing a lively flow of ideas and information. Be alert to new ideas about your topic, ideas that are fresh and potentially fruitful. You will revise and edit later.

Try writing the body in two stages. First, concentrate on the paragraphs and look at each individually. Do you provide enough details and examples? Second, look at the paragraphs as a group. Do the paragraphs work together as a unit? Do you need transitions to connect the individual parts logically and make them flow smoothly?

As you write the draft, be mindful of your outline but do not become a slave to it. You may find yourself departing from the outline because you discover something new about your subject through writing about it. Let this happen, but make an "X" or a note in the margin indicating that you may be deviating from your plan. These notes will remind you of what you were thinking as you wrote and allow you to reconsider those thoughts when revising.

 C-Tip

### *Triple-spacing for revision*

If you triple-space between lines, you can easily make handwritten revisions on a printout (hard copy). Carry your hard copy with you to read at odd moments; sometimes when you are relaxed and not feeling pressed to produce, you will get new insights into your topic. Before printing out a final copy, type in changes, reformat, and double-space your file.

## COMP 3c   Pay special attention to your beginning and ending.

The beginning of your paper, or the *lead* as journalists refer to it, is like a personal greeting; it attracts and holds the reader's attention.

You might consider using one of the following beginnings:

1. an incident, anecdote, or illustration
2. historical background
3. a quotation
4. a broad, general thesis statement
5. a contradictory or ironic statement
6. a surprising fact or idea
7. a statement
8. a rhetorical question

No matter how you attract the reader's attention, however, your introduction should clearly relate to your thesis. For this reason, even though the temptation is to get it just right from the outset so you feel you are off to a good start, you may find it best to draft a workable beginning and then revise it after you have written and revised the body of your composition. When the body is in final form, you may have a better idea how to introduce it to your readers.

A good conclusion does more than indicate the end of your composition. You may use it to inspire your readers to some action or new way of thinking, or you may want to drive home a point you made in your introduction by giving another particularly apt example or by repeating a key word or phrase to remind your readers of where you began your composition. You may also use your conclusion to summarize what you have written, but never in a mechanical way and not with such expressions as *In summary, In conclusion,* or *As you can see.*

See the essays on pages 1–2 and 30–33 of this chapter for examples of good beginnings and endings.

# COMP 4 _____
## REVISING

When you have finished writing your draft, give it an honest appraisal. Focus on the large issues of thesis, purpose, content, organization, and paragraph structure that affect your entire composition. It would be counter-productive to look at grammar and punctuation, for example, if the elements that make an essay "go" need work. Suppose you inherit an old car. Anyone can see that it badly needs a new paint job, but should you spend the money to have the work done if you do not know whether the car runs? What if you discover after you have invested in a paint job that the engine needs extensive repairs or, worse yet, is not worth fixing at all? So it is with writing. First you revise—work on the large issues that clarify your purpose and improve your organization—and then you **edit**—check for correctness and style.

No one—*no one*—produces perfect prose on the first draft. Be prepared to revise and, in the words of one Canadian critic, "be prepared to revise your revision, and when your revision is revised, prepare yourself for the final revision. Then revise it again."

## COMP 4a    Revise the largest elements of your composition first.

Revision is best done by asking yourself questions about what you have written. Otherwise, you can stare at a draft for a good long time, wondering what you should be looking for. Begin by reading, preferably aloud, what you have written. Reading aloud forces you to pay attention to every single word; you are more likely to catch lapses in the logical flow of thought. Then ask yourself the questions in the checklist that follows. Use the cross-referenced sections for help.

### Checklist for Revising Large Elements

1. Is my topic well focused? (See COMP 2c.)
2. Does my thesis statement clearly state the point of my composition? (See COMP 2e.)
3. Are my paragraphs effective? (See PARA 1 and 3.) Do my topic sentences relate to my thesis? Do they support my thesis?
4. Do I have enough supporting details, and are my examples well chosen to support my thesis? (See PARA 2a.)
5. Is my organizational pattern the best one given my purpose? Have I tried alternative patterns of organization? (See PARA 2b.)
6. Do I accomplish my purpose? (See COMP 2f.)
7. How effective is my beginning? Ending? (See COMP 3c.)
8. Do I have a good title? (See COMP 3a.)

In answering these questions you may discover that parts of your paper bear little or no relationship to your thesis and purpose. You may need to rearrange your examples for greater impact. Or, perhaps you need a transition between paragraphs. All this is good. Revision is a process, and effective writing is the result of thoughtful revision.

## COMP 4b    Revise your sentences and diction.

Having revised the largest elements of your composition, turn next to the sentences themselves. Again, the best approach is to ask yourself specific questions. Use the following checklist.

### Checklist for Revising Sentences

1. Do my sentences convey my thoughts clearly? (See SENT 4.)
2. Do I subordinate less important ideas to more important ones? (See SENT 5.)
3. Do my sentences emphasize the most important part of the thought? (See SENT 6.)
4. Are my sentences varied? (See SENT 7.)
5. Are my sentences complete sentences? Have I unintentionally written any sentence fragments? (See EDIT 5.)
6. Are any of my sentences comma splices or run-ons? (See EDIT 6.)

You may find that some of your sentences are long and rambling and that others are short and choppy, giving the impression that your thoughts are disconnected. Perhaps you shifted focus within some sentences or used the same sentence pattern throughout most of your composition. Sentence problems like these may drive you to reconsider paragraphs you previously thought were effective. Again, all this is good. Writing is recursive, moving back and forth between larger and smaller elements and among the various stages.

 C-Tip

## *Saving material*

You never know when sections of text (more than a few phrases or sentences), references, or quotations you wish to delete from a draft may later prove useful, sometimes even after you have completed an assignment. Block off the material you want to delete, and move it to the end of your file in a section labelled "Supplementary Material." When you are finished writing, print only up to that point, saving the file with the supplementary material intact.

Now look at your **diction** or use of words. Do you use the word *tedious* when you mean *dull*? Do you use *man* when you mean *human*? Do you use three words when one would do? To revise for diction, ask yourself the questions in the following checklist. Use the cross-referenced sections for help.

### Checklist for Revising Diction

1. Is my diction exact? Does each word mean precisely what I think it does? (See WORD 1.)
2. Do I engage my readers with concrete nouns and strong action verbs? (See WORD 1c and 4e.)
3. Do I use appropriate language, avoiding slang, regional language, pompous language, and doublespeak? (See WORD 2.)
4. Is my language unbiased? (See WORD 3.)
5. Is my writing fresh and forceful or burdened by unnecessary words? (See WORD 4.)

Following is an early draft of Andy Pellett's opening paragraph of the Annotated Student Essay in COMP 6. It shows how he revised his sentences and diction.

As a ˄sports fan~~, who thinks of himself as a sports purist,~~ I am ~~wary~~ of
<sup>purist and a</sup> <sup>suspicious</sup>
changes ~~that occur~~ in pastimes, ~~that I love,~~ namely, baseball and football.
<sup>my favourite</sup>
~~and~~ in the past two decades, there have been many new developments —
Some ~~of these have been~~ good and some ~~not so good.~~ The most disturbing
<sup>s</sup> <sup>bad. But t</sup>
change ~~I have seen, however, has been~~ the use of artificial turf as a surface,
<sup>is</sup> <sup>introduction</sup> <sup>playing</sup>
~~on which to play~~ because it makes the games unnatural and causes injuries.

Some aspects of editing allow for personal choice. Another writer, for example, might have changed the opening of the first sentence to *As a sports fan who is also a purist.* Both revisions solve the problem of wordiness. Certain revision changes, however, are questions of correctness and thus are not open to choice. These are questions of grammar, punctuation, and mechanics (capitalization and spelling).

## COMP 4c  Ask for peer evaluation.

An excellent way to improve an essay is to read it and then discuss it at a conference with a fellow student or friend. In turn, you can sharpen your critical skills by reading your classmate's essay.

Follow these guidelines if you are critiquing someone's work:

- When the writer gives you a copy of the paper, set aside the time to read it. Make notes directly on the paper to refer to during the conference you arrange.
- Be sure you understand the essay. Read it carefully. If you are confused, ask yourself whether the problem is in the essay or whether you're missing something.
- At the beginning of the conference, ask the writer to briefly state the purpose of the essay and point out the thesis statement. If you and the writer disagree, discuss possible reasons.
- Rather than dictate changes, ask questions that lead the writer to reconsider parts of the draft.
- Ask the most important questions first so if time is limited you can be the most help in the shortest time. For example, tackle problems with the purpose and thesis before discussing transitions or a particular word choice.

- Be supportive. The way you word your comments is as important as the comments themselves (not "this is a dumb example" but "this example is not as good as the others"). At the same time, you should be honest or you won't be much help.

Follow these guidelines if your essay is being critiqued:

- Give a copy of your paper to your reviewer in advance of your meeting.
- As the conference proceeds, take brief notes on your copy of your paper ("rephrase thesis statement," "clarify paragraph 3," "consider reworking title").
- Be attentive and listen carefully. Don't waste time arguing over issues. Take everything in and evaluate comments later.
- If your reader misunderstands something, ask why—don't just explain what you meant. Trying to understand your reader's point of view will help you rewrite more clearly.
- Consider all your reader's comments carefully, but make only the changes that you agree with. Retain ownership of your work.
- Show your appreciation for the time your reader took to help you improve your work. ("Thanks, I found this session worthwhile.")

# COMP 5 _____
## EDITING

Having revised your paper, you are now ready to edit it. In other words, having made it right, you now want to make it correct.

## COMP 5a    When you edit, check grammar, punctuation, and mechanics (capitalization and spelling).

How do editing errors creep into your composition? Two ways: first, there are the inadvertent errors. You know how to capitalize proper nouns, but rushing to get down your thoughts you write *spanish* instead of *Spanish.*

Second, there are errors pointed out by friends, fellow students, or teachers. The best way to catch errors of this sort is to know yourself as a writer. That means (1) taking seriously the feedback you get from friends and teachers, and (2) using your handbook. If you know you have trouble remembering how to use punctuation with quotation marks, you are on your way to correcting the problem. Simply check your handbook during editing. For easy access to the information you need, use the tab indicators, the table of contents, or the index.

The more you know yourself as a writer, the more, too, you will develop a sense of what does not seem to sound or look quite right. Which is correct, *none are* or *none is*? Is *receive* spelled *ei* or *ie*? Turn to the appropriate section of this handbook for the answer.

## COMP 5b    Prepare the final copy.

Having revised and edited your work, you are ready to prepare the final copy of your composition. Consult FORMAT 2 for details. The sample essay in COMP 6 shows what your final draft should look like.

## COMP 5c    Proofread the final copy.

Always proofread thoroughly. Your readers cannot tell whether *recieve*, for example, is a spelling error or a typographical error. Many such seemingly small matters add up. If you are aware that you frequently make particular kinds of errors (in comma usage or subject-verb agreement, for instance), read your manuscript once for each specific problem.

The following checklist contains questions to ask yourself as you proofread your composition.

---

### Checklist for Proofreading

1. Did my manuscript print out as I expected it to? Is it properly line-spaced? Is all the text legible?
2. Have I left out words or unnecessarily repeated words or phrases? Have I overlooked any errors in grammar or punctuation?
3. Has my spell-checker approved a word that is properly spelled but has the wrong meaning for this context? (See MECH 6, C-Tip: Spell-checker.)
4. Will I need to reprint my composition, or will my instructor allow me to handwrite in minor corrections?

---

Check for spelling slips by reading lines of your manuscript backwards. This allows you to read the words out of context and to view them separately, so your eye picks up errors you ordinarily pass over when reading for content.

Always proofread on hard copy rather than on the computer screen. You cannot go back and forth as easily on the screen as you can on hard copy when you want to compare style, grammar, and usage in parts of your essay, and your eye tends to skip over errors on the screen. Reading your essay aloud from hard copy is a good way to detect errors; we tend to "hear" errors that we miss when we read. If it doesn't "sound right," it's likely wrong.

Finally, it is a good idea to keep your notes and early drafts along with a copy of your submitted manuscript until your graded assignment is returned.

# COMP 6 _____
## ANNOTATED STUDENT ESSAY

Student Andy Pellett was asked to write an argument on a topic of his own choosing. He knew from past experience that to write a good paper he should write about something he cares about. He also knew that he should allow himself a reasonable amount of time to find such a topic and gather his ideas. An avid sports fan, Andy decided to write about some aspect of sports. He considered and rejected several possibilities—including professional salaries, Olympic hockey teams, and sports heroes in advertising—before he decided that his topic would be artificial playing surfaces. From what he had read in the popular press and from his own observations, Andy disliked artificial playing surfaces, and he thought he could develop his essay on the thesis that such surfaces are bad for athletes and sports. His purpose would be to argue against their use.

Having focused on a topic, Andy began brainstorming on his computer for ideas, facts, examples, arguments, and counterarguments—anything that came to mind. When he felt he had amassed enough information, he began to sort it out. He saw that his material essentially broke down into two categories, pro and con. So, in making a rough outline of an organizational pattern, he decided to first demonstrate the weaknesses of the arguments put forth in favour of artificial turf, and then present his own strong arguments against the use of artificial turf.

Andy was ready to write his first draft. He wrote quickly, keeping his organizational plan in mind, but aiming primarily to get down his thoughts with no concern for spelling or grammar. Now, with something drafted, he was in a position to assess how it could be improved. In reading his first draft, Andy realized he had failed to mention an important objection to artificial turf (the high cost of installation and replacement). He saw that his second and third paragraphs were really on the same topic, so he combined them. He also found places where he could add phrases to make his meaning clearer. Finally, he rearranged the sentences in his fifth paragraph, and decided to save his argument about injuries until the very end.

Next, Andy turned to his title. He wanted a title that would arouse curiosity, that would make people want to read what he had to say. He checked the list of titles he had made when he first started his paper and chose "The Perils of Astroturf." He also thought about the way his essay began and concluded. He was happy with his beginning but decided to lighten his ending by adding an amusing comment made by Richie Allen.

When he was satisfied with his revisions, Andy began to edit. He referred to his handbook to delete several vague words that had crept into his essay and to fix subject-verb agreement and comma-splice problems. Before printing a final copy, Andy proofread his paper and then used his spell-checker (see MECH 6, C-Tip: Spell-checker).

The final draft of Andy's paper appears on the following pages. We have annotated it to highlight features that may be helpful to you as a writer. The paper may not be perfect, but Andy can be proud of learning the steps in the composing process. He now knows how to move systematically from large conceptual issues to smaller technical matters, saving him time and frustration. No longer does he wonder where to start and what to do next. With more practice, Andy will make the process, if not always quicker and easier, at least more familiar and rewarding.

Pellett 1

The Perils of Astroturf

Andy Pellett

*Heading:* States author's surname and indicates page number.

*Title:* Indicates main idea of essay in a catchy way.

As a purist and a sports fan, I am suspicious of changes in my favourite pastimes, namely, baseball and football. In the past two decades, there have been many

*Thesis statement:* Sets up a clear expectation in the reader's mind.

new developments—some good and some bad. But the most disturbing change is the introduction of artificial turf as a playing surface, because it makes the games unnatural and causes injuries.

*Diction:* Changing *artificial turf* to *fake grass* is calculated (no one likes "fake" things).

This fake grass first appeared on the sporting scene in 1966. The grass in the Houston Astrodome was dying, so in desperation it was replaced by artificial turf. This new surface, manufactured by the Monsanto Company, was

*Audience:* Andy provides background information for his general audience.

appropriately called Astroturf. Since then, the living grass in the stadiums and playing fields everywhere has been replaced with one form of artificial turf or another, usually made of green nylon fibres stitched over a cushioned polyester mat. Astroturf is still the most common.

What's so great about artificial turf? If real grass was good enough for the sports heroes of yesteryear, why shouldn't it be good enough for those of today? The

*Organization:* Andy announces two basic arguments.

proponents of artificial turf have at least two basic arguments.

The first argument uses a familiar line of reasoning: artificial turf saves money. The field needs less

Pellett 2

maintenance, and rain water drains easily through small holes in the mat. Also, the field can be used for more than one sport. A football game won't tear up the turf, making it possible to play a baseball game on the same field a day later.

This argument, however, overlooks several important problems. The cost of laying down a new synthetic field is very high—close to a million dollars. In addition, artificial turf deteriorates in appearance and condition. Tobacco juice spit onto the ground soaks in; on Astroturf it makes an ugly stain that gives groundskeepers fits. In 1971, the artificial turf in Miami's Orange Bowl was decoratively painted for the Super Bowl. After the game, the paint couldn't be removed and remained on the field for months. For these and other reasons, older fake fields may have to be resurfaced. Such resurfacing increases, not decreases, the cost of field maintenance.

*Transition:* The use of *however* sets up Andy's refutation.

*Paragraph development:* Andy supports his argument with specific examples.

The second argument proponents of Astroturf make is that traction is increased by artificial turf, thereby making it easier to play in inclement weather. But why should we make it easier to play in bad weather? A game like football is a tough sport, and playing in horrible conditions exemplifies that toughness. Most fans enjoy watching two football teams battle it out, with mud covering every part of their uniforms. Baseball, like football, was meant to be played outside on the grass,

Pellett 3

*Organization:*
Transitional
paragraph
bridges the
two halves of
Andy's compo-
sition; it looks
back, restating
that the argu-
ments for
Astroturf are
weak, and
ahead, promis-
ing two strong
arguments
against it.

*Diction:* Figura-
tive language
(a simile)
creates a vivid
image to drive
home how
artificial turf
makes the
whole game
artificial.

*Dialogue:*
Speech makes
the debate
more realistic
and captures
the reader's
attention with
its unexpected
use in a
straight prose
piece.

and, if we take the natural element out of the sport, we lose a sense of drama.

It is evident that arguments in favour of artificial turf ignore some important facts. Furthermore, these arguments appear even weaker when compared to the arguments put forth by the detractors of Astroturf. Opponents of artificial turf make essentially two arguments: artificial turf causes the ball to bounce unnaturally, which affects team statistics and strategy, and artificial turf causes injuries to players.

In the major leagues, the baseball diamond has been turned into a basketball court by the hard surface. The ball rockets off the turf as if being fired from a cannon. It rolls faster and farther than on natural grass, allowing for more extra-base hits.

"Great," some fans will say. "We like to see more offence." But a baseball player's performance is measured by statistics. So it really isn't fair for a weak hitter to acquire more extra-base hits just because he plays on artificial turf. Strategy is also affected. An outfielder must play back to prevent the ball from caroming over his head. This allows cheap bloop singles that ordinarily would be caught. And what about when the batter grounds the ball into the turf in front of home plate? Normally this play should be an out; but by the time the ball comes down, the batter is standing on first with a "Monsanto single."

Pellett 4

The other problem with Astroturf is injuries. Athletes have complained that artificial turf is responsible for everything from friction burns to broken bones. Because of the hard surface, athletes must make adaptations in their running style, which can often result in painful foot ailments. Also, the increased traction of Astroturf means that when a player plants a foot, it won't slide at all. Therefore, if a player who is in an awkward position with feet planted gets hit, serious knee injuries can result. Artificial turf has been blamed for a rash of season-ending injuries in the Canadian Football League, and it's hard to find an outfielder on either the Toronto or Montreal baseball teams who hasn't come up with both the ball and "turf burn" after a diving catch.

My fervent, yet probably unrealistic, hope is that artificial turf will be banned. There was never any controversy when real grass was the only surface on which outdoor games were played. If we stick with natural substances, we can't go wrong. Trying to improve on nature only causes trouble. Richie Allen, a former baseball player, probably said it best: "If my horse can't eat it, I don't want to play on it."

*Organization:* Andy ends with player injuries because he feels it is his strongest argument.

*Paragraph development:* Andy has specific examples to support his point.

*Conclusion:* A natural outgrowth of the arguments against artificial turf.

# COMP 7 _____
## SPEAKING SKILLS

Many of your courses might have a component that calls for an oral presentation. For many students, this oral composition or "speech" is approached with fear and uncertainty. It is certainly true that a good writer is not necessarily a good speaker: although writing and speaking have many of the same components, such as an identifiable thesis, a clear purpose, an appeal to the interests of the audience, and a definable structure, the very fact that your speech is a public presentation before an audience rather than a private, one-on-one document for your teacher, causes anxiety in most students.

The secret to a successful oral assignment rests on the same principles as a successful written assignment—prepare well, know your audience, understand your topic, and deliver your speech with confidence.

## COMP 7a    Task, purpose, and audience

Consider how much time you have to prepare your presentation, consider its length, and decide on the types of visual materials or handouts you need. A group presentation assignment will mean that you need time to decide on the tasks of each member of your group, and that extra time will have to be allowed for practice.

The purpose of your presentation will demand a great deal of careful thought. The contents of your presentation or the approach you take to your topic will differ if you intend to lead a discussion rather than present a proposal, or if you intend to give a report rather than make a persuasive argument. These are only a few examples of potential purposes for your oral presentation, and each must be approached differently. Determining the nature of your audience is also important in your approach to your topic. You have to consider the audience's familiarity with the topic, any opinions the members of the audience may have about the topic, and what the audience needs to know if it is to understand the point of view you take in your presentation.

## COMP 7b    The introduction and conclusion

The most important parts of any oral presentation are the beginning and the ending. The audience will usually remember what you say in the introduction or the conclusion, so make sure that you make an impact in these sections. Start with an opinion, a question, a quotation, a startling statement, or an anecdote, for instance, and relate your topic, which should be brought out clearly in the opening section of your presentation, to the interests and experiences of your listeners. The conclusion should be more than a summary; it should challenge the audience to take action or to see your point of view so clearly and accurately that the position you have taken in your presentation cannot be challenged.

## COMP 7c    Structure and language

Your entire oral presentation should be delivered in such a way that you continue to support the thesis—your point of view—that you make in your introduction. Organize your presentation carefully and clearly, and pause between the major supporting points you make in your presentation in order to emphasize them. Transitions are important to point out the shifts between your supporting statements (transitional words and phrases can be found in PARA 3b and PUNCT 1f). Avoid long, complicated sentences, and be sure to use concrete verbs and nouns in your presentation rather than abstractions.

## COMP 7d    Visuals

You can use charts, graphs, overheads, or other graphics to enhance and reinforce the important points in your presentation. These visuals must be large enough to be seen clearly by your entire audience, and they must be used to help the audience focus on your presentation rather than to distract them.

## COMP 7e    Practice

A good oral presentation takes practice. Prepare your presentation, including your visuals, far enough in advance that you can practise it more than once. Speak into a tape recorder and play it back, give your presentation in front of a mirror, or make your presentation to a small group of friends—all of these methods will help you fine-tune your presentation and put you at your ease when it comes time to speak in front of your audience. Be sure to keep within your time limit. As a rule of thumb, people generally speak 250 words per minute in everyday conversation. This guide will help you determine whether you are speaking too quickly or too slowly, or whether you have too much or too little material to fill your allotted time. When you are speaking, maintain eye contact, allow time for any questions, and remember to thank your audience when you're finished.

# PARA

## Paragraphs

### *Learning Objectives*

After reading this section, you should

1. understand what makes a paragraph unified,
2. be able to use various strategies to develop your ideas,
3. know different ways of achieving coherence within and between paragraphs.

# PARA

## Paragraphs

In many ways the paragraph is an essay in miniature. The paragraph has a topic sentence that states the main idea of the paragraph in the same way that the thesis statement presents the main point of the essay. Like the well-written essay, the well-written paragraph is *unified*—all sentences relate to the main idea (PARA 1); it is well *developed*—there is apt and sufficient supporting detail (PARA 2); and it is *coherent*—ideas and sentences flow logically and smoothly (PARA 3).

The following paragraph on the life cycle of neighbourhoods, by Kevin Cunningham, a university student, is an example of a well-written paragraph.

> Neighbourhoods are often assigned human characteristics, one of which is a life cycle: they have a birth, a youth, a middle age, and an old age. A neighbourhood is built and settled by young, vibrant people, proud of their sturdy new homes. Together, residents and houses mature, as families grow larger and additions get built on. Eventually, though, the neighbourhood begins to show its age. Buildings sag a little, houses aren't repaired as quickly, and maintenance slips. The neighbourhood may grow poorer, as the young and upwardly mobile find new jobs and move away, while the older and less successful inhabitants remain.

Cunningham provides a clear topic sentence that explains what he means by a life cycle. He then goes on to describe the stages of that cycle and the process by which one stage leads to the next. Cunningham maintains unity by excluding anything that does not directly relate to the concept of the life cycle. He achieves coherence by ordering his sentences to flow smoothly without breaks in rhythm or meaning and by using transitional words (*and, as, eventually, while*).

# PARA 1 _____
## UNITY

The **topic sentence** presents the main idea of the paragraph. It is also called the *controlling idea* because it limits the subject of the paragraph and, like the thesis statement, suggests ways of developing the thought. The topic sentence of each paragraph should be an outgrowth of the thesis statement (see COMP 2e).

| TOPIC SENTENCE | IMPLIED DEVELOPMENT STRATEGY |
|---|---|
| There were three classes of people in Medieval society. | You will *name* the three classes and *describe* each one. |
| What is a "best friend"? | You will *define* "best friend." |
| After I bought a computer, the grades I received for my English essays were much better than they had been. | You will *contrast* your grades before and after you bought a computer. |

In a unified paragraph all sentences relate to the topic sentence by explaining it with facts, examples, and supporting details. You should eliminate all sentences that stray from the point of the topic sentence.

## PARA 1a    Write a topic sentence.

No matter where you finally decide to place your topic sentence, begin with one in mind. Then, as you write, you will zero in on what you want to say in this portion of your paper. Usually, the topic sentence is at, or near, the beginning of the paragraph; this way, the writer lets the reader know the direction of thought and function of the other sentences in the paragraph. The topic sentence may, however, be placed anywhere in the paragraph, particularly if you want to create a special effect.

In the following paragraph the topic sentence (shown in italics) comes first, and the anecdote that follows illustrates how bees astonish us.

> *Bees are filled with astonishments, confounding anyone who studies them, producing volumes of anecdotes.* A lady of our acquaintance visited her sister, who raised honeybees. They left their car on a side road, suited up in protective gear, and walked across the fields to have a look at the hives. For reasons unknown, the bees were in a furious mood that afternoon, attacking in platoons, settling on them from all sides. Let us walk away slowly, advised the beekeeper sister, they'll give it up sooner or later. They walked until bee-free, then circled the fields and went back to the car, and found bees there, waiting for them. —Lewis Thomas, "Clever Animals"

The topic sentence may be most effective at the end of the paragraph when the writer wishes to create a sense of drama or suspense, or when, as in the following paragraph, the main idea is introduced by a convincing example.

> Consider, for a moment, the variety of Canada's forests. This country is home to 31 species of coniferous trees, including the pine, hemlock, cedar, and the majestic Douglas fir of the West coast. In addition, we have over 100 species of deciduous trees, among which are numbered 10 varieties of maple in our vast forests, four of oak, and five of hickory. *If these forests aren't*

*preserved, future generations will know the grandeur of our forests as nothing more than cold statistics.*

Often the topic sentence is preceded by a transitional sentence or contains a transitional clause or phrase referring to the previous paragraph. In the next paragraph, a transitional phrase leads into the topic:

> *After years of looking for inspiration, Lucy Maud Montgomery finally found the basis for one of Canada's most enduring literary characters, Anne of Green Gables.* Montgomery had noted in an early journal, "Elderly couple apply to orphan asylum for a boy; by mistake a girl is sent them." Years later, she developed this idea into one of the most widely read Canadian books ever written, and Anne Shirley, the red-haired orphan from Prince Edward Island, became known and loved around the world.

The first part of the topic sentence looks back: *After years of looking for inspiration*; the clause *Lucy Maud Montgomery finally found the basis for one of Canada's most enduring literary characters, Anne of Green Gables* shapes and controls what follows. By providing this transition, the writer easily develops the line of thought in the paragraph. Lucy Maud Montgomery looked for an idea for years, found that she had already written this idea in a journal, and *developed this idea into one of the most widely read Canadian books ever written*, telling the reader that Anne *became known and loved around the world.*

Topic sentences are explicitly stated in most paragraphs, but on occasion, particularly in narrative or descriptive paragraphs, a writer may merely *imply* a controlling idea. In the following paragraph, the writer carefully chooses details that will lead the reader to the main idea without the writer's having to state it specifically. Leading the reader along until the point dawns on him or her can often have a much greater impact than a straightforward statement.

> You are standing on the threshold of time in as sacred a place as any in the world. It's where the life of the land and the life of the water converge in biological blur. These are the wetlands—the swamps and the mudflats that sometimes smell like rotten eggs. These are the marshes, clogged with weeds, swarming with bugs, teeming with beautiful life. This is where the moon moves the water in shallow ebbs and floods; where the sun pierces down to the ooze and the nutrients flow in a strange and marvelous way. Nowhere else except here in these sopping grounds is there so much life in so much concentration. But the life is dwindling. And as these lands start to go—you do, too.          —Sierra Club, "Threshold of Time"

Through cumulative detail that strongly appeals to the senses, this writer conveys the controlling idea that marshes and wetlands are fascinating and ecologically important, and people ought to be concerned about them. The controlling idea is conveyed even though it is not explicitly stated.

### C-Tip

## *Boldfacing topic sentences*

To check for unity and coherence while drafting your paragraphs, boldface or underline the topic sentence in each of your paragraphs. By calling special attention to each topic sentence, you see how the other sentences in the paragraph relate to the topic sentence and to each other.

## PARA 1b    Relate all sentences to the controlling idea.

A paragraph is unified when all its sentences develop, or expand on, the central idea in some way. No sentence is off the topic.

Notice how every sentence in the following paragraph develops the topic sentence; it is a unified paragraph.

> My husband and I often joke that the reason we have stayed married for so long is that we continually mystify each other with responses and attitudes that are plainly due to our different backgrounds. For years I frustrated him with unpredictable silences and accusing looks. I felt a great reluctance to tell him what I wanted or what needed to be done in the home. I was inwardly furious that I was being put into the position of having to *tell* him what to do. I felt my femaleness, in the Japanese sense, was being degraded. I did not want to be the authority. That would be humiliating for him and for me. He, on the other hand, considering the home to be under my dominion, in the North American sense, did not dare to impose on me what he wanted. He wanted me to tell him or make a list, like his parents did in his home.
>
> —Jeanne Wakatsuki Houston, "Living in Two Cultures"

The plan of the paragraph is clear: Houston's first sentence states her belief that culture shapes our attitudes and responses. Then she gives reasons:

1. She could not tell her husband what she wanted, so she remained silent and gave accusing looks.
2. She did not want the authority of having to tell him what to do.

3. Her femaleness, in the Japanese sense, was threatened by his attitude.
4. He considered, in the North American sense, that the woman ran the house.
5. He did not want to impinge on her role.
6. He wanted to be told what to do or be given a list.

 C-Tip
### Testing for unity

If you think that there are sentences in any of your paragraphs that may be unnecessary and might be eliminated, block them off, move them out of the paragraph, and read the new paragraph. If the paragraph is tight, with no gaps in logic, eliminate the sentences permanently.

# PARA 2 _____
# DEVELOPMENT

Whether it is first or last or someplace in the middle, whether it is explicitly stated or merely implied, the topic sentence is the point of departure for writing an effective paragraph. How you **develop**—clarify and support—your topic sentence depends on how you answer the question, "Why or how is this so?" Consider, for example, the following topic sentence:

Neat people are especially vicious with mail.

Applying the question, "Why or how is this so?" suggests a strategy for development: the writer needs to tell how "neat people are especially vicious with mail."

*Neat people are especially vicious with mail.* They never go through their mail unless they are standing directly over a trash can. If the trash can is beside the mailbox, even better. All ads, catalogues, pleas for charitable contributions, church bulletins, and money-saving coupons go straight into the trash can without being opened. All letters from home, postcards from Europe, bills, and paycheques are opened, immediately responded to, then dropped in the trash can. Neat people keep their receipts only for tax purposes. That's it. No sentimental salvaging of birthday cards or the last letter a dying relative ever wrote. Into the trash it goes.

—Suzanne Britt, "Neat People vs. Sloppy People"

## PARA 2a  Develop paragraphs fully.

In expository prose (prose that explains), a paragraph typically contains 100-150 words. Longer paragraphs appear in professional journals that discuss new or highly complex information requiring in-depth explanation and evidence. Paragraphs are shorter in newspapers and magazines where the print column is narrow and needs to be broken more often, and where the subject matter is less demanding of the reader.

Occasionally a paragraph is too long and needs to be divided or restructured for clarity. The more common problem is the underdeveloped paragraph that leaves the reader wanting more information.

UNDERDEVELOPED

> It is considerably easier to forge a cheque in your name than you might think. Forgery is a form of fraud, and the number of fraud-related offences has climbed considerably over the past 10 years. It's also easy for a fraud artist to use your credit card number.

The topic sentence in the preceding paragraph sets up an idea and a plan for developing it, but more information is needed to convince the reader to be careful when writing cheques. A fully developed version of the paragraph follows. The writer adds details about cheque forgery, showing how easy it is to forge a name or an amount on a cheque.

WELL DEVELOPED

> It is considerably easier to forge a cheque in your name than you might think. Many people make it a lot easier for the forgers by not paying attention to proper procedures for protecting themselves. For instance, a pickpocket is able to obtain a copy of your signature when your wallet is stolen, and can easily forge this signature on a blank cheque made out to Cash. Cheques that have been filled out and signed can be altered with little difficulty: simply add zero to $20, for example, if you have left room for extra figures on your cheque. This type of forgery is common: the number of fraud-related offences in Canada climbed from 875 250 in 1991 to nearly 2 000 000 by the late 1990s. So be careful when writing your cheques: someone may be waiting to take advantage of your carelessness.

To be sure you have provided enough information to enlighten and convince the reader—and thus communicate all you intend—ask a friend to read your composition and point out anything that is not explained clearly or fully enough.

A paragraph may be only a sentence or two long and still be well developed. Such paragraphs often function as transitions from one section of a composition to another. Sometimes, too, as in the following example, a very short paragraph is used to emphasize a point.

From modest beginnings more than two decades ago, computer networks have spread to form an enormous global web. Many users log on to Internet, a system of tens of thousands of networks crammed with scientific and scholarly information as well as thousands of discussion forums or news groups. —Mark Nichols, "Welcome to Cyberspace"

In his next paragraph, one of normal length, Nichols continues by discussing the spread of Internet across Canada and the world.

## PARA 2b    Use the strategy implied in your topic sentence to develop your paragraph.

### Narration

To **narrate** is to tell what happened. Because narration is story-telling, it usually follows a chronological pattern, as in the following example. However, the sequence of events can be rearranged for special effect (see PARA 3a).

One thing that I remember clearly about my early youth was the day that my family got its first dial telephone. We lived in the country, in a small southwestern Ontario village named Mitchell's Bay, and whenever we wanted to call someone in those days, we picked up the telephone and waited for the operator to answer.

"Number, please," the operator would say.

"754-W1," I'd answer. That was the number of my friend Brian, who lived about a mile away.

We were on a party line, which we shared with four other families, each with its own ring. When the phone rang twice, it was for us: "ring-ring, ring-ring, ring-ring." One, three, or four rings signalled a call for one of our neighbours. But even when the phone rang twice, you could be sure that other people would listen in. I guess that there wasn't much else to do back then on a winter's day in the country.

But the dial phone changed all that. One ring, one family on the line. The day of the party line was finished. I was so excited about this new dial phone the first day that it went into service that I called my friend at six in the morning. His father answered.

"Just trying it out," I said.

Like I mentioned, there wasn't much else to do in the country back then, especially at six in the morning.

### Description

To **describe** is to create a verbal picture of a person, place, thing, or even a mood or idea. Description relies on specific and concrete details to create sensory impressions for the reader (see WORD 1c and PARA 3a,

Spatial order). In the following paragraph, Harry Bruce describes the ferry *Trillium*:

> As she edged away from her slip and picked up speed in the shiny green waters of Lake Ontario, you heard the *plosh, plosh, plosh* of her paddle wheels. In the railings, in the slats of her wooden benches burnished over the years by a million rumps, you felt the steady, comforting shudder of her engines. The *Trillium's* sides were white as a swan, and she was a vision of beauty and business.                    —Harry Bruce, "Floating Around Canada"

### Examples and illustration

One of the best ways to convince a reader of the validity of a generalization in the topic sentence is to provide **examples**—specific instances of what you are talking about. In the following paragraph, the author enumerates examples to support the topic sentence that "Canadians know very little about their own history."

> It has been said that Canadians know very little about their own history. In fact, very few high school students ever take Canadian history as part of their curriculum, since it is no longer a required subject in most schools, and there are many more interesting options available to help pass the hours between the first and last bells of the school's day. Does anyone care about the fact that Sir John A. Macdonald, whose picture is on the $10 bill, in 1867 became Canada's first prime minister? Does it matter that Her Majesty Queen Elizabeth II is the Queen of Canada and Canada's head of state? How important is the fact that thousands of Chinese came to Canada in the late 1800s to help build the final section of the Canadian Pacific Railway? We should care, it does matter, and it is important. Without an understanding of our history, we remain strangers in a strange land, a nation unable to grasp the identity we search for in our quest to come to terms with our differences.

Sometimes a single, extended example—called an **illustration**—is more effective.

> I have always wondered why my best friends were so important to me; but it wasn't until recently that something happened to make me really understand my relationship with my best friends. My father died, and this was a crisis for me. Most of my friends gave me their condolences. But my best friends did more than that: they actually supported me. They called long distance to see how I was and what I needed, to try to help me work out my problems or simply to talk. Two of my best friends even took time from their spring break and, along with two other best friends, attended my father's memorial service; none of my other friends came. Since then, these are the only people who have continued to worry about me and talk about my

father. I know that whenever I need someone, they will be there and willing to help me. I know also that whenever they need help, I will be ready to do the same for them.      —Howard Solomon, Jr., student

## Facts, statistics, and reasons

A **fact** is a piece of information with objective reality. **Statistics** are numerical facts. A **reason** is a statement offered as a logical explanation or justification. Facts, statistics, and reasons can be used singly or in combination, as in the following example.

> The whale is the most astonishing animal the earth has ever known. It does not merely inspire superlatives—it is a living superlative. Some whales are much larger than the gigantic dinosaurs of the Mesozoic. It would take 25 elephants, or 2000 human beings, to equal the weight of a single blue whale; its tongue alone weighs as much as an elephant. The blue whale is as long as four buses placed end to end. The skeleton weighs 18 tons, its blubber 30, its meat 44. When it blows at the ocean's surface, the spout looks for all the world like a new cloud in the sky.
>     —Jacques-Yves Cousteau and Yves Paccalet, *The Assault on Whales*

## Definition

Depending on your audience, or sometimes your subject, you may need to **define** key words in your composition. Sometimes this can be done in a sentence or two, or even parenthetically. Occasionally you may want to provide an extended definition (as in the example that follows). To define a term, first place it in a class of similar items and then show how it is different from the others in that class. For example, a *wrist watch* is in the class of *devices for telling time* and differs from other items in this class because it is relatively small and *worn on the wrist.*

> A cough is a reflexive action that clears the airways of mucus, phlegm, or other blockages. There are two types of coughs, productive and dry. The productive cough, producing phlegm, unblocks the airways, while the dry cough, usually caused by a viral infection, irritates the nasal passages. Medication is often the only way to relieve a dry cough, while medication for a productive cough should be avoided.

## Process analysis

There are two types of process analysis: *informational* and *instructional.* **Informational process analysis** explains how something works—how blood moves through the circulatory system or how tides occur. The following explanation of how champagne was first made and how it has been made ever since is informational.

The next time you find an excuse to break open a bottle of champagne—be it New Year's, a wedding, or a whim—you might raise your effervescent glass in solemn thanks to one blind Benedictine monk who made it all possible. Three centuries ago there lived in northern France a great blender of wines, Dom Perignon, who served as cellar-master at the Benedictine Abbey of Hautvillers for 47 years. For some reason that we may never know, this monk decided one day to seal his bottles with cork instead of the usual cloth soaked in oil. The carbon dioxide that is produced during fermentation could pass through the cloth, but was imprisoned by the new stopper. The result: a sparkling wine.

—Caroline Sutton, "How Did They Discover Champagne?"

**Instructional process analysis** gives directions on how to do something and usually follows a time pattern—first you do this and then you do this (see PARA 3a, Chronological order). Gladstone's paragraph is instructional, telling step-by-step how to build a good fireplace fire.

Though "experts" differ as to the best technique to follow when building a fire, one generally accepted method consists of first laying a generous amount of crumpled newspaper on the hearth between the andirons. Kindling wood is then spread generously over this layer of newspaper and one of the thickest logs is placed across the back of the andirons. This should be as close to the back of the fireplace as possible, but not quite touching it. A second log is then placed an inch or so in front of this, and a few additional sticks of kindling are laid across these two. A third log is then placed on top to form a sort of pyramid with air spaces between all logs so that flames can lick freely up between them.

—Bernard Gladstone, "How to Build a Fire in a Fireplace"

## Comparison and contrast

The purpose of any **comparison and contrast** is to make clear the superiority of one thing over another or explain something unfamiliar by comparing it to something familiar. A comparison-contrast follows one of two basic patterns: AA/BB or AB/AB. In the first pattern all the characteristics of A are presented, followed by all the characteristics of B. In the second pattern one characteristic of A is compared or contrasted with its counterpart in B, the next characteristic of A with its counterpart in B, and so on. Use the AA/BB pattern if you think the reader can remember all the points of A while reading about B; if not, the AB/AB pattern is probably a better choice.

In the following paragraph, the AA/BB pattern is used to compare career interruptions for women in the 1950s and the 1990s.

A study suggests that Canadian women in the 1990s marry, have children, and return to work with what women 30 years ago would have considered barely a short break. In the 1950s, only one percent of women in Canada went back to work within two years of having their first child. It was common for women to quit work for years to raise children. In the 1990s, 56 percent of new mothers returned to work within two years of having their first child. For most women, returning to work relatively quickly is simple economic necessity.

In her essay on communicating with family and friends, Goodman uses the AB/AB alternating pattern of development.

> Sometimes I think the telephone call is as earthbound as daily dialogue, while a letter is an exchange of gifts. On the telephone you talk; in a letter you tell. There is a pace to letter writing and reading that doesn't come from the telephone company but from our own inner rhythm.
> —Ellen Goodman, "Life in a Bundle of Letters"

## Analogy

An **analogy** is a special kind of comparison. It points out certain similarities between a difficult concept and another that is more familiar and concrete to enable the reader to understand the difficult one.

In the following paragraph, the game of hockey is described by using a war analogy.

> Ice hockey is war—war on skates, maybe, or war on ice—but war nevertheless. From the time the puck is dropped at centre ice, the troops on both sides flash up and down the ice in their colourful uniforms, eliminating each other from the play with crushing body checks and intricate manoeuvres with skate and stick. The forwards, the front line troops, pressure the defenders into conceding territory, into abandoning the puck, into surrendering that one good shot on goal that will lead to victory. The general stands calmly behind the bench, directing his old war horses and green recruits, calling for the rear guards to tighten the line, sending in reinforcements to hold the trenches. Make no mistake, hockey may be only a game, but the only goal is to defeat the enemy at the other end of the rink.

## Classification

To **classify** is to categorize, to group people, ideas, facts—anything—on the basis of some system. The *basis of classification* is an integral part of the process. In the following paragraph, Cleary, a student, places all stereo buyers into four categories on the basis of why they buy. (In subsequent paragraphs he discusses the four in detail.)

> As stereo equipment gets better and prices go down, stereo systems are becoming household necessities rather than luxuries. People are buying stereos by the thousands. During my year as a stereo salesman, I witnessed

this boom firsthand. I dealt with hundreds of customers, and it didn't take long for me to learn that people buy stereos for different reasons. Eventually, though, I was able to divide stereo buyers into four basic categories: the wattage buyer, the quality buyer, the price buyer, and the looks buyer.

—Gerald Cleary, student

## Cause and effect

A **cause-and-effect** paragraph shows the relationship between events. The focus may be on cause by indicating it in the topic sentence and following with its effects. Or the focus may be the other way around, with an effect given in the topic sentence followed by its causes.

The following paragraph on sleep begins with an effect, and follows with the reasons for it.

Why do students who get a good night's sleep before a test or exam seem to do better than those who regularly pull "all-nighters"? The reason probably involves the fact that your brain is hard at work while you're sleeping, even if you aren't. Studies conducted by the Better Sleep Council in the United States indicate that the brain may actually be more active when you are asleep than when you are awake. Deep sleep and dreaming are reported to be important to learning and memory—the brain seems to store information acquired during waking hours and to organize it while you sleep. Canadian studies indicate that "all-nighters" don't produce good results next day. So get a good night's sleep before your next exam—but don't forget to study.

## Mixed strategies

Often logic dictates that you use a combination of strategies to develop your topic sentence. In the paragraph that follows, Smith uses cause and effect, informational process analysis, statistics, and a hypothetical case in point (a kind of example) to develop her topic sentence, *They [cockroaches] reproduce at a truly amazing rate.*

Cockroaches give credence to the old adage that there is safety in numbers. They reproduce at a truly amazing rate. About two months after mating, a new generation of cockroaches is born. One cockroach can produce about two dozen offspring each time it mates. To get some idea of their reproductive power, imagine that you start with three pairs of cockroaches that mate. Approximately three weeks after mating the females lay their eggs, which hatch some 45 days later. If we assume two dozen eggs from each female, the first generation would number 72 offspring. These roaches would continue to multiply geometrically so that by year's end the colony's population would total more than 10 000 cockroaches. Stopping the process is almost impossible because even if we annihilate the adult population, a new generation still in egg form would be in the making.

—Courtney Smith, student

# PARA 3
## COHERENCE

When something *coheres* it fits together, it makes sense. **Coherence** in a paragraph is achieved when the sentences flow smoothly from one to another without awkward breaks in rhythm or meaning.

Coherence is achieved by arranging sentences in the most effective order, using transitional words and phrases, repeating key words and phrases, and using parallel structures. These techniques knit the sentences of a paragraph into a tight structure. Coherence is also a feature of the essay as a whole and is achieved by using transitions to link paragraphs. As originally written the following paragraph lacked coherence; it jumped from idea to idea. In the revision, coherence is achieved by (1) repositioning a sentence, (2) repeating a key phrase, and (3) adding a transition.

The term "badlands" is usually associated with that part of the western

United States commonly seen in cowboy movies, where the outlaw runs to

escape the pursuing posse. Canada *also* has its own badlands, mainly in south-

ern Alberta. This area is barren and deeply eroded, with little vegetation

and characterized by steep, rocky slopes and narrow, winding gullies. It is

thought that the French, the first explorers in the interior of North America,

gave the badlands its name by combining the French terms <u>terres</u> (lands) and

<u>mauvaises</u> (bad), a reflection of the barren landscape that they discovered.

The *barren* areas around Drumheller, Alberta, and Dinosaur Provincial Park in

southern Alberta are the best examples of badlands in this country.

## PARA 3a   Arrange sentences in the most effective order.

Basically, coherence in a paragraph comes from organizing the ideas and facts in a sensible pattern. Sentences in a paragraph are usually arranged according to one of three patterns: (1) a *chronological (time) order,* (2) a *spatial order,* or (3) a *logical order.* The most suitable arrangement depends on your purpose, subject, and audience. Whichever pattern you choose, follow it consistently and thoughtfully to knit the ideas and elements of your paragraph into a seamless whole that your readers can easily follow.

## Chronological order

**Chronological order,** or *time order*, presents events as they occurred. A personal story, a report on an automobile accident or historical event, and the steps in a process, for example, would naturally be told in chronological order. In the following paragraph Ming-Yee Wai uses chronological order to tell about a disturbing memory.

> I clearly remember my sixth birthday because Dad was in the hospital with pneumonia. He was working so hard he paid very little attention to his health. As a result, he spent almost the entire summer before I entered the first grade in the hospital. Mom visited him nightly. On my birthday I was allowed to see him. I have memories of sitting happily in the lobby of the hospital talking to the nurses, telling them with a big smile that I was going to see my dad because it was my birthday. I couldn't wait to see him because children under 12 were not allowed to visit patients, so I had not seen him in a long time. When I entered the hospital room, I saw tubes inserted into his nose and needles stuck in his arm. He was very, very thin. I was frightened and wanted to cry, but I was determined to have a good visit. So I stayed for a while, and he wished me a happy birthday. When it was time to go, I kissed him good-bye and waited until I left his room to cry.
>
> —Grace Ming-Yee Wai, "Chinese Puzzle"

## Spatial order

**Spatial order** is used to describe a person, place, or thing. The writer begins at a particular point and moves methodically in one direction, say, from top to bottom, left to right, far to near, front to back, outside to inside, or, as in the following paragraph, from the perimeter of the yard toward its centre.

> My backyard, compared to others in the neighbourhood, wasn't large. It measured 70 metres in length and about 45 metres in width. In the winter, all of my mother's gardens, which lined our lot, were covered with snow. The old clothesline, where my mother hung our laundry to dry in the summer, stood at the back of the lot, unused and lonely. The only thing that was important to me in our backyard, right in the middle, was the tiny skating rink my father made for me and flooded every night. In my dreams, this rink was the first step toward the National Hockey League.

Logical order

A **logical** pattern of organization can take many forms, depending on the subject matter and the writer's purpose. In organizing a paragraph, it may be most logical to move from the easiest to understand aspects of the subject to the most difficult, from the least important examples to the most important, from the specific to the general or from the general to the specific, or from the least controversial elements to the most controversial, to name just a few possible patterns.

The following paragraph begins with a strong but general topic sentence; each sentence thereafter narrows the subject until the last zeros in on the writer's point.

> There is scarcely a corner of human affairs that Shakespeare doesn't touch upon, nor a topic for which he fails to supply a memorable quote. All of this has led, predictably, to every trade and profession claiming him for their own. There have been any number of attempts to prove that before he turned his hand to writing plays he was a lawyer, a soldier, a physician, an astronomer, a printer, a sportsman, a gardener, and heaven alone knows what else. And of all of these guesses as to what he did at Stratford before coming to his London career, one that seems nearest the mark is gardening. This does not mean, of course, that he would tramp off of a morning, spade and hoe slung over his shoulder like a pikeman's weapons, to delve in the soil of Lord So-and-so's gardens and orchards. What it does imply is that Shakespeare was a countryman long familiar with the growth of plants in woodlands, fields, and cottage and kitchen gardens. He may well have tended a garden of his own.
> —Frank J. Anderson, "Shakespeare in the Garden"

## PARA 3b  Use transitional words and phrases.

Transitional words and phrases connect units of thought—within a sentence, between sentences, and among paragraphs. In other words, **transitions** signal relationships, and thus can be categorized by their functions. In revising your composition (see COMP 4a), check that you use a transition everywhere one is needed to establish a logical connection between ideas, and that you use the correct transitional word. For example, do not use *also* (showing an addition) when you really want *similarly* (to compare two things), or *however* (showing contrast) when you really need *although* (to show concession).

The following list presents some of the more common transitional words and expressions categorized by meaning. (Some words are listed in more than one category because their meaning varies with context.)

ADDITION  and, again, too, also, in addition, further, furthermore, moreover, besides

CAUSE AND EFFECT  therefore, consequently, thus, accordingly, as a result, hence, then, so

CLARIFICATION  that is, in other words, in simpler terms, to put it differently, simply stated, partly, actually, in fact

COMPARISON  similarly, likewise, by comparison

CONCESSION  although, to be sure, granted, of course, it is true, to tell the truth, certainly, with the exception of, although this may be true, even though, naturally

CONTRAST  but, however, at the same time, in contrast, on the contrary, on the other hand, yet, nevertheless, after all, in spite of, conversely, still

EXAMPLE  for example, for instance, one case of

PLACE  elsewhere, here, above, below, farther on, there, beyond, nearby, opposite to, around

SEQUENCE  first, second, third NOT firstly, secondly, and so on, next, finally, following, then, in time

SUMMARY  in conclusion, to conclude, to summarize, in brief, in short

TIME  afterward, later, earlier, subsequently, at the same time, immediately, this time, until now, shortly, currently, lately, in the meantime

The transitional words and phrases in the following paragraph are italicized. To test how important they are in showing relationships among ideas in the paragraph, try omitting them or substituting others.

> Your only reason for starting your own business, *in the first place*, is to work for yourself and to make money. *In other words*, you are ambitious, desire a good income, and are eager to climb the ladder to success. Your success will depend on your goals, your skills, and your determination. *However*, your formula for success must be put into practice. *Therefore*, get started! *Later*, you'll be able to look back at this time in your life and realize that, *right now*, you've made a decision that has started you on the road to financial security and personal independence.

## PARA 3c  Repeat key words and phrases.

**Repetition** is another way of knitting together a paragraph. A sprinkling of key words and phrases improves coherence by keeping the main point in front of the reader in the most obvious way. The repeated key word is italicized.

Tears of hurt and frustration pricked at the corner of my eyes as the now-familiar pain seared my leg. I sat down and looked around the colour-less room: *beige* walls, *beige* ceiling, *beige* floor tiles. In one corner was a small cot with a *beige* bedspread, and in the opposite corner a sink, mirror, and *beige* waste basket. The shades were drawn and the lights were much dimmer than they had been in the hall. Gradually I relaxed and waited.

—Laura LaPierre, student

## PARA 3d  Use parallel structure.

**Parallel structure** is repetition of a certain kind; it is repetition in a series. Parallelism can occur on the word, phrase, clause, or whole-sentence level (see SENT 1a). In the following paragraph Ardrey's use of parallelism knits the sentences into a seamless whole; sentences one through four use one pattern of parallelism, and sentences five and six another. The parallel structures are italicized.

(1) *The male herring gull is a creature of sufficient* ingenuity that if he picks up a mussel with a shell too hard for his beak to break, he will carry it to a height and drop it on a hard rock. (2) *He is a creature of sufficient* loyalty and perception to guarantee that he will never attack his own mate, and will recognize her among dozens flying into the colony at a distance to defy human binoculars. (3) *He is a creature of sufficient* social sophistication that, while many arrive in the spring already paired, definite areas in the colony which Tinbergen calls "clubs" will be set aside as meeting places for the unpaired. (4) *He is a creature* also, as we have seen, of such sensitive social adjustment that the arriving flock will make "decisions" of mood and readiness as if it were one being. (5) *So dependent is the herring gull* on the community of his citizenship that he would probably be unable to breed were he to return in the spring to the wrong gull town. (6) *So powerful and incomprehensible is his attachment* for home that, like the albatross, a pair may return year after year to nest in precisely the same spot, although the North Sea's winter storms will have effaced all landmarks to guide his eye.

—Robert Ardrey, "Herring Gull"

## PARA 3e  Use transitions to link paragraphs.

Just as transitions are used to link sentences within a paragraph, so are they used to link paragraphs themselves. Because each new paragraph indicates a further progression of thought in the composition, transitions help the reader follow along. In the passage that follows, transitions are used to link the first and second paragraphs and the second and third paragraphs; the transitions are italicized.

The age of television began in Canada in 1952, five years behind the United States, when a station in Montreal, and one in Toronto two days later, signed onto the Canadian Broadcasting Corporation. A third station in Vancouver went on the air three days later.

*However,* television broadcasting in the 1950s was a far cry from what it is today. Shows were in black and white (Canada didn't begin colour broadcasting until 1966), they were broadcast live and, as you might suspect, there were more than a few bugs to work out of the system.

*Currently,* television is a staple of Canadian life. Ninety-nine percent of Canadian households have at least one television set, and Canada's longest running show, *Hockey Night in Canada,* has been on the air over 40 years.

 C-Tip

## *Testing for transitional words*

Test the coherence of your composition by boldfacing or underlining the transitional words and phrases. If you have only a few, strengthen the connections between your thoughts by adding transitions, both within paragraphs and between them.

# GRAM

## Grammar Essentials

### *Learning Objectives*

After reading this section you should

1. be able to identify the parts of speech in a sentence,
2. be able to identify the subject and predicate of a sentence,
3. recognize different kinds of phrases and clauses,
4. be able to classify sentences by structure or purpose.

# GRAM

## Grammar Essentials

Studying grammar will help you to write better in two ways. First, because there is never just one way to write a sentence, but many ways to present the same thought, knowing the parts of speech and how they function in sentences gives you the power to write exactly what you mean. Second, if you understand how words function in sentences, you are better able to identify why a sentence is confused, awkward, or not as clear as you had hoped. Studying grammar, then, allows you to look at sentences in a new light, both when you compose and when you revise.

# GRAM 1 
## PARTS OF SPEECH

Because English has more than 600 000 words, we group them in categories that share common characteristics in order to make it easier to talk about language. In grammar, these groupings are called **parts of speech**. English has eight parts of speech: *verbs* (V), *nouns* (N), *pronouns* (PRO), *adjectives* (ADJ), *adverbs* (ADV), *prepositions* (PREP), *conjunctions* (CONJ), and *interjections* (INTJ). A word may be a member of more than one category, however, depending on its use in a particular sentence.

ADJ
She had a *sound* plan.

N
They sailed across the *sound*.

V
The driver will *sound* the car's horn.

## GRAM 1a    Verbs

A **verb** (V) expresses action (*run, think*) or a state of being (*is, become, seem*). A complete verb is composed of the **main verb** (MV) itself and any **helping verbs** (HV) that may be used with it. The most commonly used helping (auxiliary) verbs are the nine **modals**: *may, might, shall, will, would, must, should, can, could.* Modals express how the writer feels about an action. Modals express probability, necessity or obligation, or ability (see ESL 1a).

HV MV
He *may wash* the dishes.   [probability]

HV MV
He *should wash* the dishes.   [obligation]

HV MV
He *can wash* the dishes.   [ability]

Other helping verbs include the forms of *have, be, do, used to,* and *ought to.*

HV MV
He *is washing* the dishes.

HV MV
He *did wash* the dishes.

HV MV
He *used to wash* the dishes.

## Forms of verbs

All verbs have five forms, with the exception of *be,* which has eight forms. The first three of the five verb forms are called the *principal parts of a verb.*

| | | | |
|---|---|---|---|
| 1. | BASE FORM OR INFINITIVE | *(to) talk/write* | *(to) be* |
| 2. | PAST TENSE | I *talked/wrote* | *was, were* |
| 3. | PAST PARTICIPLE | I *have talked/written* | *been* |
| 4. | -s FORM OR PRESENT TENSE | *He/she/it talks/writes* | *am, is, are* |
| 5. | PRESENT PARTICIPLE | I *am talking/writing* | *being* |

The infinitive is made up of *to* and the base form (*to see, to believe*).

Most verbs in English are **regular** (*talk, talked, talked*), but a few are **irregular** (*write, wrote, written*). (See EDIT 2a.)

## Intransitive, transitive, and linking verbs

A verb can be *intransitive, transitive,* or *linking,* depending on whether it takes an object or complement and, if so, what kind (see GRAM 2c and 2d).

An **intransitive verb** has a **subject** (S) but does not require an object or complement to complete its meaning.

S V
Nobody *cares.*

A **transitive verb**, as its name indicates, transfers its action from the subject to the object of the sentence. Transitive verbs always take a **direct object** (DO) and sometimes an **indirect object** (IO) to complete their meaning.

S     V         DO

The waves *lashed* the shore.

S     V      IO    DO

Maria *gave* her mother flowers.

A **linking verb** (LV) connects the **subject** to a **predicate noun** (PN), which renames the subject, or a **predicate adjective** (PA), which describes the subject.

S     LV   PN

My brother *is* a writer.

S    LV PA

The grapefruit *is* sour.

## Common linking verbs

be (is, am, are, was, were)
act
appear
become
grow
look
seem
feel
taste

## Verbals

Sometimes a verb does not function as a verb in a sentence. In this case, it is called a **verbal**. There are three types of verbals: *gerunds, participles* (both past and present), and *infinitives*. Verbals are usually used in phrases (see GRAM 3b).

**GERUND**

N

*Swimming* is my favourite sport.

**PRESENT PARTICIPLE**
ADJ
*Swimming* out to the raft, he got a cramp.

**PAST PARTICIPLE**
ADJ
His *cramped* leg still aches.

**INFINITIVE**
N
Ali is learning *to swim.*

## GRAM 1b    Nouns

A **noun** (N) is the name of a person, place, thing, quality, action, or idea.

George, Brazil, chair, beauty, flight, mercy

Most nouns are made plural or possessive or both by *inflections*, or changes in form.

| SINGULAR | PLURAL | SINGULAR POSSESSIVE | PLURAL POSSESSIVE |
|---|---|---|---|
| boy | boys | boy's | boys' |
| woman | women | woman's | women's |
| tennis | — | tennis's | — |
| society | societies | society's | societies' |
| Regina | — | Regina's | — |

Nouns can be divided into the following subclasses.

**Proper nouns** name specific people, places, and things and they are capitalized (see MECH 1a).

Mary Cameron, South Africa, CN Tower

**Common nouns** name all items that are not proper nouns.

dog, paper, stoves

**Abstract nouns** name ideas, qualities, and other intangibles (see WORD 1c).

fear, freedom, neglect

**Concrete nouns** name tangible items (see WORD 1c). We know concrete nouns through the five senses (sight, hearing, touch, taste, and smell).

bottle, telephone, letters

**Collective nouns** name groups. If a collective noun refers to the group as a whole, it takes a singular verb. If it refers to the individual members of that group, it takes a plural verb. (See EDIT 1d.)

army, communities, herd

**Count nouns** name items that can be counted. Count nouns are frequently accompanied by an adjective indicating how many are referred to.

one dollar, eight pills, a half-dozen sandwiches

**Noncount nouns** name items that come in quantities that are not capable of being counted (see ESL 2a). Most of these nouns fall into certain categories.

*Food:* butter, flour, milk, sugar
*Nonfood bulk materials:* asphalt, gold, oxygen, snow
*Abstractions:* anger, love, pity, stress

## GRAM 1c   Pronouns

A **pronoun** (PRO) is a word that takes the place of a noun in a sentence. Although there are vast numbers of nouns in English, there are considerably fewer pronouns. The noun that a pronoun replaces is called its **antecedent** (see EDIT 3a and 3b). Pronouns are divided into the following groups.

**Personal pronouns** refer to specific persons, places, or things. The **case** of a personal pronoun refers to its function in a sentence (see EDIT 3c).

*Singular:* I, me, you, he, she, him, her, it
*Plural:* you, we, they, them, us

**Possessive pronouns** show ownership by persons, places, or things.

*Singular:* my, mine, your, yours, his, her, hers, its
*Plural:* our, ours, your, yours, their, theirs

**Demonstrative pronouns** point out the nouns that they replace.

this, that, these, those

**Indefinite pronouns** refer to nonspecific persons or things (see EDIT 1f).

all, any, anybody, anyone, anything, both, everybody, everyone, everything, few, many, no one, nothing, somebody, someone, something, several, some

**Interrogative pronouns** introduce questions.

who(ever), whom(ever), whose, which(ever), what(ever)

**Relative pronouns** join a dependent clause to a noun.

who(ever), whom(ever), whose, which, that

**Intensive** and **reflexive pronouns** consist of a personal pronoun plus *-self* or *-selves.* An intensive pronoun refers back to a noun or another pronoun for emphasis (I did it *myself*); a reflexive pronoun refers back to the subject for emphasis or to complete the meaning (I washed *myself*).

*Singular:* myself, yourself, himself, herself, itself
*Plural:* ourselves, yourselves, themselves

## GRAM 1d    Adjectives and articles

An **adjective** (ADJ) is a word that modifies or qualifies a noun or pronoun. An adjective tells what kind, how many, or which one.

N
*brass* trombones    [what kind]

N
*seventy-six* trombones    [how many]

PRO
*the older* one    [which one]

Adjectives change form when *-er* or *-est* is added or when they are preceded by *more* or *most* to form the comparative and superlative (see EDIT 4e).

| POSITIVE | COMPARATIVE | SUPERLATIVE |
|---|---|---|
| silly | sillier | silliest |
| powerful | more powerful | most powerful |

**Articles** are considered to be adjectives. There are two types of articles: **definite** (*the*) and **indefinite** (*a, an*).

You can send *the* parcel by Canada Post.

The signing of *the* Proclamation of 1763 was *a* historical event.

See WORD 7 for additional use of articles.

## GRAM 1e    Adverbs

An **adverb** (ADV) modifies a verb, an adjective, or another adverb. Adverbs tell where, when, how, why, under what circumstances, and to what extent.

He drove *nearby*.    [where]

He drove *yesterday*.    [when]

He drove *carefully*.    [how]

He drove *because* he had to.    [why]

He drove *while* tired.    [under what circumstances]

He drove *quite* carefully.    [to what extent]

Adverbs are frequently made from adjectives by adding *-ly* (*roughly, quickly*), but not all adverbs end in *-ly* (*first, not, very*). Like adjectives, adverbs can also signify degrees of comparison (*-er/-est, more/less,* and *most/least*). (See EDIT 4e.)

| POSITIVE | COMPARATIVE | SUPERLATIVE |
|---|---|---|
| near | nearer | nearest |
| frequently | more frequently | most frequently |

Adverbs of frequency

| | | |
|---|---|---|
| never | often | sometimes |
| seldom | always | even |

Adverbs of degree

| | | |
|---|---|---|
| even | extremely | more |
| just | much | quite |
| only | surely | too |
| very | | |

## GRAM 1f    Prepositions

A **preposition** (PREP) comes before a noun or pronoun to create a phrase that modifies another word in the sentence. The noun or the pronoun is called the **object of the preposition** (OP), and the phrase that is created is called a **prepositional phrase**. Prepositions show relationships between objects and ideas in a sentence (see GRAM 3a).

            PREP OP
She spilled the drink *on him*.    [*On him* is the prepositional phrase.]

Here is a list of the most common prepositions.

| | | | |
|---|---|---|---|
| about | beside | near | than |
| above | between | next | through |
| across | but | of | till |
| after | by | off | to |
| along | concerning | on | toward |
| among | considering | opposite | under |
| around | despite | out | underneath |
| as | down | over | unlike |
| at | during | past | until |
| before | except | respecting | upon |
| behind | for | round | with |
| below | in | since | without |

## GRAM 1g    Conjunctions

A **conjunction** (CONJ), like a preposition, shows the relationship between parts of a sentence. There are four kinds of conjunctions: *coordinating, subordinating, correlative,* and *conjunctive adverbs*.

A **coordinating conjunction** connects words, phrases, and clauses of equal rank.

| | | | |
|---|---|---|---|
| and | for | or | yet |
| but | nor | so | |

Leslie *and* Hal caught three rock bass, *but* they didn't get any lake trout *or* pike.

A **subordinating conjunction** introduces a subordinate clause (SC) and connects it to a main clause (MC). (See GRAM 4.)

| | | | |
|---|---|---|---|
| after | before | so | when |
| although | even if | than | where |
| as | if | that | whereas |
| as if | in order that | though | wherever |
| as though | rather than | unless | whether |
| because | since | until | while |

    SC         MC           SC

*Unless* we hurry, we won't arrive *before* the concert starts.

**Correlative conjunctions** work in pairs to connect words, phrases, clauses, and whole sentences.

| | | |
|---|---|---|
| both/and | neither/nor | not only/but also |
| either/or | not/but | whether/or |

We will be *neither* swayed *nor* delayed in our deliberations.

**Conjunctive adverbs** can function in two ways. First, they can serve as transitional expressions to connect units of thought (see PARA 3b and PUNCT 1f).

*Meanwhile,* Todd was home making Lisa's favourite dinner.

[*Meanwhile* connects Todd's actions to the previous statement.]

Conjunctive adverbs can also link main clauses (MC) (see PUNCT 2b).

MC

Lisa thought she'd surprise Todd by picking up a pizza for dinner;

MC

*meanwhile,* Todd was home making her favourite—fried chicken.

Here is a list of common conjunctive adverbs.

| | | | |
|---|---|---|---|
| accordingly | finally | likewise | specifically |
| also | furthermore | meanwhile | still |
| anyway | hence | moreover | then |
| besides | however | nevertheless | thereafter |
| certainly | incidentally | now | therefore |
| consequently | indeed | otherwise | thus |
| conversely | instead | similarly | undoubtedly |

## GRAM 1h    Interjections

An **interjection** (INTJ) is a word or phrase used to express emotion or attract attention. Interjections are independent units not grammatically connected to a sentence, and they are always followed by an exclamation point (see PUNCT 6c) or a comma (see PUNCT 1i).

*Hey*! There's a parade coming.

*Oh well,* maybe we can do better next time.

# GRAM 2

## PARTS OF SENTENCES

A **sentence** is a group of words expressing a complete thought. A sentence has two basic parts, a *subject* (S) and a *predicate* (P). The predicate includes the *verb* (V), *direct object* (DO), *indirect object* (IO), *predicate noun* (PN), *predicate adjective* (PA), and *object complement* (OC).

Most English sentences follow one of these six patterns:

```
        P
  S  | V |
Speed kills.
```

```
        P
  S  | V   DO |
Birds eat berries.
```

```
            P
  S  | V   IO   DO |
Dad wrote me a letter.
```

```
          P
  S  | V    PN      |
She is a firefighter.
```

```
           P
  S  | V  PA |
The soldier is brave.
```

```
            P
  S  | V   DO OC|
The movie made us sad.
```

## GRAM 2a    Subjects

The **subject** (S) of a sentence is the person or thing the sentence is about.

*Fear* eroded our confidence.

The **simple subject** is the noun or pronoun alone.

A *Camaro* is my first choice.

The **complete subject** is the simple subject and all words associated with it.

A *teal green Camaro with leather interior* is my first choice.

A **compound subject** is made up of two or more simple subjects.

*Sticks and stones* broke his bones.

## GRAM 2b  Predicates

The **simple predicate** of a sentence is made up of the verb and any helping verbs (see GRAM 1a).

The ship *was turning* in the harbour.

The **complete predicate** of a sentence is the simple predicate and its modifiers and complements.

The ship *was turning in the harbour*.

The **compound predicate** is made up of two or more predicates that have the same subject.

Canada's national symbols *are the maple leaf and the beaver.*

## GRAM 2c  Objects

A **direct object** (DO) is the noun, pronoun, or verbal (see GRAM 1a) that receives the action of the verb.

He kissed *her*.

An **indirect object** (IO) is the noun, pronoun, or verbal that tells *to* whom or *for* whom something is done.

The coach gave *Melissa* another chance.

To test whether a word is a direct or indirect object, insert *to* or *for* into the sentence. If the sentence makes sense, the word is an indirect object.

The coach gave another chance *to Melissa*.

## GRAM 2d  Complements

A **complement** is a word or word group that completes the sense of a verb and adds to the meaning of a subject. There are two types of complements: subject complements and object complements.

A **subject complement** (SC) is a noun which renames the subject (predicate noun) or an adjective which describes the subject (predicate adjective), and is used in a sentence with a linking verb (see GRAM 1a).

|  |  |
|---|---|
| **Predicate noun** | She is a *doctor*. |
| **Predicate adjective** | The Lake Superior region is *rugged*. |

An **object complement** (OC) is an adjective in the predicate of a sentence which follows the direct object of a sentence and describes or renames the direct object.

**Object complement**    I consider *Roberta Bondar* to be a *hero* for our time.

# GRAM 3 _____
## PHRASES

The phrase is the most common word group we use in writing. A **phrase**, unlike a clause, does not have a subject and a predicate. A phrase is used as a single part of speech; that is, as a noun, a verb, an adjective, or an adverb. There are four kinds of phrases: *prepositional, verbal* (including gerund, participle, and infinitive phrases), *appositive*, and *absolute*.

## GRAM 3a  Prepositional phrases

A **prepositional phrase** consists of a preposition (a word such as *to, with, after, on, in, by,* or *between*) and its object, which is always a noun or pronoun. In sentences prepositional phrases usually function as adjectives or adverbs, but in some instances they can function as nouns.

ADJ

The chapter *on photosynthesis* is fully illustrated.

ADV

Many Canadians go to Florida *in the winter.*

N

*After two o'clock* would be most convenient for me.

## GRAM 3b    Verbal phrases

When a verb does not function as a verb in a sentence, it is called a verbal (see GRAM 1a). Verbals are usually used in phrases. There are three kinds of verbal phrases: *gerund, participial,* and *infinitive.*

A **gerund phrase** consists of an *-ing* form of a verb *(brewing, flying, joking, studying)* with any modifier(s) and/or object(s). A gerund phrase always functions as a noun in a sentence. It can, therefore, serve as a subject, a predicate noun, a direct object, an indirect object, or an object of a preposition in a sentence.

S

*All this fancy cooking* takes time.

PN

Chan's main recreation is *lifting weights.*

OP

I believe in *telling the truth.*

A **participial phrase** consists of a present participle (*-ing* form of a verb) or past participle (*-ed* form of a verb) with its auxiliary, modifier(s), object(s), and complement(s). A participial phrase always functions as an adjective in a sentence.

ADJ

The girl *riding the mountain bike* is my cousin.

ADJ

*Having finished his work for the day,* the carpenter went home.

An **infinitive phrase** consists of the word *to* and the base form of the verb *(stop, attempt, march, liberate)* with its modifier(s) and object(s), if any. An infinitive phrase can function as an adjective, an adverb, or a noun in a sentence.

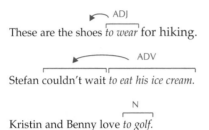

These are the shoes *to wear* for hiking.

Stefan couldn't wait *to eat his ice cream.*

Kristin and Benny love *to golf.*

## GRAM 3c   Appositive phrases

An *appositive* is a noun or noun equivalent. An **appositive phrase** is a noun or noun equivalent, together with any modifier(s), that directly follows (or precedes) another noun or noun equivalent. Unlike an adjective, which modifies a noun or noun equivalent, an appositive phrase identifies or explains. Most appositive phrases contain non-essential or parenthetical information and are, therefore, set off by commas.

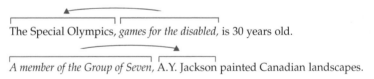

The Special Olympics, *games for the disabled,* is 30 years old.

*A member of the Group of Seven,* A.Y. Jackson painted Canadian landscapes.

## GRAM 3d   Absolute phrases

An **absolute phrase** is a noun or noun equivalent, followed in most cases by a participial phrase. An absolute phrase modifies a clause or sentence, not just a word as all other types of phrases do.

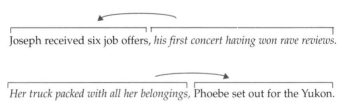

Joseph received six job offers, *his first concert having won rave reviews.*

*Her truck packed with all her belongings,* Phoebe set out for the Yukon.

# GRAM 4

## CLAUSES

A **clause** is a group of words that contains a subject and a predicate. A **main clause**, or **independent clause**, can stand alone as a complete sentence.

Jane bought Ted's old Volkswagen.

It had a good engine but a rusted body.

A **subordinate clause**, or **dependent clause**, in contrast, cannot stand alone as a sentence because it is an incomplete thought.

*When I cook*, I use a lot of garlic.

*If you don't like garlic*, you can substitute onions.

## GRAM 4a    Adjective clauses

An **adjective clause** (also called a **relative clause**) modifies a noun or pronoun. Usually it immediately follows the word or words modified and is introduced by a relative pronoun—*who, whom, whose, which, that, whoever, whomever,* or *whatever* (see GRAM 1c)—or by the subordinating conjunction *when* or *where* (see GRAM 1g).

Ted's old Volkswagen, *which had a badly rusted body,* still ran like a dream.

My grandmother remembers a time *when Volkswagens were not on the market.*

If the relative pronoun or subordinating conjunction (the subordinator) introducing an adjective clause does not function as the subject of the subordinate clause, you can omit it. In fact, omitting it picks up the pace of the sentence.

The Volkswagen ~~that~~ Jane saw at the car show was completely restored.

If the subordinator is the subject of the adjective clause, you can usually rewrite the sentence to eliminate unneeded words.

marble
A statue of Louis Riel, ~~which is made of marble,~~ is in front of City Hall.

## GRAM 4b    Adverb clauses

An **adverb clause** modifies a verb, an adjective, or an adverb. It is always introduced by a subordinating conjunction, such as *if, after, when, though, since, where, while* (see GRAM 1g). An adverb clause answers the questions posed by the words *when, where, why,* or *how.*

The children looked for coins under the bleachers *after the game was over.*

## GRAM 4c    Noun clauses

A **noun clause** can function in the same way that a noun does—as a subject, a predicate adjective, a predicate noun, a direct or an indirect object, an object complement, an object of a preposition, or an appositive (A) (see GRAM 1b). A relative pronoun *(who, whom, whose, which, that, whoever, whomever, whatever)* usually introduces a noun clause.

S
*Whoever said so* must be telling the truth.

DO
No one knows *what his name is.*

PN
One condition of Guido's employment was *that he shave off his beard.*

A
The news *that both sides had called a ceasefire* took everyone by surprise.

# GRAM 5 _____
## TYPES OF SENTENCES

Sentences can be classified by the kinds of clauses they contain (grammatically) or by their purpose (rhetorically). Becoming aware of this allows you to vary your writing style to suit your audience, content, and purpose. You will find, too, that sentence variety holds the reader's interest. How boring it is to read all simple sentences! In contrast, after many longer sentences, a short, punchy one adds force to a key point.

## GRAM 5a  Classification by clause structure

### Simple sentences

A **simple sentence** consists of one main clause and no subordinate clauses.

> Reading and writing are the primary goals of early education.

A simple sentence is not necessarily short, however, because the subject or the predicate—or both—may be compound or have many modifiers. The following example consists of one main clause; the subject is *The Order of Canada* and the verb is *is.* The rest of the sentence is made up of details.

> The Order of Canada, an award instituted on July 1, 1967, to honour Canadians for outstanding achievement and service to their country and humanity at large, is often given to Canadians in the fields of the arts, sciences, or politics.

### Compound sentences

A **compound sentence** consists of two or more main clauses and no subordinate clauses. The main clauses may be joined by a coordinating conjunction (*and, but, or, for, nor, so,* or *yet*) and a comma; by a semicolon; by a semicolon and a transitional word (*however, nevertheless, therefore*); or by a correlative conjunction such as *either/or, both/and.*

MC
The Supreme Court of Canada is this country's highest court of law, but

MC
there are other courts of law in the Canadian judicial system.

### Complex sentences

A **complex sentence** consists of one main clause and one or more subordinate clauses.

SC                                          MC
If you take a trip to Quebec, I suggest you visit the Eastern Townships.

## Compound-complex sentences

A **compound-complex sentence** consists of two or more main clauses and at least one subordinate clause.

$$\overset{\text{SC}}{\overbrace{\text{Even though many cities and towns along the river were prepared,}}} \overbrace{\text{the flood}}$$

$$\overset{\text{MC}}{\overbrace{\text{waters were devastating,}}} \text{and } \overset{\text{MC}}{\overbrace{\text{many lives were lost.}}}$$

## GRAM 5b   Classification by purpose

A **declarative sentence** makes a statement. In expository prose, most sentences are declarative. An **interrogative sentence** asks a question. It customarily ends with a question mark. An **imperative sentence** gives a command, makes a request, or offers advice. Usually *you* is the understood subject. An **exclamatory sentence** indicates intense emotion or excitement and ends with an exclamation point. Sometimes exclamations are not complete sentences.

| | |
|---|---|
| DECLARATIVE | Sumiko bought new running shoes. |
| INTERROGATIVE | Did Bharati get a job as a lifeguard? |
| IMPERATIVE | Please pass the salt and pepper. |
| EXCLAMATORY | What a movie! |

# ESL

## ESL Basics

### *Learning Objectives*

After reading this section, you should

1. have greater mastery of auxiliary verbs,
2. better understand the use of nouns, quantifiers, articles, adjectives, and adverbs,
3. have greater mastery of prepositional phrases,
4. be more proficient in using word groups and writing different kinds of sentences in English.

# ESL

## ESL Basics

Mastering a language, whether it is your own or a second language, is an ongoing process. This chapter is designed to help students of English as a second language (ESL) with the most frequent problems in writing grammatically correct, idiomatic English.

# ESL 1 _____
## VERBS

Verb constructions formed with helping verbs (auxiliaries) can be troublesome for people whose first language is not English. This section provides additional information about these verb forms. (See GRAM 1a for more about verbs.)

## ESL 1a    Use modal auxiliaries correctly.

**Modals** (M) are verbs that are used with a main verb (MV) to suggest various judgments by the writer or speaker about the action of the main verb. (See GRAM 1a for more about modals.)

M    MV
You *should* see a doctor.

[The modal *should* expresses the writer's feeling that the action is necessary or urgent.]

Modals express the following ideas about an action or event:

PROBABILITY OR LIKELIHOOD    may, might, would, should, could

NECESSITY OR OBLIGATION    must, should

ABILITY    can, could

Follow these six rules for writing verb phrases with modals.

### 1.  Use the base form of the main verb after modals that express ideas about the present or the future.

The modals *can, could, may, might, must, should,* and *will* can be used with the base form of the verb to write about the present or the future. [*Will* expresses the most certainty of a future event, and *might* expresses the least.]

swim                                    compete
Marc can ~~swimming~~ very well. He should ~~competes~~.

**2. Do not omit *shall* or *will* to express the future, even in sentences with adverbs that indicate future time.**

The coach <sub>∧</sub> phone Bob soon. I am sure he <sub>∧</sub> get to play first base this year.
> *will* ... *will*

You can also use *going to* or the present progressive to express the future (see EDIT 2c).

**3. Use only one modal with each main verb.**

The following sentence expresses two ideas that are normally suggested by modals. However, the expression *be able to* must substitute for the modal *can*.

I might ~~can~~ join the swimming team this year.
> *be able to*

The following phrases can be used with modals. Their meanings are similar to modals.

| | |
|---|---|
| *have to* | They may *have to* leave early. |
| *be obliged to* | He might *be obliged to* pay that bill. |
| *be able to* | I will *be able to* get to the theatre by 8 p.m. |

**4. Use *could, was able to, had to,* and *was obliged to* plus the base form of the main verb to write about the past.**

Two years ago he ~~cannot~~ read.
> *could not*

**5. Use *would* plus the base form of the main verb to write about a habitual action in the past.**

When I was a child, I ~~will~~ always try to go barefoot in summer.
> *would*

See ESL 6d for how to use *would* and *might* in reported speech.

**6. When the modal is followed by a main verb in the perfect or progressive tense, use the base form of the auxiliaries *have* or *be*.**

Laila should not ~~had~~ quit school. She must ~~is~~ looking for a job now.
> *have* ... *be*

## ESL 1b    Form the perfect tenses correctly.

The **perfect tenses** in English are useful for talking about two moments or periods of time in the same sentence. The perfect tenses are created by combining a form of *have* with the past participle of the main verb. (See EDIT 2c for more information about perfect tenses.)

PRESENT PERFECT    Use present perfect or talk about an action that was begun in the past and continues into the present, or to talk about an action that was completed in the past but still affects the present.

Luis and Lupe *have lived* here for 10 years.    [They still do.]

SIMPLE PAST

Luis and Lupe *lived* here for 10 years.    [They don't any more.]

PAST PERFECT    Use past perfect to talk about one past action that occurred *before* another past action.

We already *had started* dinner when the Smiths arrived.

[We started before they arrived.])

SIMPLE PAST

We *started* dinner when the Smiths arrived.

[First they arrived, then we started.]

FUTURE PERFECT    Use future perfect to talk about one future action that will occur before another future action.

All the snow *will have melted* by April.

[The focus is on the process of the melting and the sentence encompasses all the time between now and April.]

SIMPLE FUTURE

All the snow *will melt* by April.

[The focus is on the completion of the melting in the future.]

Sometimes, as in the present perfect example above, the difference in meaning is clear. Often, however, there is no difference at all or the difference is very slight. When you're not sure which tense is correct, ask a native English speaker for an opinion.

## ESL 1c  Form and use the progressive tenses correctly.

The **progressive tenses** usually refer to action that is in progress. The present progressive is also useful for speaking about the future and referring to temporary conditions. Progressive tenses use a form of the auxiliary verb *be* (*am, is, are, was, were, being, be,* or *been*) plus the present participle of the main verb. (See EDIT 2c for more information about progressive tenses.)

**PRESENT PROGRESSIVE**

Haroon *is building* a new house.   [action in progress]

Arletha's parents *are moving* to California next year.   [future action]

I *am riding* the bus this week while the mechanic fixes my car.   [temporary condition]

**PAST PROGRESSIVE**

Sheila *was washing* her hair at midnight.

**FUTURE PROGRESSIVE**

We *will be travelling* to Alberta soon.

The following four points will help you form the progressive tenses correctly.

1. **Use a form of *be* with the progressive.**

   is
   Yu Wen working in the lab all afternoon today.

   are
   Several of us working on the same project.

2. **Make sure the auxiliary verb *be* agrees with its subject.**

   were
   The librarians was helping Uma find books for her report.

   is
   The number of work-study scholarships are increasing.

(Review subject–verb agreement in EDIT 1.)

## 3. Use the auxiliary verb *have* in the present perfect progressive.

<u>has</u>
Ari been cooking all day for the party.

<u>have</u>
Elliot and Craig been restoring an old Chevy on weekends.

## 4. Learn which verbs are usually not used in the progressive.

Certain verbs are *typically* (although there are exceptions) not used in the progressive tenses. These verbs fall into the following categories:

LINKING VERBS AND VERBS THAT INDICATE QUALITIES OR STATES OF BEING   appear, be, become, have, seem

<u>seemed</u>
Cheng ~~was seeming~~ sick all morning.

VERBS THAT SHOW INTELLECTUAL STATES, EMOTIONS, OR ATTITUDES believe, disagree, dislike, hate, imagine, intend, know, like, pity, prefer, realize, suppose, think, understand, want, wish, wonder

<u>know</u>
I ~~am knowing~~ those formulas perfectly.

VERBS THAT SHOW SENSE PERCEPTIONS   feel, hear, see, smell, taste

<u>smells</u>
The milk ~~is smelling~~ sour.

## ESL 1d   Form the passive voice correctly.

The **passive voice** of a verb (V) consists of a form of *be* (*am, is, are, was, were, being, be,* or *been*) plus the past participle of the main verb. In a sentence in the passive voice, the subject (S) *receives* the action; it does not *do* the action. (Read about the passive voice in SENT 3d and 6c, EDIT 2f, and WORD 4e.)

S ⤶ ⌐ V
Diamonds and gold *are mined* in South Africa.

Keep the next three points in mind to form the passive voice correctly.

## 1. Use the past participle, not the base form or past tense, to form the passive voice.

Pay particular attention to past participles of irregular verbs (see EDIT 2a).

> manufactured
> Many electronic parts are ~~manufacture~~ in Southeast Asia.

> worn                                         given
> Clothing was ~~wore~~ by all three children and then ~~gave~~ to the church.

## 2. Identify the subject and make sure the auxiliary verb *be* agrees with it.

> were
> Coffee and dessert ~~was~~ *served* at the poetry reading.

## 3. Use only transitive verbs in the passive voice.

A **transitive verb**, unlike an **intransitive** one, always takes a direct object (DO). (Review transitive and intransitive verbs in GRAM 1a.)

**TRANSITIVE**

> S        V        DO
> The plumber *fixed* the sink.

[The direct object, *sink,* receives the action of the verb *fixed.*]

In the passive voice, the object of the action becomes the grammatical subject of the sentence.

> S        V
> The sink *was fixed* by the plumber.

**INTRANSITIVE**

> V
> Sylvia *seems* forgetful lately.

[The verb *seems* has no direct object. *Forgetful* is a predicate adjective that describes the subject, *Sylvia.*]

Since intransitive verbs have no direct object, you cannot form the passive voice with them. If you are not sure whether a verb is transitive, check your dictionary.

## ESL 1e    Use two-word verbs correctly.

**Two-word verbs** consist of a main verb plus a particle (a preposition or adverb). Note that the particle changes a verb's meaning completely.

let down    [disappoint]

let out    [free]

These combinations of verb + particle are **idiomatic**; that is, the separate meanings of the verb and the particle do not predict their meaning when they are combined into a two-word verb. (See WORD 1d.)

Like other verbs, two-word verbs may be either transitive or intransitive.

TRANSITIVE    come across [find], let down [disappoint], tell off [rebuke]

INTRANSITIVE    catch on [understand], crop up [occur], give in [yield]

Transitive two-word verbs are either **inseparable** or **separable**. The verb and particle of inseparable two-word verbs are never separated by the direct object. However, the verb and particle of separable two-word verbs are sometimes separated by the direct object. You cannot tell which two-word verbs are inseparable and which are separable except by noting how a writer handles the object of these verbs. You must, therefore, note this distinction when you learn each new two-word verb.

Follow these four rules in placing the direct object of transitive two-word verbs.

**1.  Do not separate the verb and particle of inseparable two-word verbs. Place the noun or pronoun after the particle.**

DO

Lucy does not *take after* her older sister.

DO

Lucy does not *take after* her.

**2.  When the object of a *separable* two-word verb is a noun, place it either between the main verb and the particle or after the particle.**

DO

We *turned* the offer *down*.

DO

We *turned down* the offer.

**3. When the object of a separable two-word verb is a pronoun, place the object only between the verb and the particle.**

DO

We *turned* it *down* because it came too late.

**4. Learn some common separable and inseparable transitive two-word verbs.**

SEPARABLE

*fill out* an application/*fill* it *out*   [to complete]

*give up* smoking/*give* it *up*   [to quit]

*look up* some words/*look* them *up*   [to find, usually in a book]

*put out* a fire/*put* it *out*   [to extinguish]

*tear down* a house/*tear* it *down*   [to destroy or demolish]

*throw away* the paper/*throw* it *away*   [to put in the garbage]

*try on* some clothes/*try* some *on*   [to put on and examine]

*turn down* the TV/*turn* it *down*   [to reduce]

*turn up* the volume/*turn* it *up*   [to increase]

INSEPARABLE

*call on* a student/*call on* her   [to ask someone to speak]

*come across* an article/*come across* it   [to encounter something by chance]

*get over* a cold/*get over* it   [to recover]

*hear from* an old friend/*hear from* him   [to receive a communication]

*look after* his mother/*look after* her   [to take care of]

*look through* an encyclopedia/*look through* it   [to browse]

*pick on* someone smaller/*pick on* someone   [to harass or bother]

*run into* a neighbour/*run into* her   [to encounter someone by chance]

*take after* a grandparent/*take after* him   [to resemble]

## ESL 1f  Learn which verbs are followed by an infinitive and which ones by a gerund.

**Infinitives** and **gerunds** are *verbals*, words formed from verbs. **Verbals** can function in a sentence as nouns, adjectives, or clauses (see GRAM 1a). Infinitives and gerunds can both be used as nouns and, therefore, can follow main verbs as direct objects. Some main verbs can be followed by either an infinitive or a gerund. However, some must be followed by an infinitive and others must be followed by a gerund.

The following six rules list common verbs and phrases associated with each of these verbals. They also give help in correctly using infinitives and gerunds as objects.

1. **Use an infinitive with *to* after these common verbs:**

| | | | | |
|---|---|---|---|---|
| agree | come | have | mean | refuse |
| arrange | decide | hope | offer | wait |
| beg | deserve | intend | plan | want |
| claim | expect | manage | promise | wish |

Keith refused ~~participating~~ in the discussion.
*(to participate)*

2. **Learn which verbs are followed by a noun or pronoun object and an infinitive with *to*.**

Some verbs are followed by two objects—a noun or pronoun that receives the action of the verb and then the infinitive. The following verbs have a noun or pronoun object as well as an infinitive object:

| | | | | |
|---|---|---|---|---|
| advise | convince | invite | persuade | tell |
| allow | forbid | order | remind | urge |
| cause | instruct | permit | require | warn |

We persuaded to come with us.
*(our neighbours)*

The embassy invited to attend a reception in the Princess's honour.
*(us)*

The following verbs may either take a noun or pronoun object or be followed directly by an infinitive:

| | | | | |
|---|---|---|---|---|
| allow* | cause | force | help | want |
| ask | expect | get | need | would like |

I *would like* dessert.

I *would like* it.

I *would like* to go.

\*EXCEPTION:  When *allow* does not have a noun or pronoun object, it is followed by a gerund.

Many companies no longer allow *smoking* on their premises.

### 3. Use *let, make,* and *have* correctly.

When *let* means "allow," *make* means "force," and *have* means "cause," they are followed by a noun or pronoun object (O) and the infinitive without *to.*

Customs officials *let* Gina *pass* through without inspecting her luggage.
<br>*(O over "Gina")*

They did not *make* her *show* them her briefcase, either.
<br>*(O over "her")*

Tadashi *had* the barber *cut* his hair much shorter this time.
<br>*(O over "the barber")*

### 4. Use a gerund after the following verbs:

| | | | | |
|---|---|---|---|---|
| admit | delay | imagine | postpone | resist |
| allow* | deny | keep | practise | risk |
| appreciate | discuss | mind | prevent | stop |
| avoid | enjoy | miss | regret | suggest |
| consider | finish | permit | remember | tolerate |

I enjoyed ~~to meet~~ *meeting* your family.

The government no longer allows ~~to smoke~~ *smoking* in government offices.

\*NOTE:  *Allow* is followed by an infinitive when it has a noun or pronoun
object.

I don't allow anyone ~~smoking~~ *to smoke* in the house.

### 5. Use a gerund after certain verbs plus a preposition.

The following phrases are frequently followed by gerunds:

| accuse someone of | be responsible for | feel like |
| apologize for | be tired of | insist on |
| approve of | be used to | look forward to |
| be afraid of | believe in | object to |
| be capable of | depend on | talk about |
| be interested in | dream of | think about |

Sue *is responsible for* preparing the financial data.

See EDIT 3c4 for gerunds modified by a possessive pronoun.

### 6. Use either an infinitive or a gerund after the following verbs:

| begin* | hate | love | start* |
| continue | like | prefer | |

The store cannot *continue to raise* prices.

The store cannot *continue raising* prices.

> *NOTE: When *begin* and *start* are used in the progressive tenses, they can only be followed by an infinitive.

Lani is beginning ~~enjoying~~ *to enjoy* her dance class.

After some verbs, such as *remember, stop,* and *try,* the infinitive and the gerund have different meanings.

Sid remembers *going* to the bank on Friday.

[Sid remembers that he went to the bank last Friday.]

Sid remembers *to go* to the bank on Friday.

[He remembers to go to the bank every Friday.]

# ESL 2 _____

# NOUNS, QUANTIFIERS, AND ARTICLES

Two important categories of nouns are *noncount nouns* and *count nouns*. **Noncount nouns** name things that cannot be counted separately, such as *air* and *water*. **Count nouns** name things that can be counted separately, such as *students* and *chairs*. (See GRAM 1b for more about noncount nouns and count nouns.) This section contains information about some features of noncount and count nouns. It also gives help in using quantifiers (such as *a little* and *a few*), the indefinite article *a/an*, and the definite article *the*.

## ESL 2a    Identify and use noncount nouns correctly.

Most noncount nouns fall into one of several categories. Learning these categories and some of the nouns associated with each one will help you recognize and use these nouns correctly.

### 1.  Learn to identify noncount nouns.

Many nouns in the following categories are noncount nouns.

FOODS   beef, bread, cauliflower

LIQUIDS, POWDERS, GRAINS   milk, dust, sand

AREAS OF KNOWLEDGE   biology, economics, history

IDEAS AND EMOTIONS   beauty, hatred, truth

OTHER NONCOUNT NOUNS   (These are not obvious, so you must learn them.)   clothes, furniture, information, machinery, money, news

### 2.  Do not make noncount nouns plural.

I checked my ~~luggages~~ *luggage* at the airport.

A **partitive** is a phrase that indicates the units of something; for example, *a piece of* luggage, *a pound of* sugar, *a litre of* gasoline. When a partitive is used with a noncount noun, the noun itself remains singular, even when the partitive is plural.

I had two pieces of luggage~~s~~ with me.

### 3.  Do not use the indefinite article *a/an* with noncount nouns.

Use no article when the noun has a general meaning.

~~An~~ *A* ir needs to be put into tires when they are flat.

Use *some* or *the* when the noun has a specific identity that is known to your reader.

I bought ~~a~~ *some* gasoline yesterday.

## ESL 2b   Use the correct quantifiers for noncount nouns and count nouns.

A **quantifier** is a word or phrase that tells how much or how many of something. It can be used instead of an article.

### 1.  Use the appropriate quantifiers for noncount and count nouns.

| NONCOUNT NOUNS | COUNT NOUNS |
|---|---|
| *a little* salt | *a few* students |
| *too much* poverty | *too many* cars |
| *a great deal of* confidence | *three* instructors |

### 2.  Learn which quantifiers can be used with both noncount and count nouns.

| NONCOUNT NOUNS | COUNT NOUNS |
|---|---|
| *enough* money | *enough* quarters |
| *some* furniture | *some* chairs |
| *a lot of* bread | *a lot of* oranges |

To ask questions regarding quantity, use "How much?" with noncount nouns and "How many?" with count nouns.

*How much* salad should I make?

*How many* foreign cars were sold in Canada last year?

## ESL 2c   Use the indefinite article *a* or *an* before a singular count noun when you do not specify which one.

It's hot in here. Please open *a* window.   [any of several windows]

Use *a* before words beginning with a consonant sound and *an* before words beginning with a vowel sound.

| a *user* | an *hour* from now |
|---|---|
| an *advertising* agency | a *happy* family |

Notice that *an* is used before a silent *h* (*hour*) and *a* is used before an *h* with a consonant sound (*happy*).

## ESL 2d Learn when to use the definite article *the*.

The following six rules explain when to use the **definite article** *the*.

**1. Use the definite article before nouns that refer to something the reader already knows about or that is obvious from the context.**

Please open <u>the</u> window.   [The reader knows which window.]

**2. Use the definite article after the first time a noun is mentioned.**

FIRST MENTION

Fill a large pot with *water.*

SUBSEQUENT MENTION

Bring <u>the</u> water to a boil.

**3. Use the definite article for items of unique reference.**

British Columbia borders on <u>the</u> Pacific Ocean.

<u>The</u> Mackenzie River is the longest river in Canada.

**4. Use the definite article with the superlative form of adjectives.**

<u>The</u> best way to paint a house is to hire a professional to do it.

**5. Use the definite article with nouns that are described by restrictive phrases or clauses.**

**Restrictive phrases** and **restrictive clauses** answer the question "Which one?" or "Which ones?" about the noun they modify.

<u>The</u> woman *on the left* is the chairperson.

<u>The</u> first woman *to become Prime Minister of Canada* was Kim Campbell.

## 6. Do not use the definite article for the following:

**PEOPLES' NAMES**

Please tell ~~the~~ Tina to come into my office.

**ABBREVIATIONS FOR UNIVERSITIES AND BUSINESSES**

Tan works for ~~the~~ UBC.

**GENERALIZATIONS**

Vegetables
~~The vegetables~~ are good for you.

**LANGUAGES OR SUBJECTS OF STUDY**

Charles is taking ~~the~~ history this semester.

**SPORTS**

Is ~~the~~ hockey or ~~the~~ lacrosse Canada's national sport?

**HOLIDAYS OR RELIGIOUS OCCASIONS**

~~The~~ Easter is in April this year.

**PHRASES WITH *BED, CHURCH, CLASS, SCHOOL, TOWN,* OR *WORK***

Kyoko goes to ~~the~~ work in the afternoon.

**CONTINENTS, COUNTRIES,\* PROVINCES (OR STATES), CITIES, TOWNS, LAKES, OR STREETS**

Many tourists visit ~~the~~ Ottawa each year.

**\*EXCEPTIONS:** Countries whose name includes *of*: *The United States of America, The Commonwealth of Independent States, The People's Republic of China, The Republic of the Philippines.*

~~The~~ Australia is the smallest continent.

# ESL 3 _____

# ADJECTIVES AND ADVERBS

*Adjectives* and *adverbs* modify or describe other elements in a sentence. An **adjective** shows the quality or number of a noun. An **adverb** modifies a verb, an adjective, another adverb, or a clause. This section gives information about placing adjectives and adverbs in sentences. (See GRAM 1d and 1e for more about adjectives and adverbs.)

## ESL 3a   Use correct word order when you modify a noun with more than one adjective.

a small oval
an ~~oval small~~ gem

tall red brick
five ~~red brick tall~~ buildings

The following word order is typically used when more than one adjective precedes a noun:

1. Article, possessive adjective, or other quantifier: *a/an, the, my, people's, five, some*
2. Number or comparative or superlative form of the adjective: *two, first, older, slowest*
3. Evaluative adjective that can be modified by *very*: *beautiful, committed, delicious*
4. Size: *big, small, long, short*
5. Shape: *round, square, triangular*
6. Age: *modern, nineteenth-century, ancient, new, old*
7. Colour: *red, green, mauve*
8. Nationality: *German, Chinese, Mexican*
9. Religion: *Protestant, Jewish, Muslim, Buddhist*
10. Material: *wood, brick, gold*
11. Noun used as an adjective: *student* lounge, *music* program, *dining room* furniture

NOTE:   Using more than two or three adjectives to modify a noun is usually awkward. Focus on the most important qualities and choose your descriptive words carefully.

## ESL 3b   Learn the different meanings of present and past participles.

Present participles and past participles are verbals that are often used as adjectives. (See GRAM 1a for more about verbals.) Their meanings are quite different:

PRESENT PARTICIPLE

My friend Jake is *annoying*.   [Jake causes annoyance.]

**PAST PARTICIPLE**

My friend Jake is *annoyed*.* [Jake experiences annoyance.]

*NOTE: This sentence is in the present tense. The past participle, which is an adjective in this sentence, does not indicate past tense.

When you use participles to describe moods or feelings such as the following, check a dictionary or ask someone whose first language is English for help.

| | |
|---|---|
| annoying/annoyed | exhausting/exhausted |
| boring/bored | interesting/interested |
| confusing/confused | frightening/frightened |
| depressing/depressed | refreshing/refreshed |
| discouraging/discouraged | surprising/surprised |
| exciting/excited | tiring/tired |

interesting
Our tour of the Roman ruins was ~~interested~~.

interested
I am very ~~interesting~~ in learning to play the piano.

exhausting                                     refreshed
Fatima's trip was ~~exhausted~~, but she returned ~~refreshing~~ by the experience.

## ESL 3c    Place adverbs correctly in sentences.

The position of an adverb in a sentence depends on what element of the sentence the adverb modifies. There are two basic types of adverbs: adverbs of *frequency* tell *how often* and adverbs of *manner* tell *how*. Remember these five rules for placing adverbs in a sentence.

**1. Place adverbs of frequency, such as *always, often, never,* and *usually,* after the verb *be*.**

Céline Dion's songs are *usually* very romantic.

**2. Place adverbs of frequency before verbs other than *be*.**

Unknown evils *always* lurk in the cemetery at midnight.

**3. Some adverbs modify adjectives (ADJ) or other adverbs (ADV). Place these adverbs of manner in front of the adjective or other adverb that they modify.***

Icy roads are *extremely* dangerous, day or night.

We were driving *too* fast for the road conditions.

> ***EXCEPTION:*** The adverb *enough* follows the adjective or adverb that it modifies.

We were not careful *enough* on such icy roads.

**4. Other adverbs may be placed before or after the verb, or at the beginning or end of the sentence.**

Mina *tactfully* avoided the subject.

Pay equity legislation passed *easily.*

*Slowly* and *carefully,* he eased the car out of the parking space.

Check with someone whose first language is English if you are not sure where to place the adverb in a sentence.

**5. Do not place an adverb between a verb and its direct object.**

We signed ~~gladly~~ his petition to get on the ballot.
gladly

# ESL 4 _____

# PREPOSITIONS AND PREPOSITIONAL PHRASES

A preposition (PREP) shows a relationship between objects or ideas in a sentence. The relationship can be in space (spatial), in time (temporal), or in manner.

SPATIAL   Ravi's room is *next to* the candy machine.

TEMPORAL    Dr. Bey has her office hours *before* class.

MANNER    They eat french fries *with* lots of ketchup.

A **prepositional phrase** contains a preposition followed by one of the items in the relationship, usually a noun or noun phrase. (See GRAM 1f and 3a for more about prepositions.)

## ESL 4a    Learn the correct prepositions for the meanings you want to convey.

Not all languages have prepositions. Languages that do have them usually have fewer prepositions than English does, and the meanings of prepositions in other languages often do not correspond to the meanings of English prepositions. Moreover, most English prepositions have more than one meaning. (He left *at* 4:00 a.m. I live *at* 28 DeForest Heights.) Therefore, English prepositions can be difficult to learn. When you are unsure of which preposition to use, consult your dictionary.

      *at/in*
Yesterday I worked all day ~~to~~ the library.

[*To* is used to show direction with motion verbs, as in the sentence *I go to school every day. Work* does not show motion.]

    *in*
Susan and Frank live ~~at~~ Medicine Hat.

[*At* is used with exact addresses, as in the sentence *Susan and Frank live at 55 Summit Street. In* is used with the names of cities and provinces. Medicine Hat is a city.]

## ESL 4b    Do not omit necessary prepositions.

Prepositions are needed at the beginning of prepositional phrases. Without them, nouns that are not direct objects can be mistaken for direct objects. In addition, important information can be lost.

    *in*
My father has been living ˄ this house for many years.

[A preposition is needed in front of *this house* to show that it is not the direct object of *has been living*. The preposition *in* helps explain where *my father* has been living.]

Yesterday we went *to* the store.
^

[A preposition is needed in front of *the store* to show that it is not the direct object of *went*. The preposition *to* helps explain where we went.]

## ESL 4c   Do not add extra words to prepositional phrases or create prepositional phrases when you do not need them.

A prepositional phrase is not always necessary to complete the meaning of a sentence. When one is necessary, it should contain only a preposition followed by its object. Subjects and verbs should not be included in prepositional phrases.

Faisal is learning English by ~~he~~ listening to the radio.

[This prepositional phrase contains a preposition, a subject, and an object. Only a preposition and an object are necessary.]

## ESL 4d   Remember that infinitives cannot be used as the objects of prepositions.

The object in a prepositional phrase is always a pronoun or some form of noun, such as a noun phrase (*the dog*), noun clause (*what the dog wanted*), or gerund phrase (*barking*). Infinitives (*to bark*) cannot be used as objects of prepositions.

These heavy boots are especially designed for *hiking* ~~to hike~~.

## ESL 4e   Learn some common compound prepositions.

Some prepositions are only one word. Others consist of two or more words. Prepositions of two or more words are called **compound prepositions** (C PREP).

PREP
I like to walk *by* myself.

C PREP
I walk *next to* the sea.

COMMON COMPOUND PREPOSITIONS

| | | |
|---|---|---|
| according to | contrary to | next to |
| along with | due to | on behalf of |
| apart from | for the purpose of | on top of |
| as a result of | in addition to | out of |
| as far as | in back of | prior to |
| aside from | in contrast to/with | regardless of |
| as well as | in favour of | subsequent to |
| away from | in front of | together with |
| because of | in spite of | up to |
| by means of | instead of | with regard to |

## ESL 4f   Learn some common adjective + preposition combinations.

Certain adjective + preposition combinations have special meanings and are very common.

Marta is *fond ~~for~~* chocolate.
<br>*of*

Andrei is *interested ~~about~~* Russian history.
<br>*in*

COMMON ADJECTIVE + PREPOSITION COMBINATIONS

| | | |
|---|---|---|
| (un) accustomed to | conscious of | (dis) pleased with |
| associated with | dedicated to | proud of |
| aware of | different from | qualified for |
| based on | equal to | (dis) satisfied with |
| (in) capable of | fond of | surprised by/about |
| committed to | interested in | (un) worthy of |
| composed of | (un) known for | |

# ESL 5

# PARTS OF SENTENCES

Every sentence has a subject and a predicate (see GRAM 2a and 2b).

## ESL 5a  Every sentence must have a verb, even when the meaning is understood.

English requires a main verb in each clause or sentence, even when the meaning is clear without it. Sentences need *be* (*is, are,* etc.) to link a subject with a prepositional phrase or a predicate adjective.

       is                                             are
The conference in Winnipeg this year. Manitobans very friendly.

## ESL 5b  Each sentence or independent clause has one, and only one, subject.

The weather, which started out cloudy, it improved later in the day.

[Even though the subject, *weather,* is separated from the verb *improved* by a descriptive clause, it should not be repeated.]

                                                      It h
The Northwest Territories has a national park called Aulavik. Has another one called Auyuittuq.

## ESL 5c  Use expletives correctly.

In most English sentences, the subject is first and the verb and other parts of the predicate follow it. (Review parts of sentences in GRAM 2.) However, a subject may not appear until later in the sentence. In this case, an **expletive** (*there, here,* or *it*) at the beginning of the sentence substitutes for the postponed subject. (See EDIT 1g for more about expletives.)

Expletives are used in the following ways:

*There* is a common expletive used to indicate that a particular phenomenon exists.

                      S
*There* is a large Chinese community in Vancouver.

[The subject, *a large Chinese community,* is placed after the verb.]

The expletive *here* usually introduces information.

                 S
*Here* are a few ways to be an effective language learner.

The pronoun *it* often functions as an expletive when the deferred subject is a noun clause or phrase.

S

*It* is tragic to watch the world's tropical rain forests disappearing.

[The subject is the entire noun phrase.]

S

*It* is not enough that we have good intentions.

[The subject is the noun clause *that we have good intentions*.]

Follow these three guidelines for writing correct sentences with expletives.

**1. When you use *there* or *here* as an expletive, check that the verb agrees with the deferred subject.**

Singular subjects require singular verbs; plural subjects require plural verbs.

SING.    PLURAL

Here is a turkey sandwich for your lunch, and here are some cookies.

**2. Use the expletive *it* when talking about a condition or when there is no other subject.**

It i
~~As~~ wonderful to see you.

It i
~~As~~ raining again.

**3. Remember to use a form of the verb *be* with expletives.**

are
There ~~have~~ many Canada Geese at Jack Miner's bird sanctuary.

# ESL 6 _____

## SPECIAL PROBLEMS

This section gives information on word order and verb tenses in questions, reported speech, and conditional sentences. (See GRAM 4 for additional information on clauses.)

### ESL 6a    Use the correct word order for questions.

In English, word order in questions is very important and follows predictable patterns. Questions that take a yes/no answer begin with an auxiliary. When there is one verb in a basic tense, use a form of *do* (*do, does, did*), followed by the subject.

*Does* Simone play the piano?

*Do* her brothers also play?

"Yes/no" questions in progressive or perfect tenses, or ones that have modals, begin with the appropriate auxiliary or modal, followed by the subject.

*Have* you bought your books yet?

*Can* you swim?

When there is a question word (*who, what, where, when, why,* or *how*), it comes first, followed by the auxiliary. (See ESL 6b for *who* or *what* questions that do not require an auxiliary.)

*Where does* Professor Long's class meet?

This is the basic word order for questions; the items in parentheses are optional.

| (question word) | auxiliary | subject | (main verb) | (everything else) |
|---|---|---|---|---|
| | Are | they | | hungry? |
| How long | has | Eun | worked | for IBM? |
| Who | | | teaches | calculus? |
| Who | is | | teaching | calculus? |

## ESL 6b  Use the correct word order and helping verbs for questions with *who, whom,* and *what.*

*Who* and *what* can be used in questions as either subjects or objects. However, notice the differences in the ways questions are formed when *who* and *what* are used as subjects and when they are used as objects.

**1. In questions with *who* or *what* as subjects, use the word order of declarative sentences. Do not use a helping verb.**

QUESTION                        DECLARATIVE SENTENCE

S
*Who* saw him?

S
*We* saw him clearly.

S
*What* causes lower
  back pain?*

S
*Weak stomach muscles* cause it
  in most cases.

*NOTE:  *Who* and *what* are always treated as singular and take singular verbs.

**2. In questions with *who(m)* or *what* as objects, use forms of *do* as helping verbs and use an interrogative word order with the object at the beginning.**

O
*Whom do* they usually *hire?*

O
They usually hire *students.*

O
*What did* they *decide?*

O
They decided *to approve the project.*

## ESL 6c  Use correct word order in indirect questions.

Review declarative and interrogative sentences in GRAM 5b. When direct questions become part of another declarative sentence, they are called **indirect questions**.

DIRECT QUESTION                    INDIRECT QUESTION

Does it rain a lot in Rimouski?    I am not sure *whether it rains a lot
                                     in Rimouski.*

| DIRECT QUESTION | INDIRECT QUESTION |
|---|---|
| Could First Nations peoples use tools at that time? | Archaeologists do not know *if First Nations peoples could use tools at that time.* |
| Where were the First Nations peoples from? | This article discusses *where the First Nations peoples were from.* |
| Where did they go? | The map shows *where they went.* |

When you use indirect questions in your writing, watch for the following three differences between indirect questions and direct questions.

**1. For indirect questions, use the word order of declarative sentences, not the word order of direct questions.**

The article discusses where ~~were they~~ from.
        they were

**2. Introduce indirect "yes/no" questions with *if* or *whether* and use the appropriate form of the main verb.**

Do not use *do, does,* or *did* and the base form of the verb, as you would with a question.

I don't know ~~did they explore~~ North America.
     if they explored

Introduce indirect questions that have modal verbs with *if* or *whether.*

The author is not sure ~~could First Nations Peoples~~ navigate by the stars.
     whether First Nations peoples could

**3. Use the punctuation that is correct for the entire sentence.**

No First Nations peoples remember why their tribes built the mounds~~?~~.

[This is a declarative sentence, so punctuate it with a period.]

## ESL 6d   Use the correct verb tense in reported speech.

Writers report someone else's words either by direct quotation or by reported speech. In **direct quotation**, the writer reproduces the speaker's exact words, enclosed in quotation marks. In **reported speech** (indirect quotation), the writer restates the speaker's words and puts them in a clause. (Review tense in EDIT 2d and shifts between direct and indirect quotations in SENT 3e.) Changing a speaker's exact words into reported speech requires the following changes.

## 1. Change present tense in direct quotations to past tense in reported speech.

Change auxiliary verbs *do* and *does* to *did*.

| DIRECT QUOTATION | REPORTED SPEECH |
| --- | --- |
| "I *assign* several short essays," Professor Lyons told us. | Professor Lyons told us that he *assigned* several short essays. |
| "I *do not require* a research paper," Professor Lyons assured us. | Professor Lyons assured us he *did not require* a research paper.* |

*NOTE: You may omit *that* at the beginning of the clause for reported speech.

## 2. Change present perfect or past tense to past perfect.

| DIRECT QUOTATION | REPORTED SPEECH |
| --- | --- |
| Petra said, "I *have studied* acting for four years." | Petra said that she *had studied* acting for four years. |
| Greg said, "I *lost* my car keys." | Greg said he *had lost* his car keys. |

## 3. Change present progressive to past progressive.

| DIRECT QUOTATION | REPORTED SPEECH |
| --- | --- |
| "I *am working* part time to earn money for tuition," I said. | I said I *was working* part time to earn money for tuition. |

## 4. Change *can* to *could*, *will* to *would*, and *may* to *might*. Do not change other modals.

| DIRECT QUOTATION | REPORTED SPEECH |
| --- | --- |
| The mayor said, "We *can't* raise taxes." | The mayor said that the town *couldn't* raise taxes. |
| "I *will* try to obtain federal funds," he told the audience. | He told the audience that he *would* try to obtain federal funds. |

| | |
|---|---|
| "However," he cautioned, "I *may* not be successful." | However, he cautioned that he *might* not be successful. |

## 5. Report "yes/no" questions with *if* or *whether.*

DIRECT QUOTATION

"Can we expect to know soon?" asked one reporter.

REPORTED SPEECH

One reporter asked *if* we could expect to know soon.

## 6. Report "or" questions with *whether.*

DIRECT QUOTATION

He asked, "Are you going to meet here or in Saskatoon?"

REPORTED SPEECH

He asked *whether* the mayor was going to meet here or in Saskatoon.

## 7. Use the infinitive with *to* to report commands.

DIRECT QUOTATION

The mayor told the reporter, "*Wait* until next week for that announcement."

REPORTED SPEECH

The mayor told the reporter *to wait* until next week for that announcement.

## ESL 6e    Use the correct verb tense in conditional sentences.

In a **conditional sentence**, if a certain fact exists, then another related fact may also exist.

When population increases, the demand for health services also increases.

[An increase in population is one cause of an increase in the demand for health services.]

There are usually two clauses in a conditional sentence, a *main clause* (MC) and a *subordinate clause* (SC) that begins with *if, when, whenever,* or *unless.* The verb in these clauses can be confusing because the normal meanings of the tenses do not always apply. In one type of conditional sentence, for example, the past is used to speculate about events in the future.

```
       SC                    MC
┌──────────────┐ ┌─────────────────────┐
```
If you wear my size, you can borrow my jacket.

[The present tense is used to speak about the present.]

SC | MC

If you wore my size, you could borrow my jacket.

[The past tense is used to speak about the future.]

Here are some rules to help you write correct conditional sentences.

1. **Determine what kind of condition you are writing about.**

First, determine the time frame—past, present, or future. Then determine whether the conditions you are describing are real or unreal. The most common types of conditional sentences are presented here.

In **present** and **past real conditions**, the conditions stated in both the subordinate and the main clause actually exist or existed.

SC | MC

When air warms, it rises.

SC | MC

Whenever the pollen count increased, my brother got hay fever.

**Future real conditions** predict situations that are likely to occur if a condition is met.

SC | MC

If you travel by freighter, expect an adventure.

**Present** and **future unreal conditions** speculate about untrue or unlikely situations in the present or future.

SC | MC

If I were* on vacation, we could spend more time together.

[I am not on vacation, so we can't spend more time together.]

*NOTE: With the verb *be*, use *were* for all subjects in the *if*-clause.

**Past unreal conditions** speculate about situations in the past that did not occur.

SC | MC

If the plumber had fixed the leak, the basement would not have flooded.

[The plumber did not fix the leak, and the cellar flooded.]

**2. For present and past real conditions, use the same verb tense in both clauses.**

$\overbrace{\phantom{xxxxxxxxxxxxxxxxxx}}^{\text{SC}}$ $\overbrace{\phantom{xxxxxxxxxxxxxxxxxx}}^{\text{MC}}$

If Tina *reads* for a long time, she *gets* a headache.

$\overbrace{\phantom{xxxxxxxxxxxxxxxxxx}}^{\text{SC}}$ $\overbrace{\phantom{xxxxxxxxxxxxxxxxxx}}^{\text{MC}}$

Whenever Trudeau *spoke,* the audience *was* spellbound.

**3. For future real conditions, use the following verb tenses:**

| SUBORDINATE CLAUSE | MAIN CLAUSE |
|---|---|
| *If* or *unless* + present tense* | *can, may, might, should,* or *will* + base form |

$\overbrace{\phantom{xxxxxxxxxxxxxxxxxx}}^{\text{SC}}$ $\overbrace{\phantom{xxxxxxxxxxxxxxxxxx}}^{\text{MC}}$

If you *leave* by eight o'clock, you *can* still catch your plane.

*NOTE:     For future real conditions, use the present tense, not the future, in the subordinate clause, even though this clause expresses a future condition.

**4. For present and future unreal conditions, use the following verb tenses:**

| SUBORDINATE CLAUSE | MAIN CLAUSE |
|---|---|
| *If* + past tense* | *could, might,* or *would* + base form |

$\overbrace{\phantom{xxxxxxxxxxxxxxxxxx}}^{\text{SC}}$ $\overbrace{\phantom{xxxxxxxxxxxxxxxxxx}}^{\text{MC}}$

If I *had* my dictionary, I *could* check the spelling for you.

[Since I do not have my dictionary, I will not be able to check the spelling.]

$\overbrace{\phantom{xxxxxxxxxxxxxxxxxx}}^{\text{SC}}$ $\overbrace{\phantom{xxxxxxxxxxxxxxxxxx}}^{\text{MC}}$

If I *were*** in charge, things *might* be different.

[Since I'm not in charge, things will probably stay the same.]

$\overbrace{\phantom{xxxxxxxxxxxxxxxxxx}}^{\text{MC}}$ $\overbrace{\phantom{xxxxxxxxxxxxxxxxxx}}^{\text{SC}}$

Jorge *would* get up on time if he *set* his alarm clock at night.

[Since Jorge does not set his alarm, he does not get up on time.]

*NOTE: For present and future unreal conditions, past verb forms do not express action in the past. Instead, the past form is used to show that events are unlikely or imagined.

**NOTE: With the verb *be*, remember to use *were* for all subjects in the *if*-clause.

5. **For past unreal conditions, use the following verb tenses:**

| SUBORDINATE CLAUSE | MAIN CLAUSE |
|---|---|
| *If* + past perfect* | *could have, might have*, or *would have* + past participle |

|   SC   |   MC   |
|---|---|

If I *had done* my laundry, I *would have had* clean socks.

[I did not do my laundry, so I do not have clean socks.]

*NOTE: In past unreal conditions, the past perfect does not have its usual meaning of an event prior to another event in the past. Instead, it is used to speculate about something that did not occur or that was unreal in the past.

# ESL 7 _____

## CONFUSING WORDS AND PHRASES

Some words and phrases in English are particularly confusing to ESL learners. Two of these are *do* and *make*. *Do* usually means "to complete" or "to perform." *Make* usually means "to create," "to construct," or "to produce." Both are verbs.

The children *do* their homework before going outside.

[The children *complete* their homework first.]

Greg *makes* dinner almost every night.

[Greg *creates* or *puts together* the dinner.]

Two other particularly confusing words are *too* and *very*. *Too* implies a negative result. *Very* does not imply a negative result. Both are adverbs.

> This book is *too* long to read in one day.
>
> [It is *impossible* to read the book in one day.]
>
> This book is *very* long, but I must read it all today.
>
> [It is *possible* to read the book in one day.]

Certain words and phrases are also usage problems for native speakers. Some of the most common are presented in the Glossary of Usage in WORD 7.

# SENT

## Sentences

### *Learning Objectives*

After reading this section, you should

1. write more unified, logical, and varied sentences,
2. be able to use parallelism, subordination, and coordination to express your ideas,
3. be familiar with different ways of achieving emphasis in your writing,
4. recognize problems with modifiers,
5. recognize inappropriate shifts (e.g., in verb tense).

# SENT

## Sentences

# SENT 1

## PARALLELISM

Improve the coherence and effectiveness of your sentences by using **parallelism**; that is, by balancing ideas of equal weight (either similar or contrasting ideas) in grammatical structures of equal weight. You can balance a word with a word, a phrase with a phrase, or a clause with a clause. You can balance entire sentences by repeating the pattern of one sentence in a subsequent sentence.

### SENT 1a   Use parallel construction to improve coherence at all levels of sentence construction.

#### BALANCE A WORD WITH A WORD

His idea was *poorly conceived, poorly timed,* and *poorly presented.*

#### BALANCE A PHRASE WITH A PHRASE

I was *a junk dealer,* then I became *a scrap dealer,* then *a secondary materials engineer,* and now I'm in recycling. But the job hasn't changed.
—Chester Waxman

#### BALANCE A CLAUSE WITH A CLAUSE

Manitoba is known as the Land of 100 000 Lakes; Manitoba is also the most important source of hydroelectric power in the prairie region.

### SENT 1b   To emphasize parallel structures, repeat an article (*a, an, the*), a preposition, the sign of the infinitive (*to*), or the first word of a long phrase or clause.

Parmesh wanted both a promotion and _a_ salary increase.

Kim had real doubts—to go or _to_ stay.

## SENT 1c   Use parallel constructions with correlative conjunctions (*either/or, neither/nor, not only/but also, both/and, whether/or*).

He was neither a good host nor ~~someone who could tell a good story~~ *a good storyteller.*

The couple behind us who kept whispering were both inattentive and ~~not showing good manners,~~ *rude.*

## SENT 1d   Use parallel constructions in comparisons that use *than* or *as.*

I would rather resign than ~~agreeing~~ *agree* to an unethical solution.

Seeing is as good as ~~to believe,~~ *believing.*

# SENT 2 _____

# MISPLACED AND DANGLING MODIFIERS

The words, phrases, and clauses that function as modifiers in a sentence can usually be moved around, so place them carefully to avoid unintentionally confusing—or amusing—your reader. There are basically two types of problems that arise with modifiers: the **misplaced modifier** and the **dangling modifier**.

MISPLACED    The waiter brought a steak to the young man *covered with mushrooms.*    [*Covered with mushrooms* is misplaced.]

REVISED    The waiter brought a steak *covered with mushrooms* to the young man.

[The steak, not the man, was covered with mushrooms.]

DANGLING    *Flying over the mountain tops,* several herds of deer could be seen.    [*Flying over the mountain tops* is dangling.]

REVISED    *Flying over the mountain tops,* we could see several herds of deer.    [We, not the deer, were flying.]

Because most English sentences depend heavily on word order for meaning, modifiers should be placed as close as possible to the word or words they modify. We see this in the preceding sentences. Notice, in the following sentences, how the position of one word—*just*—can change the meaning.

*Just* he said that he dented the fender.    [No one else said it.]

He *just* said that he dented the fender.

[He said it just now, or he said no more.]

He said *just* that he dented the fender.    [He said no more.]

He said that *just* he dented the fender.    [No one else was involved.]

He said that he *just* dented the fender.

[He dented it just now, or he did not do more damage.]

He said that he dented *just* the fender.

[He dented no more than the fender.]

# SENT 2a    Place modifiers where they will be most effective.

**1.  Place adverbs such as *just, only, even, hardly, nearly,* and *merely* directly before the words they modify.**

nearly
He missed his appointment. ~~nearly~~
        ^

**2.  Place prepositional phrases used as adjectives after the words they modify (see GRAM 3a).**

with holes in it
Zena wore an old shirt for painting. ~~with holes in it~~
        ^                    ^

**3.  Place prepositional phrases used as adverbs near the words they modify (see GRAM 3a).**

in a hurry
Mary left for a vacation ~~in a hurry~~.
        ^            ^

**4. Place adjective clauses near the words they modify (see GRAM 4a).**

who was wearing a black bathing suit

The actress was walking the poodle. ~~who was wearing a black bathing suit~~

**5. Be alert for squinting modifiers.**

A **squinting modifier** looks in two directions; that is, it appears to modify both the word it follows and the word it precedes.

badly

The passenger who was hurt ~~badly~~ needed help.

[Placed after *hurt, badly* modifies both *hurt* and *needed*. When *badly* is placed before *hurt*, the sentence says several passengers were hurt and one seriously.]

badly.

The passenger who was hurt ~~badly~~ needed help

[Moving *badly* to modify *needed* communicates that only one passenger was hurt seriously.]

**6. Keep the main verb and all auxiliaries and modals as close together as possible (see GRAM 1a).**

have

We ~~have~~ never before had such a tremendous interest in the right-to-die issue.

[The complete verb is *have had*.]

**7. Avoid splitting infinitives (see GRAM 1a).**

if you have time.

Try to ~~if you have time~~ return the VCR movies

## SENT 2b    Connect a dangling modifier to the main part of the sentence.

A **dangling modifier** occurs when a participle, a gerund, an infinitive phrase (see GRAM 3b), or an **elliptical clause** (one with some words implied rather than stated) does not logically relate to the main part of the sentence. Dangling modifiers are usually at the beginning of a sentence; the doer of the action is unstated. To eliminate a dangling modifier, (1) state the subject immediately after the dangling phrase, (2) give the dangling phrase a subject, or (3) revise the sentence by changing the subject.

*Walking on the ceiling,* ~~he noticed~~ a very large insect, was noticed by him.

[The subject has been stated immediately after the dangling participial phrase. However, since the new sentence is in the passive voice and awkwardly phrased, it would be a good idea to revise further.]

~~*Walking on the ceiling,* he noticed~~ A very large insect, was walking on the ceiling, he noticed.

[The dangling participial phrase has been given a subject.]

~~*Walking on the ceiling,*~~ He noticed a very large insect, walking on the ceiling.

After eating lunch, we left in the little plane. ~~left~~

[The implied subject of the dangling gerund is explicitly stated.]

To run well, you need good running shoes ~~are needed.~~

[The implied subject of the dangling infinitive phrase is explicitly stated.]

Keep beating the eggs until they are fluffy.

[Here, *they are* substitutes for "the eggs are," which is implied but not stated in this elliptical clause.]

# SENT 3 _____
## SHIFTS

Abrupt or inappropriate **shifts**—changes from past to present tense, from first person to third person, or from informal to formal diction (see WORD 2a), for example—weaken the logic of your writing or obscure your meaning. At the very least, such inconsistencies confuse and therefore slow down your reader. Inappropriate shifts most often occur within a sentence, but sometimes they happen between one sentence and the next.

## SENT 3a    Use pronouns consistently.

Shifts in **person** most commonly occur between first-person (*I, we, me, us, my, our*) and second-person pronouns (*you, your, yours*) and between second-person and third-person pronouns (*he, she, it, they, him, her, them, his, hers, its, their, theirs*).

First-person pronouns highlight the writer and are appropriate for writing based on personal experience. Second-person pronouns, on the other hand, focus attention on the reader and are appropriate for directions and other how-to types of writing. Third-person pronouns highlight the subject and are used in most informative writing situations, including academic writing (see COMP 2f).

> *we*
> When we asked about tour trips, we learned ~~you~~ could take a whitewater rafting tour down the Fraser River.

[Because the writer is not addressing the reader directly, the shift from first-person *we* to second-person *you* is inappropriate.]

> *you*
> If you eat sensibly and watch your fat intake, ~~most people~~ should be able to
> *your*
> maintain ~~their~~ desired weight.

[The shift from second-person to third-person pronouns causes confusion. Because the writer is addressing the reader directly, *you* is appropriate throughout.]

Sometimes, in an effort to be formal or scholarly, writers use the indefinite pronoun *one*, as in "Nothing makes one realize the mystery of nature so much as viewing the Northern Lights." Because most people find such phrasing unnatural—even pretentious (see WORD 2c)—they often find themselves shifting between *one* and first person or second person.

> *me*
> Viewing the Northern Lights makes ~~one~~ realize the mystery of nature, and knowing the scientific explanation makes me appreciate the spectacle all the more.

[It is much more natural to speak in the first person throughout.]

Most shifts in **number**—the singular and plural forms of nouns and pronouns—occur when a plural pronoun is used to refer to a singular noun or vice versa (see EDIT 1i).

students take
When a student takes an exam, they should read all the questions carefully.

[By changing *student takes* to *students take,* the writer eliminates the unnecessary shift in number and avoids the *he/she* issue (see EDIT 3a).]

The Organization of American States, which Canada joined in 1990, has not

it has
achieved economic unity in the Western Hemisphere; they have succeeded

in other areas, however.

[Because *Organization of American States* is singular, the pronoun in the second main clause must be singular as well.]

## SENT 3b    Maintain the same verb tense.

The **verb tense** in a sentence indicates when the action is taking place. Shifting from one tense to another without a logical reason makes readers wonder what you really mean (see EDIT 2c and 2d).

found
Yvonne always stayed at the Algonquin Hotel; she finds the rooms spacious and beautifully decorated.

[Putting both verbs in the past tense clarifies that Yvonne no longer stays at the Algonquin.]

## SENT 3c    Maintain the same mood.

Verbs in English have three **moods**: the *indicative,* the *imperative,* and the *subjunctive* (see EDIT 2e). Problems with inconsistency usually occur with the imperative mood.

In learning to hit a golf ball, take a full back swing, and it is also important to keep your eye on the ball.

[Eliminating *it is also important to* avoids the unnecessary shift from the imperative to the indicative mood.]

## SENT 3d    Keep subject and voice consistent.

Inconsistencies in the subject of a sentence (see GRAM 2a) and the voice (see EDIT 2f) often go hand in hand, resulting in awkwardness and confusion.

> We could see the widespread effects of the drought as ~~the farm was~~ *we* approached~~the farm.~~

[Shifting from the active voice in the main clause to the passive voice in the subordinate clause results in the confusing shift of subject from *we* to *farm*.]

Sometimes a shift in subject and voice creates a *dangling modifier*—a modifying phrase or clause that is not logically connected to any word in the sentence (see SENT 2b).

> Exhausted, our final destination ~~could be seen~~ *we could see* clearly in the distance.

[*Exhausted* is a dangling modifier because it does not logically relate to the subject of the main clause (the destination is not exhausted); in the corrected main clause, the subject *we* explains who is exhausted.]

## SENT 3e    Avoid unnecessary shifts from direct to indirect quotation.

In **direct quotation** the writer repeats a speaker's words verbatim—that is, word for word—in quotation marks. In **indirect quotation**, or **reported speech**, the writer paraphrases or summarizes what the speaker said.

DIRECT QUOTATION

The aerobics instructor said, "Let's really raise those knees!"

INDIRECT QUOTATION

The aerobics instructor said we should raise our knees higher.

A shift from direct to indirect quotation or vice versa can be confusing.

> Our instructor said work stations had to be cleaned at the end of each lab session and ~~report~~ all test-tube breakage~~.~~ *had to be reported.*

This example can also be revised to maintain consistent direct quotation:

> Our instructor said, "Clean your work stations at the end of each lab session and report all test-tube breakage."

## SENT 3f   Keep tone and style consistent.

Unnecessary shifts in **tone**—the writer's attitude or stance toward the subject and audience—and in **style**—the writer's manner of expression—call attention to themselves and away from the intended meaning. For example, a reader would be surprised by an unexpected shift from a reverent to a sarcastic tone or from a flowery to a simple style. In most cases, such inconsistencies are matters of appropriate word choice (see WORD 2). Choose words carefully to achieve a consistent tone and style.

> The fact that some large industrial plants are not conforming to clean-
> air laws ~~ticks off~~ *angers* many people.

[*Ticks off* is a slang expression and contrasts sharply with the more formal and objective tone established at the beginning of the sentence. *Angers, worries,* or *alarms* are better word choices.]

> John and Stefano climbed into the leaky old rowboat and rowed out to the
> middle of the lake to ~~reenact the ancient rivalry in which man and fish do battle.~~ *fish.*

[*To reenact the ancient rivalry in which man and fish do battle* stylistically is too poetic or elevated for the rest of this simple, straightforward sentence.]

## SENT 3g   Maintain the same point of view.

An abrupt shift from one **point of view**—the angle from which events are viewed—to another point of view can be unsettling. An event can be viewed from any number of angles: from the inside or the outside, the front or the back, or above or below, for example. The key is to be consistent.

The audience applauded wildly at the end of the play, ~~and the~~ *while outside* taxis lined

up to take them away.

[The abrupt shift from inside to outside the theatre is disconcerting; adding *while outside* prepares the reader for the change in point of view.]

# SENT 4 _____
## UNIFIED AND LOGICAL SENTENCES

In a **unified** sentence, all parts—words, phrases, and clauses—work together to achieve the desired effect. A unified sentence is composed in such a manner that if its components were rearranged or changed, its purpose would not be achieved as effectively. Because we usually think faster than we write, however, we can easily neglect to include information that will make a sentence complete and clear. Or sometimes we do not put all the details in the best order or fail to choose the best ones to make our point. Sometimes, too, we mentally make logical connections that we do not capture in writing, leaving the reader unable to follow our line of thought. For example, in the following sentence, notice how a cause-and-effect relationship is merely hinted at in the original version, whereas the revision clearly establishes the logical relationship for the reader.

The mail-order business is growing very fast in this country, ~~and~~ *because* many people don't have time to shop.

In some sentences that lack unity, however, no logical relationship can be established between the ideas; in this case make two sentences.

DISJOINTED  The Parliament Buildings, destroyed by fire in 1916, are located on Parliament Hill, Ottawa, Ontario.

REVISED  The Parliament Buildings are located on Parliament Hill, Ottawa, Ontario. Once, in 1916, they were destroyed by fire.

## SENT 4a    Use only relevant details.

Details make writing vivid and interesting, but details that have no connection to the central idea of a sentence only obscure that idea. Irrelevant details also bore and distract your reader.

The *Apollo 16* space mission left earth on April 16, 1972, ~~with its three man~~

~~crew,~~ spent three days on the moon, and returned successfully on April 27,

1972.

## SENT 4b    Avoid mixed or illogical constructions.

Sentences can be illogical for many reasons, but certain kinds of problems occur more frequently than others. Here are some guidelines for avoiding the most common problems.

### 1. Be sure the subject and predicate are related.

Faulty predication occurs when the subject and the predicate of a sentence are not sensibly related (see GRAM 2a and 2b).

                                            *done*

The casting for the school play was ~~selected~~ by the director.

[*The casting was done* OR *the cast was selected,* but not both in the same sentence.]

### 2. Make correct use of linking verbs.

A linking verb should not be used to equate elements that cannot be equated logically.

                                      *high.*

The cost of a college education is ~~expensive~~.

[*The cost is high* OR *a college education is expensive,* but not both in the same sentence.]

A linking verb should not be used to introduce an adverbial clause (see GRAM 4b). This most often happens with *is when*, *is where*, and *the reason is because* constructions.

In a
~~A~~ double-dip recession, ~~is where~~ the economy recovers for a short time,

then dips once again.

[A *double-dip recession* is an event, not a place.]

~~The reason~~ I love math ~~is~~ because it's challenging.

[The linking verb *is* requires a subject complement, and what follows here is an adverbial clause.]

An appositive, or noun substitute (see GRAM 3c), should be equal to the noun for which it stands.

vice-presidency,
Ms. Martindale was given a promotion, a ~~vice president,~~ for being so successful in sales.

[A *vice president* is a person; what is needed here is the name of the position.]

### 3. Keep figures of speech consistent.

We mix figures of speech (see WORD 1e) more often when we speak than when we write because we do not think out an entire sentence in advance. Still, the error also occurs in writing.

rough seas.
We were sailing along smoothly, until we ran into ~~a roadblock.~~

[A *roadblock* relates to land travel and is inconsistent with *sailing*.]

### 4. Make all parts of a sentence agree in number (see SENT 3a).

she
A police officer stopped our car, but ~~they~~ did not arrest us.

[A *police officer* is singular; *they* is plural.]

### 5. Avoid double negatives.

It is a convention of standard English to use only one negative to negate. Avoid using a negative modifier (*no*, *not*, or *never*) with other negative words (such as *no one*, *nobody*, *nothing*, *none*, *neither*, and *nowhere*).

anything
You can't say ~~nothing~~ that will change his mind.

[*Not* (in *can't*) and *nothing* are the two negatives.]

A double negative is acceptable, however, if the intent is to make a positive statement in a dramatic way.

Everyone agreed that she wasn't unaware of what she was doing.

# SENT 5 _____

## SUBORDINATION AND COORDINATION

As writers we impose emphasis on what we write to distinguish the most important ideas from the least important or to convey that ideas are equally important. We use **subordination** to make one idea less important than another. We use **coordination** to balance equal ideas and give equal emphasis.

Subordination emphasizes the more important idea in a sentence by putting it in the main clause and the less important ideas in dependent phrases or clauses (see GRAM 3 and 4). In the following sentence, the author wishes to emphasize that Canadians like to watch whales, and puts this idea in an independent clause, and subordinates the reasons why whale watching is popular following the subordinating conjunction *because*.

A popular new hobby in Canada is whale watching, because many people like to observe these fascinating mammals in their natural habitat.

In the following example, the writer uses coordination to indicate that both ideas—what Luba bought and how she paid for it—are equally important; thus, each is presented in a main clause.

                               *and she*
Luba bought a classic '57 Chevy, ~~She~~ paid cash for it.
                               ^

## SENT 5a   Use subordination to group short, choppy sentences into larger units of thought.

Besides being stylistically monotonous, short, choppy sentences give equal importance to all your ideas, but only rarely are all your ideas equally important. You communicate more clearly if you show how your thoughts are related. Use one of the following four strategies for subordinating supporting details to the main idea. (See also SENT 7a.)

**1. Subordinate with an adjective or a phrase that functions as an adjective (see GRAM 1d, 3a, and 3b).**

> exhausted and covered with mud,
> The football players stood in the rain. ~~They were exhausted. They were covered with mud~~. ^

[The minor ideas, *exhausted* and *covered with mud,* are now subordinated.]

**2. Subordinate with an adverb or a phrase that functions as an adverb (see GRAM 3a and 3b).**

> After removing           and cleaning                         carefully reinstall
> ~~Remove~~ the spark plugs. ~~Clean~~ them with a wire brush, ~~Reinstall~~ them.
> ^
>
> ~~Be careful,~~

[The minor idea *carefully* has been subordinated to the main point, the instructions.]

**3. Subordinate with an adverb clause (see GRAM 4b).**

> When s                      s
>   ~~S~~he was 30 years old, ~~S~~he made her first solo flight.
>     ^                     ^
> [The less important thought, *30 years old,* has been subordinated to the main point, what she achieved.]

**4. Subordinate with an appositive or appositive phrase (see GRAM 3c).**

> The
> ~~There were two~~ winners, ~~Their names were~~ Pamela and Rajiv, ~~They~~
> couldn't attend the banquet. ^
>                            ^

[Because the main idea is that the winners couldn't attend, we're only incidentally interested in their names. Therefore, *Pamela and Rajiv* has been subordinated.]

## SENT 5b   Do not subordinate excessively.

In avoiding short, choppy sentences, do not go overboard in the other direction and subordinate excessively. Your sentence will drag on and lose its effectiveness. Eliminate excessive subordination by using modifiers—phrases as well as words—or by breaking the sentence into two.

The ship, ~~low in the water with cargo and silently creeping along~~, entered the channel, which glittered from the light of the sun. ~~that was just~~ <sup>rising</sup>

~~rising~~. Low in the water with cargo, it silently crept along.

[Breaking the sentence into two and changing the clause *that was just rising* to an adjective makes the writing more forceful.]

## SENT 5c Use coordination to put ideas of equal importance in grammatical structures of equal weight.

There are three ways to coordinate ideas in a sentence. Join the independent clauses by

1. using a comma and a coordinating conjunction (*and, but, or, for, nor, so,* or *yet*—see GRAM 1g),
2. using a semicolon (see PUNCT 2a),
3. using a pair of correlative conjunctions, such as *either/or, neither/nor, not only/but also* (see GRAM 1g).

# SENT 6 _____
# EMPHASIS

Inexperienced writers sometimes try to emphasize their most important ideas by using italics, exclamation marks, or intensifiers such as *truly* and *incredibly.* These are mechanical and unimaginative devices, however, and they actually have a numbing effect on your readers. Instead, use subordination (see SENT 5a) and a variety of other techniques presented in this section to sharpen the focus of your ideas and thereby heighten the interest of your readers.

## SENT 6a Achieve emphasis by placing the most important words and phrases at the beginning or end of a sentence.

The most emphatic part of a sentence is the end; the second most emphatic part is the beginning; the least emphatic part is the middle.

Less important ideas and qualifying phrases such as *for the most part, as I see it,* and *in a sense* should be buried in the middle of the sentence, placed at the front, or—often best—eliminated.

When our two best players were injured, our hockey team was ~~in a sense~~ defeated, ^in a sense,^

^According to experts,^ Children's carseats should be placed in the back seat, ~~according to experts.~~

## SENT 6b Place ideas that occur in a series in a logical and climactic order.

Wendell went off the road, ^lost control,~~lost control,~~ and hit a tree.

[Losing control happened first and so should be stated first.]

## SENT 6c Use the active rather than the passive voice.

The **active voice** of a verb (see WORD 4e, EDIT 2f, and SENT 3d) is emphatic because it stresses the doer of an action; the **passive voice** of a verb is less emphatic because it stresses the receiver of an action.

PASSIVE    Our sailboat was pushed by high winds onto the rocks, where it was torn to pieces by the waves.

ACTIVE    High winds pushed our sailboat onto the rocks, where the waves tore it to pieces.

Sometimes, however, the receiver of an action needs to be emphasized. In this case, of course, use the passive voice. Here, for example, how quickly the house sold is the point, not who sold it.

Our house was sold the day it went on the market.

## SENT 6d Repeat important words for emphasis.

Repeating a key word, phrase, or fact to keep an idea before the reader can be a very effective strategy. Repetition and parallelism (see

SENT 1) are frequently found together in writing, though they are not necessary to one another.

> *Victory* at all costs, *victory* in spite of all terror, *victory* however long and hard the road may be; for without *victory* there is no survival.
> —Winston Churchill

## SENT 6e    Occasionally use a short, dramatic sentence.

A short declarative sentence (see GRAM 5b), especially when it follows a longer, more involved sentence, introduces variety and thus achieves emphasis.

> He was a person who needed no introduction, who possessed immense charisma and presence, who had an international reputation for diplomacy and compromise, and whose face was as well known abroad as it was at home. *He owned any room he entered.*

## SENT 6f    Use periodic sentences for emphasis.

In a **periodic sentence**, modifying phrases and clauses build to the main idea, which is placed at the end, closest to the period (hence its name). Periodic sentences are emphatic because they keep the reader in suspense until the main idea is reached, and because they appear infrequently in modern prose.

Most sentences we write are *loose sentences*; that is, the main idea is expressed immediately, and subsequent phrases and clauses trail behind, providing details and qualifications.

LOOSE        The house was said to be haunted because a jilted lover had committed suicide in the basement more than a century ago.

PERIODIC     The house, in which a jilted lover had committed suicide in the basement more than a century ago, was said to be haunted.

Both sentences are correct, but you gain emphasis by occasionally using a periodic sentence.

## SENT 6g   Achieve emphasis by using balanced constructions.

In most **balanced constructions**, similar ideas are presented in grammatically similar constructions (see SENT 1). Emphasis can be achieved, however, by doing the unexpected—placing contrasting ideas in grammatically similar constructions.

> Hard practices are required for easy games.

> [The expectation is that a similar idea will follow in a similar construction (*hard practices/hard games*); instead, the unexpected contrasting idea (*easy games*) emphasizes the author's point.]

# SENT 7
## SENTENCE VARIETY

A series of sentences that are the same length and that follow the same basic pattern is boring. **Sentence variety** adds interest to your writing. However, you should seek variety in sentence structure not as an end in itself but as a more accurate means of reflecting your thoughts. Just as you do not think in a mechanical and monotonous way, so too you should not write mechanical and monotonous sentences (see GRAM 5).

The techniques discussed in this section are all good options for adding variety to your writing. Use them to put your thoughts into sentences that suit your purpose (see COMP 2f) and your audience (see COMP 2g).

## SENT 7a   Vary your sentences.

Both of the following passages describe the city of Vancouver. Although their content is essentially the same, the first is monotonous because it is made up of a series of simple sentences of nearly the same length; the second is interesting because it is made up of sentences of varying structure and length.

CHOPPY AND MONOTONOUS

> Water surrounds Vancouver on all sides. The snow-crowned Coast Mountains ring the city on the northeast. Vancouver has a floating quality

of natural loveliness. There is a curved beach at English Bay. This beach is in the shape of a half-moon. Residential highrises stand behind the beach. They are pale tones of beige, blue, and ice-cream pink. Turn-of-the-century houses of painted wood frown upward at the glitter of the office towers. Any urban glare is softened by folds of green lawns, flowers, fountains, and trees. Such landscaping appears to be unplanned. It links Vancouver to its ultimate treasure of greenness. The treasure is thousand-acre Stanley Park.

INTERESTING

Surrounded by water on three sides and ringed to the northeast by the snow-covered Coast Mountains, Vancouver has a floating quality of natural loveliness. At English Bay, the half-moon curve of the beach is backed by highrises in pale tones of beige, blue, and ice-cream pink. Turn-of-the-century houses of painted wood frown upward at the glitter of office towers. Yet any urban glare is quickly softened by folds of green lawns, flowers, fountains, and trees that in a seemingly unplanned fashion link Vancouver to its ultimate treasure of greenness—thousand-acre Stanley Park.

—Veronica Thomas, "Vancouver"

If you tend to write short, simple sentences, study the following five ways of combining sentences to make your writing more interesting.

## 1. Use subordinating and coordinating conjunctions to relate and connect ideas (see GRAM 1g).

~~Robert went on a tour of~~ the hospital. ~~He saw~~ many sick people. ~~He~~ had
a greater appreciation for the work doctors do. ~~He had a greater appreciation~~ for his own good health. ~~He~~ had taken ~~his good health~~ for granted.

*After touring* the hospital, *and seeing* many sick people, *Robert* had a greater appreciation for the work doctors do, *and* for his own good health, *which he* had taken for granted.

## 2. Use modifiers effectively.

Instead of writing separate descriptive statements, combine modifiers to convey a more graphic picture in a single sentence (see SENT 5a).

Suki bought the *old, dilapidated* house. ~~It was old. It was dilapidated.~~

**3. Use a semicolon (see PUNCT 2a) or colon (see PUNCT 3a) to link closely related ideas.**

This novel is not one of her better works ; ~~. I~~t is ill-conceived and badly written.

Four students won the essay contest ; ~~The winners were~~ Trang, Susan, Alfie, and Luisa.

**4. Use parallel constructions (see SENT 1).**

Georgene liked the dress. It was her favourite style and ~~The colour was also~~ her favourite colour.

**5. Use absolute constructions (see GRAM 3d).**

~~We were~~ Stuck in traffic, w~~We~~ sat for 40 minutes and ~~We~~ missed the opening face-off.

# SENT 7b  Vary your sentence openings.

More than half of all sentences in English begin with the subject (see GRAM 2a). However, if all, or nearly all, the sentences in a given passage begin this way, the effect is monotonous.

Consider the different ways in which the following sentence can be rewritten to vary its beginning and add interest.

Passengers partied in the ballroom and did not know that the ship had hit an iceberg.

**1. Begin with a participle, a gerund, or an infinitive (see GRAM 3b).**

*Partying* in the ballroom, the passengers did not know that the ship had hit an iceberg.

**2. Begin with a prepositional phrase (see GRAM 3a).**

*In the ballroom,* the passengers partied, not knowing that the ship had hit an iceberg.

3. **Begin with a subordinate clause (see GRAM 4a and 4b).**

   *As they partied in the ballroom,* the passengers did not know that the ship had hit an iceberg.

4. **Begin with a coordinating conjunction (see GRAM 1g).**

   *And* the passengers, partying in the ballroom, did not know that the ship had hit an iceberg.

5. **Begin with an expletive (see EDIT 1g).**

   *There* were passengers partying in the ballroom who did not know the ship had hit an iceberg.

Another way of changing the usual subject-verb-object order of sentences is simply to **invert**—to reverse the natural order. Do not, though, seek variety at the expense of proper emphasis.

| USUAL ORDER | INVERTED ORDER |
|---|---|
| Subject-Predicate | Predicate-Subject |
| The water gushed out. | Out gushed the water. |
| Subject-Verb-Object | Object-Subject-Verb |
| I never promised that. | That I never promised. |
| Subject-Linking Verb-Complement | Complement-Subject-Linking Verb |
| They would never be happy. | Happy they would never be. |

## SENT 7c   Do not overuse compound sentences.

A series of compound sentences (see GRAM 5a), especially with the main clauses connected by *and*, gives an impression of haste and thoughtlessness. Like a series of short, simple sentences (see SENT 7a), too many compound sentences bore the reader. When you revise, look for *and* used as a coordinating conjunction. If you find that you overuse *and*, try the following four methods to bring important ideas into focus and make it easier for the reader to follow your thoughts.

1. **Change a compound sentence into a simple sentence with a modifier(s) or an appositive (see GRAM 3c).**

   SIMPLE SENTENCE WITH A MODIFIER

   The hiking trail ,̭was nearly five kilometres long and it was wonderfully

   scenic, and it was popular with young campers.

SIMPLE SENTENCE WITH AN APPOSITIVE

My brother, is a heart surgeon, ~~and he is brilliant, and he~~ is on the staff

*brilliant*

of St. Joseph's Hospital.

## 2. Change a compound sentence into a simple sentence with a compound predicate (see GRAM 2b).

SIMPLE SENTENCE WITH A COMPOUND PREDICATE

Tony grabbed his tennis racquet/ and ~~he~~ jumped into the car.

## 3. Change a compound sentence into a simple sentence with a phrase or phrases (see GRAM 3a).

SIMPLE SENTENCE WITH A PHRASE

Canadian Tire stores have a great variety of merchandise, ~~and the prices are good.~~

*with good prices.*

## 4. Change a compound sentence into a complex sentence (see GRAM 5a).

COMPLEX SENTENCE

*Because m*

~~M~~y computer was broken, ~~and~~ I had to write my report in longhand.

# EDIT

## Editing for Grammar

### *Learning Objectives*

After reading this section, you should

1. recognize subject-verb agreement errors,
2. use verbs and pronouns correctly,
3. use adjectives and adverbs correctly,
4. recognize fragments, comma splices, and run-on sentences.

# EDIT

## Editing for Grammar

# EDIT 1
## SUBJECT-VERB AGREEMENT

In grammar, **subject-verb agreement** refers to the relationship between a verb and its subject. Every verb in a clause or sentence must agree in *number* and *person* with its subject. That is, a verb must be singular if its subject is singular; a verb must be plural if its subject is plural. Also, a verb must agree in person (i.e., the doer of the action—first person, second person, third person) with its grammatical subject.

SINGULAR SUBJECT AND SINGULAR VERB

*Overcrowding causes* many of the discipline problems in our schools.

PLURAL SUBJECT AND PLURAL VERB

*Fires destroy* millions of dollars worth of property each year.

Normally, we do not think twice about subject-verb agreement. A few constructions, however, can be troublesome. In most cases, the problem results from not having correctly identified the subject of the sentence.

### EDIT 1a   To choose the correct verb form, identify the subject of the sentence.

Sometimes intervening word groups obscure the relationship between the subject (S) and the verb in a sentence. When this happens, the culprit is usually a prepositional phrase. Mentally eliminate all the prepositional phrases in a sentence, and see what is left. One of these leftover words must be the subject because a subject never appears in a prepositional phrase (see GRAM 3a).

The first three weeks of basic training ~~is~~ *are* the worst.

[The plural subject *weeks* takes a plural verb.]

Another word group that can cause confusion about subject–verb agreement is the subordinate clause (see GRAM 4). Neither the subject nor the verb of a sentence will ever appear in a subordinate clause.

The use of mood-altering drugs, although they sometimes provide

great medical benefits, ~~are~~ *is* generally criticized by the public.

[The singular subject *use* takes a singular verb.]

A problem can also arise from the use of such expressions as *along with, as well as, in addition to, including,* and *together with.* Again, look elsewhere for the subject of the sentence.

> S                                                                    is
> The cost of medication as well as doctors' fees ~~are~~ a problem for retired Canadians wintering in Florida.
>
> [The singular subject *cost* takes a singular verb.]

Thus, if you mentally block off all the prepositional phrases, subordinate clauses, and miscellaneous expressions in a sentence, the subject and verb will stand out by process of elimination.

> Unless it rains, *I plan* on leaving as late as possible, along with all the other vacationers.

Finally, look for inverted word order, in which the subject follows the verb (see SENT 7b).

> have                                                    S
> From his research ~~has~~ come three promising anti-cancer drugs.
>
> [The plural subject *drugs* takes a plural verb.]

## EDIT 1b    Use a plural verb with most compound subjects joined by *and.*

In most cases, compound subjects are clearly plural and take a plural verb.

> S                    S    were
> Their television and their camera ~~was~~ stolen.

However, when singular subjects joined by *and* are preceded by *each, every, no, nothing,* or *many a(n),* use a singular verb.

> is
> Every chair and every couch ~~are~~ on sale this week.
>
> [Every *single* chair and every *single* couch (each) is on sale.]

> is
> No bicycling and no hitchhiking ~~are~~ permitted on Highway 20.
>
> [Neither *one,* or nothing—*no thing* (singular)—is permitted.]

If the two parts of a compound subject, whether singular or plural, express a single idea or refer to a single person, use a singular verb.

Ham and eggs ~~are~~ *is* my favourite breakfast.

[The subject *ham and eggs* is considered a single dish and takes a singular verb.]

His son and partner ~~know~~ *knows* all the facts about the incident.

[His son is also his partner. If they were different people, *know* would be correct.]

## EDIT 1c   If subjects joined by *either/or* or *neither/nor* differ in number or person, make the verb agree with the subject that is closest to it.

Neither the instructor nor the students ~~is~~ *are* satisfied with the classroom.

[One singular subject (*instructor*) and one plural subject (*students*) are joined by *nor;* make the verb agree with the closer subject (*students*), which is plural.]

Either Steffi or I ~~has~~ *have* to report the broken window.

[One third-person subject (*Steffi*) and one first-person subject (*I*) are joined by *or;* make the verb agree with the closer subject (*I*, which is first person).]

## EDIT 1d   When a collective noun used as a subject regards a group as a unit, use a singular verb. When it refers to the individual members of a group, use a plural verb.

**Collective nouns** are singular in form but have a plural meaning; for example, *band, jury, family, minority, majority* (see GRAM 1b). They may take either a singular or a plural verb, depending on whether you are considering the group as a unit or considering its individual members.

The *committee gives* its report today.

[*Committee* is considered a unit because all the members are acting as one in giving a single report; a singular verb is used.]

The *committee give* their reports today.

[The individual members of the committee will each give a report; *committee* has a plural meaning so the verb must be plural.]

To be consistent in sentences containing collective nouns, make pronoun references to the noun singular or plural as well.

The *team plans* to fly to Moncton for *its* next game.

[*Team* is considered a single entity (the members are all on the same plane); use a singular verb and a singular pronoun.]

The *team plan* to fly to Moncton for *their* next game.

[The *team* is considered as individuals travelling separately and arriving at different times; use a plural verb and a plural pronoun.]

## EDIT 1e   When a relative pronoun (*who, which,* or *that*) is the subject, make the verb agree with the pronoun's antecedent.

Usually, verb agreement is not a problem with relative pronouns (see GRAM 1c).

A *politician who votes* pro-labour gets elected.

[The singular noun *politician* is the antecedent of *who;* use a singular verb.]

*Politicians who vote* pro-labour get elected.

[The antecedent of *who* is *politicians,* which is plural; use a plural verb.]

However, when the phrase *one of the* or *only one of the* is part of the sentence, identifying the antecedent takes extra care.

She is one of the *politicians who* always *vote* pro-labour.

[The antecedent of *who* is *politicians* because the sense is that more than one politician votes a particular way; the verb, therefore, is plural.]

She is the only *one* of the politicians *who* always *votes* pro-labour.

[The antecedent of *who* is *one* because she is the only politician who votes a particular way; the verb, therefore, is singular.]

## EDIT 1f When an indefinite pronoun is the subject, choose a singular or plural verb, depending on the number of the indefinite pronoun.

Indefinite pronouns are a problem area of subject–verb agreement in English. Their usage is changing in several respects, presenting writers with new choices.

**1. Use a singular verb with a singular indefinite pronoun** (*another, anybody, anyone, anything, each, either, everybody, everyone, everything, neither, no one, nothing, one, somebody, someone, something*).

*Somebody has* to decide whether to paint the kitchen this year.

[One person (one body) will make the decision.]

**2. Use a plural verb with a plural indefinite pronoun** (*both, few, many, several*).

I spent the afternoon shopping for a camera, but *few were* reasonably priced.

[Not many, but more than one, were available.]

**3. With indefinite pronouns that can be either singular or plural** (*all, any, none, some*), **use a singular or plural verb, depending on the word the indefinite pronoun refers to.**

*All* of the *wheat is* harvested.

*All* of the *fields are* ploughed.

[Because *wheat* is singular, *all* takes a singular verb. Because *fields* is plural, *all* takes a plural verb.]

## EDIT 1g When a sentence begins with the expletive *there* or *here*, make the verb agree in number with the subject.

**Expletives** are words that stand in for a subject that is deferred until later in the sentence. In addition to *there* and *here,* the pronoun *it* can also function as an expletive, but it always takes a singular verb.

are                  S

There ~~is~~ stone, brick, and tile fireplaces in Blenheim Castle.

## EDIT 1h   Make linking verbs agree in number with their subjects, not with their complements.

A **subject complement** (see GRAM 2d) renames or describes the subject and is, therefore, sometimes confused with it.

S    is

His main interest ~~are~~ stamps.

[The subject, *interest,* is singular, so the verb must be singular; *stamps* is the complement.]

## EDIT 1i   When the subject noun is in the form of a plural but is singular in meaning, use a singular verb.

Nouns that are plural in form but singular in meaning take singular verbs. Examples of such nouns include *athletics, mathematics, measles, mumps, news, physics,* and *politics.*

S   was

Measles ~~were~~ a serious childhood disease until a vaccine was developed.

Some nouns, however, end in *s* and are singular in meaning but take plural verbs: *eyeglasses, pants, pliers, scissors, trousers, tweezers.*

S   are

The scissors ~~is~~ on the table.

If you are uncertain whether to use a singular or a plural verb with a particular noun, consult your dictionary.

## EDIT 1j   When the title of a poem, short story, play, or book is the subject of a sentence, use a singular verb, even if the title is plural in form.

S         is

*Stories of Yukon Gamblers* ~~are~~ by Rene Jallot.

## EDIT 1k   When a word used as a word is the subject, use a singular verb.

The number (singular or plural) of the word used as a word is unimportant; the sentence is about a single thing so use a singular verb.

S   is̶

*Flurries* ~~are~~ one of the terms used to describe a light fall of snow.

## EDIT 1l   When the subject of a sentence is a noun clause, use a singular verb.

S

That he actually bought a new jeep *surprises* me.

[The verb is singular because the noun clause refers to a single thing: *it* (singular) surprises me.]

Noun clauses that begin with *what* are the exception. If the subject of the sentence is plural and the verb is a linking verb, use a plural verb with a *what* clause.

*are*        S

What worries him more than anything else ~~is~~ his low grades in his major.

# EDIT 2 _____

# VERBS: FORM, TENSE, MOOD, AND VOICE

## EDIT 2a   Use the principal parts of irregular verbs correctly.

English verbs are either *regular* or *irregular* in form (see GRAM 1a). Quite simply, a **regular verb** is one that forms both the past tense and the past participle by adding *-ed* to the base form (*walk, walked, walked*). Regular verbs rarely cause problems; it is **irregular verbs** that can be tricky because they have different forms for the past tense and past participle (*sing, sang, sung*).

Canadians *sing* the national anthem before sporting events.

Roger Doucet *sang* the anthem at the Montreal Forum for many years.

Who *had sung* "O Canada" before the All-Star Game in Toronto?

The most frequently used of the approximately two hundred irregular verbs in English are identified in the following list. For some, two acceptable forms are given; they usually represent regional variations.

COMMON IRREGULAR VERBS

| Infinitive | Past Tense | Past Participle |
| --- | --- | --- |
| awake | awoke | awakened |
| be | was | been |
| bear [to carry] | bore | borne |
| bear [to give birth] | bore | born |
| become | became | become |
| begin | began | begun |
| bend | bent | bent |
| bet | bet | bet |
| bite | bit | bitten, bit |
| blow | blew | blown |
| break | broke | broken |
| bring | brought | brought |
| build | built | built |
| burst | burst | burst |
| catch | caught | caught |
| choose | chose | chosen |
| come | came | come |
| cost | cost | cost |
| cut | cut | cut |
| deal | dealt | dealt |
| dig | dug | dug |
| dive | dived, dove | dived |
| do | did | done |
| drag | dragged | dragged |
| draw | drew | drawn |
| dream | dreamed, dreamt | dreamed, dreamt |
| drink | drank | drunk |
| drive | drove | driven |
| eat | ate | eaten |
| fall | fell | fallen |
| feel | felt | felt |
| find | found | found |
| fit | fit, fitted | fit, fitted |
| fly | flew | flown |
| forbid | forbade, forbad | forbidden |

| Infinitive | Past Tense | Past Participle |
|---|---|---|
| forget | forgot | forgotten, forgot |
| freeze | froze | frozen |
| get | got | got, gotten |
| give | gave | given |
| go | went | gone |
| grow | grew | grown |
| hang [to suspend] | hung | hung |
| hang [to execute] | hanged | hanged |
| hear | heard | heard |
| hit | hit | hit |
| hurt | hurt | hurt |
| know | knew | known |
| lay [to put] | laid | laid |
| lead | led | led |
| lend | lent | lent |
| let | let | let |
| lie [to recline] | lay | lain |
| light | lighted, lit | lighted, lit |
| lose | lost | lost |
| pay | paid | paid |
| put | put | put |
| ride | rode | ridden |
| ring | rang | rung |
| rise | rose | risen |
| run | ran | run |
| say | said | said |
| see | saw | seen |
| set [to place] | set | set |
| shake | shook | shaken |
| shine | shone, shined | shone, shined |
| shrink | shrank | shrunk |
| shut | shut | shut |
| sing | sang | sung |
| sink | sank | sunk |
| sit [to be seated] | sat | sat |
| slay | slew | slain |
| speak | spoke | spoken |
| split | split | split |
| spread | spread | spread |
| spring | sprang | sprung |
| steal | stole | stolen |
| strike | struck | struck, stricken |
| swear | swore | sworn |
| swim | swam | swum |
| take | took | taken |

| Infinitive | Past Tense | Past Participle |
|---|---|---|
| teach | taught | taught |
| tear | tore | torn |
| throw | threw | thrown |
| wake | woke, waked | waked, woken |
| wear | wore | worn |
| win | won | won |
| write | wrote | written |

If you are not certain about the form of a particular verb, consult your dictionary. Most dictionaries list all three principal parts of irregular verbs and the infinitive form of regular verbs.

## EDIT 2b  Use *lay* and *lie* and *set* and *sit* correctly.

Writers often confuse the irregular verbs *lay* (to put down) and *lie* (to recline), and *set* (to put something somewhere) and *sit* (to take a seat).

| INFINITIVE | PAST TENSE | PAST PARTICIPLE |
|---|---|---|
| lay | laid | laid |
| lie | lay | lain |
| set | set | set |
| sit | sat | sat |

*Lay* and *set* are transitive verbs (see GRAM 1a) and require a direct object (DO) to complete their meaning. *Lie* and *sit* are intransitive verbs (see GRAM 1a), and therefore do not take a direct object.

   laid        DO
I ~~lay~~ the package down on the table in the hall yesterday.

       lie
I'm going to ~~lay~~ down for an hour before dinner.

     set      DO
You can ~~sit~~ the groceries on the kitchen counter.

        sit
Ms. Lane asked the class to ~~set~~ quietly.

Another pair of irregular verbs that causes problems is *hang* (to suspend an object) and *hang* (to execute a person).

The curator ~~hanged~~ <sup>hung</sup> the Iroquois masks in the entrance. <sup>DO</sup>

The prisoner was ~~hung~~ <sup>hanged</sup> at dawn yesterday.

## EDIT 2c  Use the correct verb tense to convey your meaning.

The **tense** of a verb indicates when an action is taking place. In English there are three basic tenses—*present, past,* and *future.* Each tense also has a *perfect,* a *progressive,* and a *perfect progressive* form.

### Present tense

Use the **present tense** to express an action occurring in the present, a habitual action, or a fact or general truth. Also use the present tense in describing or discussing an artistic work.

**PRESENT TIME ACTION**   Kendra *works* for the Ministry of the Attorney General in Regina.

**HABITUAL ACTION**   Tom *empties* the garbage cans every morning.

**FACT**   Water *boils* at 100°C.

**GENERAL TRUTH**   It *is* always better to be honest.

**LITERARY WORK**   Hagar *realizes* that her son Marvin and his wife Doris want to put her in a nursing home.

The **literary** or **historical present tense** refers to the use of the present tense for events that have occurred in the past. Using the present tense makes the events or fictional happenings come alive. Do not lapse into the past tense out of habit because you are writing about something that has already happened.

Both Canadians and Britons ~~surprised~~ <sup>surprise</sup> themselves with the depth of their own grief as they ~~mourned~~ <sup>mourn</sup> the death of Diana, Princess of Wales.

The present tense can also be used to indicate actions that will take place at some future time.

Susan *leaves* for Charlottetown on Saturday.

### Present perfect

Use the **present perfect tense** to describe (1) an action that occurred in the past but continues into or affects the present, or (2) an action that occurred at no specific time in the past. The present perfect is formed by combining a present form of *have* with the past participle.

She *has taught* master classes in violin for over 10 years.

Some small recording studios *have produced* big hits.

### Present progressive

To show an action that is ongoing at the time of speaking or writing, use the **present progressive**—the present participle of the verb with the present form of the helping verb *to be*.

Tom *is emptying* the garbage cans right now.

The present progressive can also be used to show actions that will take place at some future time.

We *are going* to camp at both Banff and Jasper.

### Present perfect progressive

To show the length of time an action is in progress, use the **present perfect progressive**—the present form of *have* together with *been* and the present participle of the verb.

Simone *has been working* at The Bay for three years.

### Past tense

Use the **past tense** to describe an action that occurred entirely in the past.

Shumba *filed* his income tax forms early this year.

### Past perfect

Use the **past perfect** to describe an action that preceded another action when both occurred in the past. The past perfect is formed by combining a past form of *have* with the past participle of the verb.

Everyone *had eaten* before I arrived.

## Past progressive

To show continuing action in the past, use the **past progressive**—the present participle of the verb with the past form of the helping verb *to be*.

Matthew *was visiting* his grandparents on Cape Breton Island.

## Past perfect progressive

To show the length of time an action was in progress, use the **past perfect progressive**—the past form of *have* together with *been* and the present participle of the verb.

Annika *had been playing* the piano before she took up the guitar.

## Future tense

Use the **future tense** to describe an action that will take place in the future. The future tense is formed by combining *will* with the base form of the verb.

The Goldsteins *will take* their vacation in August this year.

English has additional ways of expressing future time; see the preceding discussions of present tense and present progressive.

## Future perfect

Use the **future perfect tense** to describe an action that will be completed before another future event.

Carla *will have accumulated* 70 credits in engineering by the end of the semester.

## Future progressive

To show a continuing action in the future, use the **future progressive**—the present participle of the verb with the future form of the helping verb *to be*.

Astronomers *will be looking* for meteor showers over the southern horizon this spring.

Future perfect progressive

To show the length of time an action will be in progress, use the **future perfect progressive**—*will have been* with the present participle of the verb.

I *will have been studying* fashion arts for three years in September.

## EDIT 2d    Use sequences of tense forms that are logically related.

How do you know which tense to use? You logically relate the time expressed by verbs in the main clauses with the time expressed by verbs in subordinate clauses, infinitives, or participles.

The tiger jumped through the flaming hoop when the trainer ~~gives~~ the command.
                                                                              *gave*

Mixing tenses does not make a logical statement: you cannot have the tiger jumping in the past and the trainer giving the command in the present. Put both verbs in the past tense to show that both actions already happened, or put both verbs in the present tense to indicate a habitual action. (See SENT 3b.)

Subordinate clauses

You may use any verb tense in your subordinate clause (SC) that is compatible with the intended meaning of your sentence (see GRAM 5a).

The entrance march *will begin* after the wedding guests *have taken* their seats in the church.

[The future tense is used in the main clause (MC) to show an anticipated action; the present perfect tense is used in the subordinate clause to show that the seating of the guests will precede the march.]

Some optimistic economists *believe* that the stock market soon *will top* the 10 000 mark.

[The present tense is used in the main clause to show what economists currently believe; the future tense is used in the subordinate clause to show that the stock market's performance is anticipated at some future time.]

However, when the verb in the main clause is in the past or past perfect tense, you must also use the past or past perfect tense in the subordinate clause.

MC                    SC

The Expos *had put* the game out of reach before the Marlins *changed*

their strategy.

[The past perfect is used in the main clause to show that the Expos' action preceded the Marlins' action.]

When a general truth is presented in the subordinate clause, the present tense is used even though the main verb is in the past or past perfect.

SC

We *learned* in business ethics that power *corrupts.*

[The verb in the subordinate clause is in the present tense because *power corrupts* is a general truth.]

## Infinitives

Use the **present infinitive** (*to praise, to drink*) to express action that occurs at the same time as, or later than, that of the main verb.

Marta tried *to improve* her tennis game.

[The present infinitive is used because Marta is making an improvement at the same time as she is trying.]

Use the **present perfect infinitive** (*to have praised, to have drunk*) to express action that occurs prior to that of the main verb.

I would like *to have attended* the concert last weekend.

[The present perfect infinitive is used because attendance at the concert is in the past while the wishing or liking occurs in the present.]

## Participles

Use the **present participle** (*praising, drinking*) to express action happening at the same time as that of the main verb.

*Bicycling* across campus, Jan lost her bracelet.

[The present participle is used because Jan lost her bracelet at the same time she was bicycling.]

Use the **present perfect participle** (*having praised, having drunk*) for action occurring prior to that of the main verb.

*Having driven* 400 kilometres nonstop, Roberto stopped to stretch.

[The present perfect participle is used because the driving occurs before the stopping.]

## EDIT 2e  Use verbs in the correct mood.

The three **moods** of a verb—*indicative, imperative,* and *subjunctive*—reveal the writer's intent; that is, how the writer views a thought or action. For example, it is a verb's mood that shows the writer is making a statement and not simply expressing a wish.

Use the **indicative mood** to make a statement or ask a question. Verb tense in the indicative mood depends on context (see EDIT 2c).

Use the **imperative mood** to give an order. Verbs in the imperative mood are always in the present tense except for *be,* which is used in the base form. Usually the subject *you* is understood.

*Gargle* with salt water.

*Be* at the airport by noon.

Use the **subjunctive mood** in *that* clauses expressing demands, resolutions, or requests, and to express a condition contrary to fact or a wish. With *that* clauses, use the base form of the verb (*agree, be, farm, vote*) whether the subject is singular or plural.

The manager asked that he lists his qualifications for the job.

The coach required that players ~~are~~ be dressed one hour prior to the game.

Use *were* to express a wish and in contrary-to-fact clauses beginning with *if.*

If I ~~was~~ were younger, I would go to law school.

## EDIT 2f  Use the active voice.

**Voice** indicates whether the subject of a sentence is the actor or the receiver of the action (see SENT 6c). In the **active voice**, the subject of the sentence does the acting; in the **passive voice**, the subject is acted upon.

**ACTIVE VOICE**
The Canadian Medical Association *supports* any legislation that will improve public access to health care.

**PASSIVE VOICE**
Any legislation that will improve public access to health care *is supported* by the Canadian Medical Association.

Use the active voice in most of your writing; it is more concise, direct, and forceful than the passive voice. To change a sentence from passive to active voice, simply make the actor the subject of the sentence and eliminate unnecessary words.

The students selected
"Poverty and Homelessness" ~~was selected~~ as the theme for next year's

lecture series .~~by the students~~

When the action itself is what is important or you wish to minimize the importance of the actor, use the passive voice. The passive voice is often used in scientific and technical writing to emphasize processes and events rather than individuals.

Three drops of boric acid *were added* to the solution.

Investigative teams *were sent* immediately by the Centres for Disease Control.

When you want to highlight the recipient of an action rather than the performer, use the passive voice.

Canadian-born pitcher Ferguson Jenkins, a Hall of Famer, *was traded* by the Philadelphia Phillies early in his career.

# EDIT 3 _____
## PRONOUN PROBLEMS

A **pronoun** takes the place of a noun in a sentence (see GRAM 1c). Pronoun problems fall into three general categories: (1) Problems with agreement (a pronoun must agree with the noun to which it refers), (2) referent problems (it isn't clear what the pronoun is referring to), and (3) case problems (the wrong case is used, e.g., *I* is used instead of *me*, or *who* is used instead of *whom*). The result can be sexist language, lack of clarity, or an impression of carelessness.

## EDIT 3a   A pronoun must agree with its antecedent in gender, number, and person.

A pronoun must agree with its **antecedent**, the noun to which it refers (see GRAM 1c). Personal pronouns must agree in gender, number, and person.

### 1. Be aware of the sexist use of pronouns.

Traditionally, a masculine, singular pronoun has been used to agree with indefinite antecedents (such as *anyone, someone,* and *everyone*) and to refer to generic antecedents (such as *employee, student, patient, traveller,* or *applicant*). But *anyone* can be female or male, and women are employees (or students, patients, travellers, applicants), too. The use of masculine pronouns to refer to both females and males is unacceptable because it is **sexist**; that is, such usage leaves out women as a segment of society or diminishes their presence (see WORD 3). Instead, use *he or she, his or her.* Or, in an extended piece of writing, alternate in a balanced way the use of *he* and *she* throughout. Sometimes the best solution is to rewrite the sentence in the plural, avoiding the problem altogether.

**UNACCEPTABLE BECAUSE IT IS SEXIST**

If *anyone* wants to buy a basketball season ticket, *he* will have to sign up before Friday.

**UNACCEPTABLE BECAUSE IT IS GRAMMATICALLY INCORRECT**

If *anyone* wants to buy a basketball season ticket, *they* will have to sign up before Friday.

**REWRITTEN USING *HE* OR *SHE***

If *anyone* wants to buy a basketball season ticket, *he or she* will have to sign up before Friday.

**REWRITTEN IN THE PLURAL**

If any *students* want to buy basketball season *tickets, they* will have to sign up before Friday.

**REWRITTEN TO AVOID THE PRONOUNS**

All basketball season tickets must be reserved before Friday.

**REWRITTEN IN THE SECOND PERSON**

If *you* want to buy a basketball season ticket, *you* must sign up before Friday.

**REWRITTEN WITH A RELATIVE PRONOUN**

*Anyone* who wants to buy a basketball season ticket must sign up before Friday.

## 2. Let the meaning of a collective noun (*family, majority, choir, jury, faculty*) determine whether pronouns that refer to it should be singular or plural.

If a collective noun (see GRAM 1b) is understood as a unit, it takes a singular pronoun; if it is understood as individual members, it takes a plural pronoun.

The band started to play ~~their~~ its first number.

[The band as a unit is playing the song; use a singular pronoun.]

The band agreed to pay for ~~its~~ their own uniforms.

[The individual members came to an agreement; use a plural pronoun.]

## 3. Disregard gender and use a plural pronoun to refer to two or more singular antecedents that are connected by *and*.

Antecedents joined by *and* form a compound subject and take a plural pronoun whether the antecedents are singular or plural. Gender is not an issue.

Dinah and Chen were exhausted after ~~her and his~~ their chemistry final.

## 4. When two or more antecedents are connected by *or, nor, either/or,* or *neither/nor,* and one is singular and the other is plural, use a pronoun that agrees with the closer antecedent.

Neither the judge nor the lawyers were willing to discuss ~~his~~ their reactions to the verdict.

[Use a plural pronoun because the nearest antecedent, *lawyers,* is plural.]

When a compound antecedent has both a male and a female component, make the pronouns consistent in both gender and the order presented.

Neither Yoko nor Amir was really confident about ~~their~~ grades.
<sup>her or his</sup>

[Use *her* or *his* in that order because Yoko is used first.]

**5. Use a singular pronoun to refer to such antecedents as *each*, *anyone*, *everybody*, *either*, *sort*, *kind*, or *someone*.**

In speech and informal writing, some people use plural pronouns with these antecedents, but formal English requires singular pronouns to be grammatically correct (see pp. 146–47).

When someone doesn't understand, ~~they~~ should ask the instructor for help.
<sup>he or she</sup>

**6. Use *who* or *whom* to refer to persons; use *that* and *which* to refer to animals and things.**

The chef, ~~which~~ was trained in France, will make her famous trout amandine.
<sup>who</sup>

The bicyclist swerved to avoid the dog ~~who~~ had wandered into the street.
<sup>that</sup>

*Who* can be used for an animal with a name, however.

Burt is a friendly dog ~~which~~ likes to bark.
<sup>who</sup>

## EDIT 3b    Be sure a pronoun's referent is clear.

To avoid repeating nouns in speech and writing, use pronouns as noun substitutes (see GRAM 1c). The noun for which a pronoun is substituted is called its **antecedent** or referent.

As ~~Mai~~ opened the envelope, Mai held ~~Mai's~~ breath.
<sup>she</sup>        <sup>her</sup>

When the relationship between a pronoun and its antecedent is unclear, the message is inaccurate or ambiguous (has two or more meanings).

**1. Place a pronoun as close to its antecedent as possible.**

The more words that intervene between the antecedent and the pronoun, the more chance there is for confusion.

> *who had never had much self-confidence,*
> Cathy, was surprised she had been voted president by her classmates.
>
> ~~who had never had much self-confidence,~~

**2. Make every pronoun clearly refer to a specific antecedent.**

If a pronoun can refer to either one of two antecedents, ambiguity exists. Either repeat the antecedent or rewrite the sentence.

> *mother's*
> Liz told her mother that her sweater had a hole in it.
>
> Liz said to her mother, "Your sweater has a hole in it."

It is not acceptable to put the referent in parentheses following the pronoun.

**3. When using *it* as a pronoun referent, check that the antecedent is unmistakable.**

If there is more than one possible antecedent for the pronoun *it*, ambiguity results.

> *the car.*
> When Michel drove the car through the garage door, he badly damaged ~~it.~~

**4. Use *this, that, which,* and *such* judiciously to refer to a general idea in a preceding clause or sentence.**

If an idea is relatively simple, no confusion results from such a construction. If the pronoun refers to a broader or more general idea, however, vagueness results. To correct the problem, either substitute a noun for the pronoun or provide an antecedent to which the pronoun can clearly refer.

> *a procedure that*
> One plumber supervised while the other one did the work, ~~which~~ is normal.

**5. Make every pronoun refer to a stated, not an implied, antecedent.**

Every time you use a pronoun in a sentence, you should be able to see its noun equivalent. If you cannot, use a noun instead.

Because the flood was a potential danger to riverside communities,
inhabitants
~~they~~ were told to evacuate.

[*They* has no clearly stated antecedent; it does not refer to the flood or the communities.]

Sometimes a word or phrase, modifier, or possessive that implies a noun is mistaken for an antecedent.

Pierre Berton
In ~~Pierre Berton's~~ *The Great Depression*, ~~he~~ describes life in Canada during the 1930s.

[*He* has no clearly stated antecedent; *he* could be an unnamed narrator or, as is the case, Berton himself.]

**6. The pronouns *it*, *they*, and *you* must have an antecedent.**

In speech, we are often more involved in what we have to say than in how we say it. For example, we use *it*, *they*, and *you* loosely, without specific antecedents, and our listeners do not mind. But in written English, when these pronouns lack an antecedent, the writer gives an impression of vagueness and carelessness.

T  newscaster
~~On~~ the ~~news, it~~ said the earthquake hit 6.5 on the Richter scale.

considered
In the book, ~~they wrote that~~ the prime minister's actions were questionable.

you are
If ~~the driver is~~ not careful, you can easily miss the exit for Pointe-Claire.

## EDIT 3c    Use pronouns in the correct case.

In English the **case** or form of a personal pronoun is dictated by the grammatical function it serves in a sentence. In the **subjective case**, pronouns function as subjects or subject complements (see GRAM 1c); in the **objective case**, pronouns function as direct objects, indirect objects, or objects of prepositions; and in the **possessive case**, pronouns show ownership.

| SUBJECTIVE | OBJECTIVE | POSSESSIVE |
| --- | --- | --- |
| I | me | my, mine |
| you | you | your, yours |
| he | him | his, his |
| she | her | her, hers |
| it | it | its |
| we | us | our, ours |
| they | them | their, theirs |
| who | whom | whose |

The pronouns *I, he, she, we, they,* and *who* have different forms in all three cases, whereas the pronouns *you* and *it* have a distinctive case form only for the possessive. EDIT 3c3 explains why there are two forms of the possessive case for most personal pronouns.

1. **Use the subjective case of pronouns (*I, you, he, she, it, we, they, who, whoever*) for subjects and subject complements.**

> I
> Marge and ~~me~~ shared expenses on the trip to Mexico.
>
> [*I* is part of the compound subject of the verb *shared*.]
>
> he.
> The guy Maria dated is ~~him~~.
>
> [*He* is the complement of the subject *guy*.]

Because we are lax about using the subjective case of pronouns for subject complements in speech, you may think being grammatically correct sounds unnatural (see GRAM 2a and 2d). If so, rewrite the sentence to put the pronoun in the subject position.

> He is the guy Maria dated.

2. **Use the objective case of pronouns (*me, you, him, her, it, us, them, whom, whomever*) for direct objects, indirect objects, and objects of prepositions.**

> her
> The dean invited ~~she~~ and Miguel to represent the student body in Winnipeg.
>
> [*Her* is the direct object of the verb *invited*.]

> me
> Peter sent Alice, Diane, and ~~I~~ flowers.
>
> [*Me* is the indirect object of the verb *sent*.]

Between you and ~~I~~ *me*, Chantal's plan is best.

[*Me* is the object of the preposition *between*.]

Also see GRAM 2c and 3a.

### 3. Use one of the two forms of the possessive case of pronouns to show ownership.

When a pronoun precedes a noun, use the first form of the possessive case (*my, your, his, her, its, our, their, whose*) to show ownership.

*My* notebook has a red cover.

Use the second form of the possessive case, if there is one (*mine, yours, his, hers, ours, theirs*), when the pronoun follows a verb and does not precede a noun.

The notebook with the red cover is *mine*.

### 4. Use the possessive case of pronouns to modify gerunds.

Pronouns that modify a gerund take the first form of the possessive case (*my, your, his, her, its, our, their, whose*).

~~Him~~ *His* returning to college showed great maturity.

The car salesperson understood ~~us~~ *our* wanting a good deal.

### 5. Use the correct case for pronouns in compound constructions.

To choose the correct pronoun in a compound construction, identify its function in the sentence: Is it a subject or object? Test your choice by mentally blocking off the entire compound construction *except* the pronoun in question. Then read the remaining sentence aloud.

My three housemates and ~~me~~ *I* do the cooking.

[Read aloud: Me do the cooking. You can hear the error; revise to put the pronoun in the subjective case, *I*.]

### 6. Use the correct case for pronouns in appositives.

An **appositive** is a noun or noun equivalent that directly follows, or sometimes precedes, another noun or noun equivalent and serves to amplify its meaning (see EDIT 5c). Because an appositive has the same grammatical function as the noun or pronoun it explains, describes, or identifies, the appositive must be in the same case.

Two members of the debate team, Sara and ~~me~~ I, received certificates.

[*Sara and I* is in apposition to the subject *two members;* use the subjective case.]

Let's you and ~~I~~ me cut lab this afternoon and go shopping.

[*You and me* is in apposition to *us,* the object of the verb *let;* use the objective case.]

### 7. Use the correct case for pronouns in *as* and *than* comparisons.

When making comparisons using *as* or *than,* writers sometimes omit words because they trust their readers will readily understand what is being said.

Dag ate more hot dogs than I ~~ate hot dogs~~.

Because the comparison being made is quite clear, the rest of the clause can be omitted.

However, the case of the pronoun depends on its function in the implied clause. One way to choose the right pronoun is to supply the implied sentence parts. If the pronoun in question is the subject of the implied or understood clause, use the subjective case.

Davinder thinks about clothes more than ~~me~~ I.

[The complete understood clause is *than I think about clothes.*]

If the pronoun in question functions as an object in the implied clause, use the objective case.

My father gives my younger sister as big an allowance as ~~h~~ me.

[The complete understood clause is *as he gives me.*]

**8. Use the objective case for pronouns (*me, you, him, her, it, us, them, whom*) that function as subjects or objects of infinitives.**

**Infinitives** (*to* plus a verb) present an exception to the rule that the subjective case is used for subjects: subjects of infinitives are always in the objective case.

me
Mother asked Kurt and I to peel the potatoes.

[*Me* is the subject of the infinitive *to peel*.]

him         her.
My sister named her new baby Celeste, so I expected he to be a she

[*Him* is the subject of the infinitive *to be,* and *her* is its object; the objective case is used in each instance.]

**9. Use *who* or *whom* according to how the word functions in its own clause.**

*Who* and *whom* are interrogative pronouns (along with *whose,* not to be confused with the contraction *who's*). *Who* is the subjective case and *whom* is the objective case (see EDIT 3c1 and 3c2).

As interrogative pronouns, *who* and *whom* commonly begin questions. But which one should you use? To determine the case of the interrogative pronoun, determine its function in the clause. Sometimes it helps to recast the question in your head or to answer the question.

Who
Whom led the Allied forces on D-Day?

[Answer the question: he led the forces, not *him* led the forces, so use the subjective case *who*.]

Whom
Who is the detective speaking to now?

[Answer the question: the detective is speaking *to him,* so use the objective case *whom*.]

As relative pronouns, *who, whoever, whom,* and *whomever* are also used to introduce subordinate clauses (see GRAM 4). The case of the pronoun is determined by its function within the subordinate clause, regardless of the clause's function in the sentence as a whole. Use *who* and *whoever* for subjects; use *whom* and *whomever* for objects. Use *whoever* or *whomever* when there is no specific noun or noun equivalent referent for the pronoun. To test your choice of pronoun, mentally block off the subordinate clause in question and then read it aloud to determine whether the relative pronoun is functioning as subject or object in the subordinate clause.

He did not remember ~~whom~~ *who* was prime minister in 1982.

The Barnes Prize is awarded to ~~whomever~~ *whoever* has the highest grades in physics.

[Remember that the case of the relative pronoun is determined by its function in the subordinate clause. Here, the relative pronoun is the subject of the verb *has*, so the subjective case is required—*whoever.* The entire subordinate clause is the object of the preposition *to*.]

Frank said he would select ~~whoever~~ *whomever* he wanted.

Do not be confused by expressions such as *I believe, she thinks*, and *we know* that frequently follow *who* or *whom* in a subordinate clause. When you block off a subordinate clause containing one of these expressions, leave out the expression (*we know* in the example that follows) when reading aloud.

I plan to call only the people ~~whom~~ *who* we know will want to come.

If *whom* sounds too formal or stiff for a particular writing situation, omit the pronoun if possible.

The female vocalist ~~whom~~ I like best is Sarah McLachlan.

# EDIT 4
## ADJECTIVES AND ADVERBS

**Adjectives** and **adverbs** are modifiers—that is, they limit or qualify the meaning of other words (see GRAM 1d and 1e). There are, however, important differences between the two, and they cannot be used interchangeably.

If you have questions about the correct form of a modifier or whether a particular word is an adjective or an adverb, consult your dictionary.

## EDIT 4a  Use adverbs, not adjectives, to modify verbs, adjectives, and other adverbs.

To avoid inadvertently using an adjective when an adverb is called for, determine what is being modified. If it is a verb (V), an adjective (ADJ), or an adverb (ADV), use an adverb.

V̲‿ADV

The gold dome *shone brightly* in the dazzling sunshine.

ADV‿ADJ

It is worth a special trip to see her *really unusual* collection of masks.

In informal spoken English, *real* is often used to mean "very": We had a *real* good time last night. In formal written English, however, this construction is not acceptable (see WORD 2a).

## EDIT 4b  Use an adjective, not an adverb, after a linking verb to modify the subject.

Because the subject of a sentence is always a noun (N) or noun substitute (PRON) and only adjectives—not adverbs—modify nouns and pronouns, use an adjective after a linking verb to modify, or complement, a subject.

N ⟵――――――――――――――――――― ADJ

The *dancing* in the new National Ballet production is *spectacular.*

Commonly used linking verbs include *be, become, appear, grow, seem, remain,* and *prove.*

PRON‿ADJ

*He* seems *happy.*

N ⟵―――――― ADJ

*Sales* remained *steady* from October through December.

The verbs *feel, look, smell,* and *taste* can function as either linking verbs or action verbs (see GRAM 1a). If you are describing a state of being, the verb is functioning as a linking verb (LV) and you must use an adjective. If you are describing an action, use an adverb to modify the verb.

N     LV     ADJ

The *dentist* looked *curious.*

[In this sentence, the dentist appears inquisitive; *looked* is a linking verb and the adjective *curious* is used to describe the dentist's state of being.]

V     ADV

The dentist *looked curiously* at my chipped tooth.

[Here, the dentist is performing an action. The dentist is looking at the tooth in a curious way; *looked* is an action verb, and an adverb must be used.]

## EDIT 4c    Use *bad/badly* and *good/well* correctly.

Two commonly misused adjective/adverb pairs are *bad/badly* and *good/well.* Errors usually occur when there is a linking verb in the sentence, but you should have no trouble if you remember that *bad* is always an adjective and *badly* is always an adverb. Also, *good* is always an adjective, but *well* can function as either an adjective or an adverb.

N    LV    bad

Anne felt ~~badly~~ about not inviting Peggy and Sanjay.

[To describe Anne's state of being, use the adjective *bad;* to say she *felt badly* describes her sense of touch, which is not the issue here.]

N         LV       good

Pork chops taste especially ~~well~~ with applesauce.

[Use the adjective *good* to modify the chops; *taste* is a linking verb.]

V          well

Shake the juice ~~good~~ before drinking.

[Use the adverb *well* to modify the verb *shake.*]

As an adjective, *well* has several meanings.

All is *well* with my family.    [satisfactory or pleasing]

Elio is not a *well* man.    [sound in body and mind]

It is *well* that we did not go to the show.   [proper or fitting]

## EDIT 4d   Use the form of the demonstrative adjective that agrees with the noun it modifies.

A singular demonstrative adjective (*this, that*) is used to modify a singular noun; a plural demonstrative adjective (*these, those*) is used to modify a plural noun. Demonstrative adjectives (see GRAM 1d) rarely cause problems for writers, with one exception: phrases such as *kind of, sort of,* and *type of.* In these constructions, the demonstrative adjective modifies the noun *kind, sort,* or *type,* and so must agree with it in number.

| WITH SINGULAR NOUNS | WITH PLURAL NOUNS |
|---|---|
| this/that kind | these/those kinds |
| this/that sort | these/those sorts |
| this/that type | these/those types |

kinds
We are looking for these ~~kind~~ of apples.

sorts
Those ~~sort~~ of questions come up during orientation every year.

## EDIT 4e   Use the comparative and superlative forms of adjectives and adverbs correctly.

Adjectives and adverbs have three forms: the **positive** (used to describe: *big, vigorously*), the **comparative** (used to compare two things: *bigger, more vigorously*), and the **superlative** (used to compare three or more things: *biggest, most vigorously*).

With few exceptions, one-syllable and many two-syllable adjectives form the comparative by adding *-er* and the superlative by adding *-est.* Adjectives with three or more syllables, as well as some two-syllable adjectives, are preceded by *more* and *most,* or *less* and *least,* to form the comparative and the superlative, respectively.

| POSITIVE | COMPARATIVE | SUPERLATIVE |
|---|---|---|
| fast | faster | fastest |
| fancy | fancier OR more (less) fancy | fanciest OR most (least) fancy |
| beautiful | more beautiful | most beautiful |

A few adjectives have irregular comparative and superlative forms.

| good | better | best |
| bad | worse | worst |

Several adjectives, because of their meaning, cannot be used as comparatives or superlatives. Among them are *perfect* and *unique;* that is, a thing either is, or is not, unique or perfect.

                unusual
That's the most ~~unique~~ ring I've ever seen.

Her ring is ~~very~~ unique.

Most adverbs form the comparative and superlative by adding *more* and *most* (or *less* and *least*); a few short adverbs add *-er* and *-est*.

| POSITIVE | COMPARATIVE | SUPERLATIVE |
|---|---|---|
| quickly | quicker OR more (less) quickly | quickest OR most (least) quickly |
| safely | more (less) safely | most (least) safely |

A few adverbs have irregular comparative and superlative forms:

| well | better | best |
| badly | worse | worst |

Use the comparative form to compare two things.

                             more
Which of the two candidates is ~~most~~ qualified in your estimation?

Use the superlative to compare three or more things.

                                        least
The javelin thrower's third attempt was her ~~less~~ successful.

Be alert for double comparatives or double superlatives; that is, using *more* or *most* (or *less* or *least*) after already adding *-er* or *-est* to the adjective or adverb in question.

Tuesday was all the ~~more~~ gloomier because I failed a math quiz.

# EDIT 5 _____
## FRAGMENTS

A **sentence fragment** is a part of a sentence presented as if it were a complete sentence. That is, it begins with a capital letter and ends with a period, question mark, or exclamation point, but does not include one of the two essential elements required of a grammatically correct sentence, a subject, or a verb. A sentence fragment gives readers a "fragment" of a thought, not a complete thought. Usually fragments happen unintentionally and should be revised; under certain circumstances, however, a fragment may be used intentionally.

The most common types of sentence fragments are (1) *phrases,* (2) *subordinate clauses,* (3) *appositives,* and (4) *parts of compound predicates* capitalized and punctuated as if they were complete sentences (see GRAM 2, 3, and 4).

Sentence fragments can be eliminated in one of two ways: (1) join the fragment to a sentence nearby, or (2) develop the fragment itself into a complete sentence. In joining a fragment to a sentence, a comma, a colon, or a dash may be needed, or perhaps no punctuation at all. A dash and a colon indicate a more definite break in thought than a comma; a colon is used before items in a series (see PUNCT 3b).

REVISING WITH A COMMA

He has many hobbies, ,Including stamp collecting, bird watching, and raising tropical fish.

REVISING WITH A COLON

We had a traditional Thanksgiving dinner, Turkey with stuffing, cranberry sauce, gravy, mashed potatoes, and pumpkin pie.

REVISING WITH A DASH

Mireille washes her hair twice a day, Much too often.

REVISING WITHOUT PUNCTUATION

Tina would rather have tea, With lemon.

# EDIT  5a    Join a phrase fragment to an existing sentence or rewrite it as a sentence.

A **phrase fragment** lacks either a subject or a complete verb or both.

We left Rome and travelled northward to the picturesque little hill towns

      *We a*   *went*

of Italy. ⁀Also⁀to Florence and Venice.

Often a verbal—an infinitive, gerund, or participle—is mistaken as the verb (see GRAM 1a).

      *c*

Fourteen of us went on a mountain survival trip⁀ Climbing Mount Logan in the Yukon and living off the land.     ⁀

# EDIT  5b    Join a subordinate fragment clause to an existing sentence or rewrite it as a sentence.

A **subordinate clause** contains both a subject and a predicate, but it is introduced by a **subordinator**, either a subordinating conjunction (*after, because, rather than, as, if;* see GRAM 1g) or a relative pronoun (*that, which, who, whom, what;* see GRAM 1c), and therefore is not an independent sentence.

      *w*

I am selling back my biology books⁀, Which are in good condition.

      ⁀ *They're*

I am selling back my biology books. ~~Which are~~ in good condition.

# EDIT  5c    Make an appositive fragment part of a sentence.

An **appositive phrase** is a noun or noun equivalent that identifies or explains another noun or noun equivalent (see GRAM 3c).

      *a*

Marc read two good books during his vacation⁀, An adventure story that     ⁀

took place in Winnipeg, and a history of the Red River settlement.

## EDIT 5d   Keep a compound predicate within a single sentence.

A **compound predicate** is made up of two or more predicates that have the same subject (see GRAM 2b).

> I wanted to buy two new tires for my car, ~~But~~ had enough money to get only one.
>
> [The fragment has been made part of a compound predicate.]

> I wanted to buy two new tires for my car, ~~But~~ but I had enough money to buy only one.
>
> [The sentence has been rewritten as a compound (see GRAM 5a) by converting the fragment into an independent clause with the addition of a subject, *I*.]

## EDIT 5e   Use sentence fragments intentionally to add emphasis and to write realistic dialogue.

Sentence fragments are not always wrong. In fact, if not overused, a sentence fragment can add emphasis.

| SENTENCE | DELIBERATE FRAGMENT |
|---|---|
| Would I change my major now? No, I wouldn't. | Change my major now? No! |

Sentence fragments are most commonly used in conversation, in advertising, and in descriptive and fictional writing. To write realistic dialogue, include some sentence fragments. An actual conversation, for example, might proceed this way:

> "Go skiing yesterday?"
> "Yes."
> "Where?"
> "Wing Hollow."
> "Crowded?"
> "About a 15-minute wait for the big chair."
> "Icy?"
> "Not really—just in spots."

In descriptive and fictional writing, fragments can be used to set mood or tone. In the following passage, O'Brien uses fragments to set a mood of anticipation for the coming of winter.

A narrow road and the first tentative fall of snow. A light fall that is merely preparatory and does not yet make life cumbersome for the people or the herds. Around each clapboard house a belt of trees, and around the younger trees wooden V's to protect the trunks from the heavier snow.

—Edna O'Brien, "Ways"

In the kind of written English that appears in quality newspapers and magazines and in textbooks, referred to as **edited standard English**, certain phrases can stand alone even though they are fragments: *And now, to summarize; So much for that argument; One final example.* Except for such occasional transitional expressions, however, readers expect the sentences of expository prose to follow the usual subject-verb (object) pattern (see GRAM 2); deviations from this pattern, being unexpected, are very noticeable.

# EDIT 6 _____

## COMMA SPLICES AND RUN-ONS

A **comma splice**, or *comma fault,* occurs when two or more sentences (i.e., two or more main clauses) are incorrectly joined by only a comma.

**COMMA SPLICE**

The legislators could not agree on the bill, they had to stay in session.

**POSSIBLE CORRECTION**

The legislators could not agree on the bill. They had to stay in session.

The **run-on sentence**, or *fused sentence,* occurs when punctuation is omitted between two or more sentences (i.e., two or more main clauses) that are not joined by a coordinating conjunction.

**RUN-ON SENTENCE**

The legislators could not agree on the bill they had to stay in session.

**POSSIBLE CORRECTION**

The legislators could not agree on the bill, so they had to stay in session.

These possible corrections represent only two of the four main ways to correct comma splices and run·on sentences that are presented in the rules that follow. For example, you may want a long sentence after several short sentences, or you may want to put the emphasis on one clause rather than another.

## EDIT 6a    Separate comma splices and run-ons with a period.

**CORRECTED COMMA SPLICE**

I had to buy new sneakers. My mother threw away my old pair.

**CORRECTED RUN-ON SENTENCE**

The sun finally rose. It was light enough to see where we were.

## EDIT 6b    Connect comma splices and run-ons in sentences with a semicolon.

**CORRECTED COMMA SPLICE**

I'm taking a bike repair course; four of us are going to cycle across Prince Edward Island this summer.

**CORRECTED RUN-ON SENTENCE**

Our bike trip will be through sparsely settled country. I think I'll take a bike repair course.

## EDIT 6c    Connect comma splices and run-ons with a comma and a coordinating conjunction (*and, but, or, nor, for, so, yet*).

If the two sentences are equally important and you want to avoid two short sentences, use this method of correction.

**CORRECTED COMMA SPLICE**

It was 30 degrees in the shade, but I'd promised to mow the lawn.

**CORRECTED RUN-ON SENTENCE**

It was 30 degrees in the shade, but I'd promised to mow the lawn.

Using the right coordinating conjunction (see GRAM 1g) will also focus and clarify your meaning.

## EDIT 6d    Make one of the sentences in a comma splice or run-on a subordinate clause.

This method of correction is often the best because it offers the greatest variety of possible revisions. You can choose the subordinating conjunction that conveys exactly what you mean and put the emphasis where you want it in the sentence (see GRAM 1g and SENT 5).

**CORRECTED COMMA SPLICE**

Because t

^The fog came on suddenly, we couldn't find the dock.

[*Because* indicates a one-on-one cause-and-effect relationship.]

**CORRECTED RUN-ON SENTENCE**

When t

^The fog came on suddenly, we couldn't find the dock.

[*When* also establishes cause, but in a sense of bad timing.]

**CORRECTED COMMA SPLICE**

Even though t

^The water was murky, we found the lost anchor.

[*Even though* indicates success despite the odds.]

**CORRECTED RUN-ON SENTENCE**

Though t

^The water was murky, we found the lost anchor.

[*Though* also establishes a contrary situation, but not with the same intensity.]

Other methods of revision are also possible. Master the preceding four main methods of correcting comma splices and run-on sentences, but experiment, too. Here are some other ways the last example could be rewritten.

**OTHER POSSIBLE REVISIONS**

Regardless of the murky water, we found the anchor.

[We paid no attention to the murky water.]

The murky water did not prevent us from finding the lost anchor. [We overcame the obstacle of the murky water.]

We found the lost anchor even though the water was murky. [Emphasis is on finding the anchor.]

# WORD

## Word Choice

### *Learning Objectives*

After reading this section, you should

1. use words more exactly and appropriately,
2. be able to identify bias in writing,
3. recognize wordiness,
4. be able to use a dictionary and thesaurus to improve your writing,
5. be aware of commonly confused words.

# WORD

## Word Choice

# WORD 1

## EXACTNESS

A Canadian critic wrote: "Writing is an approximation of the writer's experience. Once read, the words have a reality of their own. Be precise, therefore, in the words you select to convey the reality of this experience." It is not enough merely to come close to saying what you want to say; imprecise **word choice**, or **diction**, not only fails to express your intended meaning but also runs the risk of confusing your reader. To use words precisely, you need not have a large vocabulary, but it is necessary that you know the correct meanings of the words you do use.

## WORD 1a  Choose words that accurately denote what you want to say.

The **denotation** of a word is its literal meaning or dictionary definition. Most of the time you will have no trouble with denotation, but problems can occur when words are close in meaning or sound a lot alike.

Bill could tell by the look on Naya's face that she was ~~disinterested~~. *uninterested.*

[*Disinterested* means "unbiased by personal interest"; *uninterested* means "having no interest."]

When our supervisor retired, many speeches were given retelling humorous ~~antidotes~~ *anecdotes* from her career.

[An *antidote* is "a medicine for countering the effects of poison"; an *anecdote* is "a short narrative concerning an interesting event."]

Consult your dictionary if you are not sure you are using the correct word (see WORD 5).

## WORD 1b  Choose words with connotations that suit your purpose.

Words have connotative as well as denotative meanings. **Connotations** are the associations or emotional overtones that words have acquired through the years. For example, the word *hostage* denotes a person who is given or held as security for the fulfillment of certain conditions or terms, but it connotes images of suffering, loneliness, torture, fear, deprivation, starvation, anxiety, and other private images based on our individual associations. Because many words in English have the same meanings—*strength, potency, force,* and *might* all denote "power"—your task as a writer in any given situation is to choose the word with connotations that best suit your purpose (see COMP 2f). Note how this writer uses connotations to suit her purpose.

Our mayor's ~~actions~~ *antics* make me think he's unfit for office.

[*Antics,* which means "ludicrous acts or actions," is a word more appropriate to the writer's purpose.]

## WORD 1c Use specific and concrete words to engage your reader.

Words can be classified as relatively general or specific, abstract or concrete. **General words** name groups or classes of objects, qualities, or actions. **Specific words** name individual objects, qualities, or actions within a class or group. For example, *dessert* is a class of food, and *pie* is more specific than dessert but more general than *pecan pie.*

**Abstract words** refer to ideas, concepts, qualities, and conditions—*love, anger, beauty, youth, wisdom, honesty,* and *sincerity,* for example. **Concrete words** name things you can see, hear, taste, touch, or smell. *Pancake, rocking chair, sailboat, music, sulfur, sandpaper, smog,* and *cow* are all concrete words.

General and abstract words fail to create in the reader's mind the kind of vivid response that concrete and specific words do. Always question the words you choose. If, for example, you are describing a party, is it enough to say the party was *wonderful*? How wonderful? Why was it wonderful? When was it wonderful? In what ways was it wonderful? Wonderful for whom? The following two paragraphs describe the same party. Based on the limited use of specific and concrete words, would you like to have attended this party?

Some friends of ours told us they went to a party a few nights ago. They had fun seeing old friends and they danced a lot, especially a new dance that everybody is doing. There was quite a bit of food. They didn't get home until late.

Canada geese sw
gic bombers.

A **metaphor** also m
jects but without *lik*

Oh, I have slippe
And danced the s

An **extended metar**
parison by using se
velop a particular co

An incidental like
essayists. It is po:
or writing well ca
perts. Almost any

In **personification**
inanimate objects.

The earthquakes
are mere coughs
earthquakes felt f
bling its words of

In each of the
municates an idea c
thing concrete and
grows out of the wr
material. Be similar
risk sounding pom
guage is not illogica

## WORD 1f  Re

Expressions tha
expressions). If an e
if you've heard it be

---

Or, would you prefer to have gone to this party?

Anna and Carl went to a great party last Friday. It was a birthday party for an old high school friend, Al Larson. They saw many old friends and met some of Al's friends they hadn't met before. They danced all night and even learned some new dances. There was a huge buffet, with platters of roast beef, turkey, and cheese, pasta, and all kinds of salads, topped off by a double-chocolate birthday cake for Al. Anna and Carl had such a good time they didn't get home until nearly three in the morning.

## WORD 1d  Use idioms correctly.

An **idiom** is an expression whose meaning cannot be explained simply by the definitions of the individual words it contains. For example, compare the meanings of the italicized words in the following sentences as individual words and as idiomatic expressions.

Julia was *beside herself* with envy.

[She wasn't having an out-of-body experience; she was extremely envious.]

Wear a hat or you'll *catch a cold.*

[You don't literally stop or restrain a cold; you become infected with cold germs.]

Idioms like these present no problems; they roll off the tongue practically as a single word (*roll off the tongue* is another idiom). Idiomatic expressions with prepositions, however, are less clear-cut. If you do not choose the correct preposition, readers will probably still know what you mean, but your sentence will sound somehow strange. Consider these examples:

Gabe was rewarded ~~by~~ *with* an "A" for the hours he put into his lab report.

We're going ~~by~~ *to* Aunt Rose's for dinner tonight.

If you are unsure of which preposition to use in an idiom, consult your dictionary under the entry for the main word, not the preposition. The following list identifies some idiomatic expressions using prepositions.

agree *in*
agree *on*
agree *to*
agree *wi*
angry *w*
concern
concern
concern
concur *i*
concur *a*
different
different
go *to*  [
obliviou
obliviou
off  [NO
parallel
parallel
rewarde
rewarde
rewarde
superior
sure *to*
try *to*  [
type *of*
vary *fron*
vary *in c*
vary *wit*
wait *for*
wait *in* l

## WORD 1

### writing

In **figur**
literal (stric
with poetry,

The way

Figurati
but also hel
figurative la
between two

---

tense and past participle of *hang,* meaning "to fasten, attach, or suspend." *Scarlet and gold banners hung from the pulpit.* See EDIT 2a.

**he/she, his/her**   See EDIT 3a for a full discussion of these pronouns and sexist language. See WORD 3 for a discussion of bias in writing.

**hisself, theirselves**   *Hisself* and *theirselves* are non-standard for *himself* and *themselves. Doug can open up the cabin by himself* [NOT *hisself*].

**hopefully**   *Hopefully* means "in a hopeful way." Do not use *hopefully* without indicating *who* is being hopeful. *The machinists look hopefully to the end of the strike.* Or, better because it is more direct, *The machinists hope the strike ends soon.* (NOT *Hopefully, the strike will be over soon.*)

**hung**   See **hanged, hung.**

**i.e.**   This Latin abbreviation for *id est* means "that is." It is used only within parentheses. *Alberta's climate in the winter is often moderated by the Chinook; that is,* [NOT *i.e.,*] *a dry, warm wind that blows from the Rockies.* (A comma is usually required after *i.e.* and after *that is.*)

**illusion, allusion**   See **allusion, illusion, delusion.**

**immanent**   See **eminent, immanent, imminent.**

**imminent**   See **eminent, immanent, imminent.**

**imply, infer**   *Imply* means "to hint" or "to express indirectly." *In her annual address the president implied she would retire soon. Infer* means "to conclude from evidence." *From what the financial officer said, students inferred it would be more difficult to get loans.*

**incredible, incredulous**   *Incredible* means "unbelievable." *Incredulous* means "disbelieving." *The judge was incredulous that the defense attorney was so incredibly unprepared.*

**individual, person**   *Individual* is a depersonalized term and should not be substituted for *person. A person* [NOT *individual*] *at high risk should get booster vaccinations.*

**infer, imply**   See **imply, infer.**

**ingenious, ingenuous**   *Ingenious* means "clever." *She offered an ingenious solution. Ingenuous* means "without sophistication." *His manner was ingenuous.*

**in regards to**   A mixture of *in regard to* and *as regards.* Use one phrase or the other. Both, however, sound very formal, if not inflated; use *about* instead. *Talk to your commanding officer about* [NOT *in regards to*] *reenlisting.*

**inside of, outside of**   Acceptable if the meaning intended is "beyond (or within) the boundaries of." *The tornado hit outside of town.* Do not use either term to mean "except" or "besides." *Except for* [NOT *outside of*] *Dr. Alvarez, the entire staff was present.*

> Canada geese sweep across the hills and valleys like a formation of strategic bombers.  —Benjamin B. Bachman

A **metaphor** also makes a comparison between dissimilar ideas or objects but without *like* or *as*.

> Oh, I have slipped the surly bonds of earth
> And danced the skies on laughter-silvered wings . . .
> —John Gillespie Magee

An **extended metaphor** takes full advantage of the richness of a comparison by using several sentences or even a whole paragraph to develop a particular comparison.

> An incidental likeness exists between food and words; or rather cooks and essayists. It is possible but unnecessary to possess natural talent. Cooking or writing well can be learned by manuals and studying the works of experts. Almost anyone can achieve a literary feast.
> —Kathleen Darlington, student

In **personification** the writer attributes human qualities to animals or inanimate objects.

> The earthquakes that occur regularly in the ocean west of Vancouver Island are mere coughs when compared to the explosions of the major destructive earthquakes felt farther south. The earth is merely clearing its throat, rumbling its words of warning to the unwary.

In each of the preceding examples, the writer more vividly communicates an idea or the essence of an object by comparing it to something concrete and familiar. In all cases, too, the figurative language grows out of the writer's thinking, reflecting the way he or she sees the material. Be similarly honest in your use of figurative language, or you risk sounding pompous or contrived. Check that your figurative language is not illogical or mixed (see SENT 4b).

## WORD 1f  Replace clichés with fresh language.

Expressions that are predictable and dull are termed **clichés** (trite expressions). If an expression comes too quickly to mind and sounds as if you've heard it before, the chances are you have. Replace clichés and overworked expressions with fresh figurative language (see WORD 1e). How many of the following clichés have you heard lately?

| | |
|---|---|
| arrived at the scene | in one fell swoop |
| at long last | it stands to reason |
| believe it or not | last but not least |
| better late than never | lodge a complaint |
| cool, calm, and collected | proves conclusively |
| crystal clear | rears its ugly head |
| few and far between | rude awakening |
| first and foremost | sadder but wiser |
| for all intents and purposes | sneaking suspicion |
| foreseeable future | step in the right direction |
| hit the spot | the bottom line |
| in no uncertain terms | the last straw |

# WORD 2 _____
## APPROPRIATENESS

In choosing how to say something, use words in keeping with your subject and be sensitive to the needs and feelings of your audience. In other words, strive for an **appropriate tone**. Ask yourself, "Does my choice of words support the seriousness of my subject?" "Do I make my subject sound more serious than it really is?" "Do I keep my audience at too great a distance from me, or do I make my readers uncomfortable because I try to get too close to them?"

Not only do you want to establish an appropriate tone, but also you want to maintain that tone consistently and not lapse into one that is more or less formal (see WORD 2a), for example, or perhaps pretentious (see WORD 2c) or voguish (see WORD 2e).

### WORD 2a    Choose a degree of formality appropriate to your subject and audience.

In **informal writing**—an e-mail message or a short memo, for example—the tone may reflect the way that people who know each other talk to one another. Informal writing is characterized by simple sentences, contractions (*can't, doesn't*), and conversational phrases (*get around to it* rather than *do it, show up* rather than *arrive*). Usually, the emphasis is more on the relationship between the writer and the audience than between the writer and the subject. Informal writing is used in the following note:

> Sorry I can't make tomorrow's meeting, Sally. I have to grab a plane this afternoon for Fredericton and troubleshoot for those guys out there. I should be back Thursday night. Talk to you Friday.

In **formal writing**—a letter of application, a class assignment, or a research report—the tone you adopt and the words you choose to create that tone should be serious and not casual. In formal writing the relationship between the writer and the subject is paramount. Unlike informal writing, formal writing does not use contractions and often employs more complex sentences and a more sophisticated—but not stilted or old-fashioned—vocabulary.

Formal writing is used in this paragraph from *Canadian Geographic*.

> To those who study them closely, beaches seem like living things. They grow, change shape, defend themselves, starve, shrink, and die. All beaches have features in common, yet each is unique. A beach is not a location or a static object, but rather a dynamic feature that is still only imperfectly understood. And it is always, always moving.
>
> —Silver Donald Cameron, "The Living Beach"

## WORD 2b  Use standard English.

**Standard English**, both spoken and written, is the English used by educators, civic leaders, and professionals in all fields, and is the language of the media.

**Non-standard English** differs from standard English in its use of fairly simple sentence structures, double negatives (*can't see no* for *can't see any*), unusual vocabulary (*spigot* for *tap*), and unconventional spelling (*nite* for *night*), pronunciation (*youse* for *you*), and grammar (*I be going* for *I am going*). Non-standard English is as acceptable and functional as standard English if it is used within social and regional contexts. It is not acceptable where standard English is required.

**Slang** is the unconventional, informal language of particular subgroups—street gangs, soldiers, or college students, for example. It is not generally known to all members of society. Moreover, the terms quickly come into and go out of existence, making communication among groups even more difficult. For example, the term *cat's pajamas*, meaning "something special," as in *He thought she was the cat's pajamas*, has long been forgotten and is not readily understood. Slang, or code words, are, therefore, unacceptable in most writing.

                             *upsetting*
Tandi said her grades were ~~a bummer~~.

**Regional expressions** are common to a specific geographical area of a country. For example, in Newfoundland a *jinker* is a person or thing that puts a jinx on someone else, "an imaginary person or creature who is supposed to bring bad luck" (*Holt Canadian Dictionary*, p. 368). Like slang, however, regionalisms, though colourful, are not widely known and can leave your reader wondering about your exact meaning, especially when the sentence provides no context.

      *miserly.*
He's ~~chintzy~~

> **NOTE:** Non-standard English, slang, and regionalisms may, of course, be used where specifically called for, especially in dialogue, to delineate character and locate the action geographically.

## WORD 2c    Be direct and clear in your writing.

To be direct and clear, avoid pretentious language, euphemisms, and doublespeak. **Pretentious language** is ornate, pompous, or falsely poetic and, therefore, inappropriate in most writing. It speaks louder than the message it is trying to convey.

| | |
|---|---|
| **PRETENTIOUS** | Of all the wondrous natural metamorphoses with which May beguiles, perhaps none is so revered as the verdant canopy of new leaves spread by the trees. |
| **DIRECT** | Of all the changes that come in May, perhaps none is as wonderful as the new leaves budding on the trees. |

**Euphemism** comes from the Greek word *euphémismos,* meaning "to speak with good words." A euphemism, then, is a mild or vague term substituted when the speaker or writer worries that more direct wording might be offensive. For example, we say *portly* or *full-figured* instead of *fat, inexpensive* instead of *cheap.* And when employers reduce the number of people they employ, they call it *downsizing.* However it is put, though, these people no longer have jobs.

Sometimes evasive language goes beyond simply trying not to hurt people's feelings. Language purposely used to hide the truth is **doublespeak**, a term first used by George Orwell in his futuristic novel *1984*. For example, the government may indicate that it will *balance the budget*. We also hear the terms *continuation of the deficit* or *decreasing the rate of increase*; the intent is to make taxpayers think that there will be *no deficit*, whereas the government really means that the deficit will *not become larger*. Similarly, when salespeople refer to a used car as *pre-owned* and advertisers offer a *free gift* with a purchase, they mean to obscure the truth rather than reveal it. Not only should we avoid using doublespeak, but also we should be wary when others use it.

## WORD 2d    Use technical language only where appropriate.

Every trade and profession has its own special vocabulary. For example, all printers know the meaning of the terms *flush left, run in,* and *extra leading,* which all refer to the position of type on a printed page. Technical terms allow professionals to communicate quickly and accurately among themselves. When technical language is used to communicate with a general audience, however, it is considered **jargon** and is inappropriate. It is far better for a doctor in communicating with a patient to use *swelling* instead of *edema, capable of preventing disease* instead of *prophylactic,* and *heart attack* instead of *myocardial infarction.*

To test for jargon, ask yourself, "Have I used the simplest terms possible without any loss in communication?"

## WORD 2e    Avoid vogue words.

**Vogue words** suddenly and frequently appear in the language of newscasters, politicians, and other public figures. We soon find ourselves using them. One reason for their popularity is that once a vogue word enters the media it is picked up by yet other members of the media who give it even greater currency. Because vogue words are used so frequently within a short time, they lose their freshness and appeal quickly, disappearing as inexplicably as they appeared. Some current vogue terms are *soccer moms, venue, edgy, factoid,* and *virtual.* Until recently the list might have included *sound bite, shock economics,* and *pushing the envelope.*

If Eric doesn't get a good grade on the course, ~~he's toast~~. he could fail.

# WORD 3 _____
## BIAS IN WRITING

A **bias**, or slanted outlook, may be favourable or unfavourable and without good reason either way. Language carries certain biases within it because of its historical development and usage. Dominant groups within cultures have often used language to maintain their superior positions and to disempower others. Calling a woman *gal, little woman, girl, the Mrs.,* or *honey* is patronizing and, in certain circumstances, abusive. Language that disempowers groups may be blatant or subtle, as the following examples show.

First Nations peoples
~~Indians~~ are taking renewed pride in their cultural traditions.

Immigrants came to Canada at the turn of the century seeking a better way

of life ~~, for themselves, their wives, and their children.~~
[Women and children were also immigrants, not lesser beings.]

Not only can language deny equality, it can deny individuality as well. Assuming that all nurses are women and all pilots are men or that the president of a company is a man and the assistant to the president is a woman may lead you astray. To assume that all young people are immature or unreasonable or reckless is no better than assuming that all middle-aged people are out-of-touch, or that all people in their later years are senile, infirm, and crotchety. To assume so is to fall prey to stereotypes, to take from people their individuality and uniqueness, to deny reality.

How can we avoid bias in language? The best way is to cultivate a sense of the equality of all people regardless of their age, gender, race, religion, country of origin, or sexual orientation.

the administrative assistant
Call the president's office and ask ~~his girl~~ to schedule an appointment.

Which player is Kate O'Flaherty ? ~~The redhead?~~

H
~~For someone in his fifties,~~ he's remarkably fit.

We must also make an effort to avoid reinforcing stereotypes, intentionally or subconsciously. Edit your writing to eliminate all inadvertent expressions and terms that promote inequality or stereo-types or that may offend your readers by making inappropriate assumptions. More specifically, learn how people want to be referred to and respect their wishes. Realize, though, that even those choices may change and sometimes rather quickly.

Most often, however, there is no need to mention a particular characteristic of a group or an individual. Simply state the idea without interjecting irrelevant comments.

Rasheeda, ~~who's physically handicapped,~~ is a good basketball player.

About 75 ~~homosexual~~ students attended the dance at the student centre.

Trudy ~~is divorced and~~ lives in Kamloops with her children.

Here is a list of some common sexist terms and alternative usages.

AVOIDING SEXIST TERMS

| Instead of | Use |
| --- | --- |
| anchorman | anchor |
| bellboy | bellhop |
| chairman | chair, head, moderator, chairperson |
| clergyman | member of the clergy |
| coed | student |
| fireman | firefighter |
| forefather | ancestor, forebear |
| freshman | first-year student, student |
| landlord/landlady | proprietor, property owner, owner |
| mailman | letter carrier, postal worker |
| male nurse | nurse |
| man, mankind | humans, humankind, humanity, people |
| manpower | staff, human resources |
| middleman | go-between |
| newsman | reporter, journalist |
| policeman | police officer, officer |
| salesman | sales associate, sales representative, salesperson |
| stewardess | flight attendant, cabin attendant |
| waitress | waiter, server |
| foreman | supervisor |

For a discussion of how to avoid using sexist pronouns, see EDIT 3a1.

# WORD 4 _____
## WORDINESS

Good writing is simple and direct. But in early drafts, intent on getting our ideas on paper, we are not always as concise and clear as we wish. Excess words are like weeds. Consider each sentence and weed out words that do not contribute to its meaning.

## WORD 4a    Eliminate redundancies.

Too often unnecessary repetition creeps into our writing and distracts the reader. Have you ever written *purple in colour, decided in my mind,* or *end result*? Redundancies come in several guises; edit by deleting words or using synonyms.

Sometimes our intent is to add emphasis, but the net effect is extra words that contribute nothing to meaning.

We reviewed the basic ~~and fundamental~~ principles of public speaking.

Sometimes we repeat an idea using different words, thinking we are being clear when really we are just saying the same thing twice, not better.

The mall ~~where people shop~~ is three miles west on Ridgewood Road.

Sometimes we repeat a noun when we could use a pronoun.

The centre passed the puck to the left winger, who shot ~~the puck~~ it at the goalie.

Sometimes we use more words than necessary; these flabby sentences need ruthless editing.

~~When~~ The Joneses ~~went camping, they~~ took a portable grill ~~with them~~ on their camping trip.

Sometimes we deliberately repeat a word in parallel structures for emphasis or as a transitional device (see SENT 6d and PARA 3c and 3d). Distinguish, though, between purposeful repetition and careless repetition.

Coming up with a solution to Juhee's problem was ~~a real problem~~ difficult.

## WORD 4b     Delete empty words and phrases.

In strong writing, every word carries its own weight. Cut empty words or phrases that add little or nothing to your meaning. Two of the worst culprits are expletives (*it, there, here;* see EDIT 1g) and adverbs (especially *really* and *very;* see GRAM 1e). Overused and imprecise, these two adverbs are virtually meaningless. Omit them entirely, or use a more precise word.

~~There were~~ F lash floods ~~following~~ followed the thunderstorm.

~~In my opinion,~~ T he orchestra performed ~~really~~ well.

Look for these other empty words and phrases as you edit:

apparently, seemingly   [unless there is a discrepancy between what something is and how it appears]
basically
essentially
for all intents and purposes
generally
in some ways
I think, I feel, I believe
it seems to me
kind of, sort of    [unless you are classifying]
tend to
various
virtually

## WORD 4c     Reduce inflated expressions to their core meanings.

Wanting to sound serious or knowledgeable, we sometimes use expressions that we think important or authoritative people use. We write *at this point in time* (instead of *now*) or *in the event that* (instead of *if*). Actually we sound pompous—as important and authoritative people do when they use inflated phrases. An expert who is also a good writer writes simply and directly. Reduce an inflated phrase to its core meaning. Often this will be a simple preposition or conjunction; at other times it may be a single, more precise word.

*of about*
He asked his cousin for a loan ~~in the neighbourhood of~~ $75.

*influenced*
Professor Trent ~~had an effect upon~~ my decision to major in English.

Other wordy expressions that can be reduced to a word or two include the following:

| WORDY | CONCISE |
|---|---|
| by means of | by |
| due to the fact that | because |
| for the purpose of | for |
| for the simple reason that | because |
| in order to | to |
| in spite of the fact that | even though, although |
| in this world of today | today |
| it is important that, it is necessary that | must |
| on the occasion of | when |
| prior to, in anticipation of | before |
| until such time as | until |
| with regard to | about |

## WORD 4d   Reduce clutter by converting clauses to phrases.

You can often eliminate needless words by converting clauses to phrases.

Orange juice ~~that is~~ made from concentrate is not as good as fresh.

[Subordinate clause converted to a verbal phrase]

Spin doctors, ~~who are~~ people who manipulate the news media, appeared after the premier gave her speech.

[Subordinate clause converted to an appositive phrase]

Sometimes a clause or phrase can be converted to a single word.

*noisy*
The spectators, ~~who had become noisy,~~ booed the referee's call.

[Subordinate clause converted to a single adjective]

## WORD 4e    Use the active voice to avoid clutter.

The **active voice** emphasizes the actor in a sentence; the **passive voice** emphasizes the receiver of the action (see SENT 3d, 6c, and EDIT 2f). Use the active voice to make your writing more concise, direct, and forceful.

In the following sentence, by changing from passive to active voice, the writer cut out unnecessary words to make a straightforward, powerful statement.

tornado flattened the

The grain elevators, ~~were flattened by the tornado~~.
      ^                    ^

# WORD 5 _____
# THE DICTIONARY

All good dictionaries—*The Gage Canadian Dictionary, Compact Dictionary of Canadian English, The Oxford Dictionary of Current English*, and *The Oxford English Dictionary*, among others—contain much useful information. It is worth spending some time learning just what your dictionary can do for you.

To use your dictionary efficiently—that is, to retrieve information quickly and accurately—become familiar with how the main entry for a word is organized. This sample entry is taken from *The Gage Canadian Dictionary*. Note the kinds of information in an entry.

DICTIONARY ENTRY

2.      3.   4.
↓       ↓    ↓

1. ——————— i•de•a [ai'diə] *n.* **1** a mental concept or abstraction: *the idea*
                        *of immortality.* **2** an opinion: *to force one's ideas on others.* **3** a
                        plan, scheme, or design: *She told them her idea for the publicity*
5.                      *campaign.* **4 ideas,** *pl.* resourcefulness; creative thinking: *a man*
                        *of ideas, full of ideas.* **5** the point or purpose: *The idea of a*
                        *vacation is to relax.* **6** a fancy or notion: *I had an idea you would*
                        *be here for dinner.* **7** *Music,* a theme. **8 a** in Hegelian philosophy,
                        the absolute truth. **b** in Platonism, the eternal archetype of a
                        class of objects; FORM (def.18).

6.

    **get ideas into** (one's) **head,** expect too much.
    **the very idea,** it is outrageous or ridiculous, etc.: *Crash the party?*
    *The very idea!* (< L < Gk. *idea* form, kind < base *id-* see). ————— 7.

8.

    ☛ Syn. **Idea,** NOTION, THOUGHT = something understood or formed in
    the mind. **Idea** is the general word applying to something existing in the
    mind as the result of understanding, thinking, reasoning, imagining, etc.:
    *Learn to express your ideas clearly.* **Notion** applies to an idea not fully,
    clearly, plainly, or completely formed or understood: *I have only a notion of*
    *what you mean.* **Thought** applies to an idea formed by reflection or
    reasoning, rather than by the imagination: *Tell me your thoughts on this*
    *proposal.*

## 1.   Spelling

The main entry word is listed with its correct spelling. If there are two different acceptable spellings (*traveller* or *traveler*), the preferred spelling is given first.

## 2.   Word division

The entry is divided into syllables, with dots used to indicate the division between syllables.

## 3.   Pronunciation

The pronunciation is written phonologically (in sound syllables), the key to which can usually be found at the bottom of the dictionary page where the entry appears. The accent mark indicates the most heavily stressed syllable.

## 4.   Part of speech

The part of speech of the entry word is indicated by an abbreviation:

| | | | |
|---|---|---|---|
| *n.* | noun | *v.* | verb |
| *adj.* | adjective | *adv.* | adverb |
| *pron.* | pronoun | *prep.* | preposition |
| *conj.* | conjunction | *interj.* | interjection |

Other abbreviations include

| | | | |
|---|---|---|---|
| *intr.* | intransitive verb | *tr.* | transitive verb |
| *sing.* | singular | *pl.* | plural |

If the word functions as more than one part of speech or has more than one meaning, those entries are listed separately with their definitions. Each meaning is usually numbered.

5.   Meanings

The main entry is defined. Definitions are usually listed in order of frequency. An example sentence usually follows the meaning.

6.   Special usage notes

This entry indicates any idiomatic expressions associated with the main entry word, as well as time labels (*Obs.* [obsolete] or *Archaic*), geographical labels (*Regional, CanF* or *CdnF* [Canadian French]) or style labels (*Informal, Non-standard, Slang*).

7.   Etymology

The etymology gives the word's origin and historical development.

8.   Synonyms

Synonyms are words similar in meaning to the main entry. Occasionally *antonyms,* words with opposite meanings, are also given.

# WORD 6 _____

## THE THESAURUS

If you are not sure you are using the best word to say just what you mean, check a thesaurus, or book of synonyms (words with similar meanings) and antonyms (words with opposite meanings). *Roget's International Thesaurus* is the classic reference work; it is available in inexpensive paperback editions as well as in software formats. Here is a typical entry:

**examination**

  [see examine]

  *evidence* 467

  undergo – 461

  **examine** 457, 461

The entry for **examination**, in the index of *Roget's*, directs the reader to the entry under *evidence* in section 467 at the front of the thesaurus, or "undergo," as in "to undergo an examination" in section 461. The entry also directs the reader to the entry for **examine** in sections 457 and 461. Entry 461 is reproduced below, in part.

> **461. Inquiry**. [Subject of Inquiry. Question.] — **N**. inquiry; request etc. 765; search, research, quest; pursuit etc. 622
>
> examination, review, scrutiny, investigation, indagation; per-quisition, -scrutation, -vestigation; inqu-est, -isition; exploration; *exploitation,* ventilation.
>
> sifting; calculation, analysis, dissection, resolution, induction; Baconian method.
>
> strict —, close —, searching —, exhaustive-inquiry; narrow —, strict- search; study etc. (*consideration*) 451.
>
> *scire facias, ad referendum;* trial.

*Roget's II: The New Thesaurus* is an easier-to-use version of the original *Roget's.* The entry for **examination** and **examine** follow:

> **examination** *noun*
> 1. The act of examining carefully: *A close examination of the knife revealed traces of human blood.*
>    *Syns:* check, checkup, inspection, perusal, scrutiny, study.
> 2. A medical inquiry into a patient's state of health: *went for an eye examination.*
>    *Syns:* checkup, exam (*Informal*).
> 3. ANALYSIS.
> 4. TEST.
>
> **examine** *verb*
> 1. To look at carefully or critically: *An expert examined the handwriting and declared it a forgery.*
>    *Syns:* case (*slang*), check, con, go over, inspect, peruse, scrutinize, study, survey, traverse, view.
>    —*Idiom* give a going over.
> 2. ANALYZE.
> 3. ASK.
> 4, 5. TEST.

As helpful as a thesaurus can be, you should use it with great care. You do not want to use a word with a denotation or connotation that does not suit your purpose. If you have doubts about the exact meaning of a word you wish to use, consult your dictionary. Also, do not use the thesaurus merely to dress up your prose. Use simple, correct words instead of inappropriate fancy words.

# WORD 7 _____
## GLOSSARY OF USAGE

The following glossary of usage is a handy reference guide to pairs of confusing words (*disinterested, uninterested*), frequently misspelled words (*their, there, they're*), words that cause agreement problems (*data, phenomena*), non-standard words and phrases (*alright, is when*), and informal usages (*lots, real*).

Many of the usage problems discussed here are also treated in other parts of the text; use the index to locate them. If you have a usage problem not covered here, consult your dictionary.

**a, an** Use *a* before words that begin with a consonant sound, even if the word begins with a vowel: *a book, a ladder, a unique choice.* Use *an* before a word that begins with a vowel sound, even if the word begins with a consonant: *an idea, an unlikely candidate, an hour.* With a word that begins with a hard *h*, use *a*: *a hotel, a hamster, a hotdog.* But with a word that begins with an unpronounced *h*, use *an*: *an hour, an honour, an honest mistake.*

**accept, except** *Accept* is a verb that means "to receive." *Except* is usually a preposition that means "other than" or "with the exclusion of." *Carla will accept all the invitations except Jason's.*

**adapt, adopt** *Adapt* means "to adjust oneself to." *Adopt* means "to choose as one's own." *We will help our adopted child adapt to life in a new country.*

**advice, advise** *Advice* is a noun and means "opinion about a course of action." *Advise* is a verb and means "to offer advice." *She advised her roommate to seek advice.*

**affect, effect** *Affect* as a verb means "to influence." *Staring at a computer screen can affect your eyesight.* *Effect* as a noun means "result." *Painting the kitchen yellow brought about the effect she wanted.* *Effect* as a verb means "to bring about." *Negotiation was the only way to effect the release of the hostages.*

**all ready, already** *All ready* means "prepared." *The swimmers were all ready to start.* *Already* means "previously or before." *We had already finished dessert when Raphael picked up his salad fork.*

**all right, alright** *All right* is always written as two words, just as *all wrong* is. *Alright* is non-standard English. *It's all right* [NOT *alright*] *if we meet at the restaurant.*

**allusion, illusion, delusion** An *allusion* is "an implied or indirect reference." *The lawyer made an allusion to a mystery by Agatha Christie.* An *illusion* is "a false concept" or "deceptive impression." *The magician was a master of illusion.* A *delusion* is "a mistaken belief," usually as a result of psychological problems. *He suffered the delusion of thinking he was Napoleon.*

**a lot, alot** *A lot* is two words, not one. *I ate a lot* [NOT *alot*] *of strawberries.*

**altogether, all together** *Altogether* means "completely." *That's altogether wrong. All together* means "in a group." *All together now, "Row, row, row your boat."*

**alumnus/alumni, alumna/alumnae** Latin masculine and feminine (singular and plural) terms for the graduate(s) of an institution. While most institutions use the singular forms to refer to a particular graduate, they refer to their graduates in the aggregate as *alumni,* leaving many women to wonder why the masculine term should prevail. Perhaps this is the reason *alum/alums* is gaining popularity. *They were both University of Lethbridge alumni* [OR *alums*].

**among, between** Use *among* for three or more persons or things. *You can choose among several research topics.* Use *between* when there are only two persons or things. *The choice is between coffee and tea.*

**amount, number** *Amount* refers to things in bulk or mass. *A staggering amount of trash is picked up in North York each day. Number* refers to things that are countable. *A number of students were given parking tickets.*

**and/or** An awkward and sometimes imprecise example of legal or business usage that is best avoided in college writing. While it appears that two choices are represented here, there are actually three: *Mr. Shah told Marcia that she would receive a promotion and/or raise.* In non-business language, write *Mr. Shah told Marcia she would receive a promotion or a raise or both.*

**anxious, eager** *Anxious* is often used when *eager* is the appropriate choice. *Anxious* means "filled with worry and apprehension." *Eager* means "looking forward with pleasure." *I am eager* [NOT *anxious*] *to see the Inuit exhibit.*

**anyone, any one** *Anyone* means "any person at all." *Any one* refers to a particular person or thing in a group. *Anyone in the room can select any one of these gifts.* The distinction also applies to *everyone/every one* and *someone/some one.*

**anyway, any way** *Anyway* means "nevertheless." *Anyway, it doesn't matter. Any way* means "by whatever means." *He'll go any way he can.*

**anyways, anywheres** Non-standard forms of *anyway* and *anywhere*. *Ted's going anyway* [NOT *anyways*].

**as, like**   See **like, as, as if**.

**awhile, a while**   Use the adverb, *awhile,* to modify a verb. *Rest awhile, if you like.* Use the article and noun, *a while,* as the object of a preposition. *We went to the park for a while.*

**bad, badly**   *Bad* is an adjective and *badly* is an adverb. *I feel bad that Cathy didn't go.* (If you felt *badly,* your sense of touch would be faulty.) *His car was badly damaged.* See GRAM 1d and 1e.

**being that, being as (how)**   Non-standard expressions used in place of the subordinating conjunctions *because* or *since*. *Because* [NOT *being that*] *Patrick had to go to work early, he couldn't give her a ride.*

**beside, besides**   *Beside* is a preposition meaning "next to" or "at the side of." *The Métis people marched beside their leader. Besides* is an adverb or a preposition meaning "in addition" or "moreover." *Besides free admission, you get a discount at the museum gift shop with your membership.*

**between, among**   See **among, between**.

**between you and me, between you and I**   The preposition *between* always takes the objective case *me: The argument is between you and me* [NOT *you and I*].

**bring, take**   Use *bring* when something is being moved toward the speaker. *Bring your calculator to class tomorrow.* Use *take* when something is being moved away from the speaker. *Would you please take these bottles to the recycling centre?*

**burst, bursted, bust, busted**   Use *burst. Bursted* is non-standard and *bust* and *busted* are slang. *The fans in the stands burst into one big cheer when Joe Carter came to bat.*

**can, may**   *Can* means "having ability." *She can play chess. May* indicates "having permission." *The children may watch television for an hour.*

**cannot, can not**   Always use *cannot*.

**can't hardly**   A double negative, this usage should be avoided. Use *can hardly* instead. *I can hardly* [NOT *can't hardly*] *wait for graduation.*

**climactic, climatic**   *Climactic* means "of or pertaining to climax." *The Canadian Open ended with a climactic hole-in-one. Climatic* means "of or pertaining to climate." *Vancouver enjoys climatic stability.*

**compare to, compare with**   *Compare to* means "to represent as similar." *The human brain is often compared to a computer. Compare with* means "to examine the character or quality of two things to see how they are similar or different." *Hank Snow's singing style has been compared with the best on the Grand Old Opry.*

**complement, compliment**   *Complement* as a verb means "to fill out or make whole." *Her lyrics complement his music. Compliment* as a verb means "to praise or congratulate." *She always compliments her students when they perform well.*

**consensus of opinion** *Consensus* means "general agreement," so the phrase is redundant. *Consensus* [NOT *of opinion*] *was reached before the deadline.*

**contact** When *contact* is used to mean "get in touch with," it is acceptable in speech and informal writing but not in formal writing. In formal writing, use the verbs *talk, write, call, e-mail, telephone. Call* [NOT *contact*] *your adviser.*

**continual, continuous** *Continual* means "recurring at intervals, intermittently." *Max continually tells the story of how we met. Continuous* means "occurring without interruption, incessantly." *She was plagued by a continuous ringing in her ears.*

**could of** Non-standard for *could have. Craig could have* [NOT *could of*] *gone to summer school.*

**criteria** *Criteria* means "standards or tests on which judgments can be based" and is the plural of *criterion. There is only one criterion for admittance, age. Professor Kim explained the criteria for receiving an A.*

**data** *Data* means "pieces of information" and is the plural of *datum,* which is now rarely used, except in formal writing. Some writers treat *data* as both singular and plural; careful writers treat it as plural only. *The national census data were gathered last year.* For the singular of *data,* many writers prefer "a piece of data" to *datum.*

**different from, different than** Use *different from* in most instances. *This chili recipe is much different from mine.* Use *different than* if a clause follows. *The exam was different than what I expected.*

**disinterested, uninterested** *Disinterested* means "free of self-interest or bias." *She was a disinterested observer at the trial. Uninterested* means "without interest." *I'm uninterested in classical music but love opera.*

**don't** *Don't* is an acceptable contraction for *do not* but not for *does not. You don't want to go, and she doesn't* [NOT *don't*] *want to stay.*

**due to** *Due to* means "owing to" or "caused by." It is acceptable as an adjective phrase following some form of the verb *to be: His death was due to natural causes. Due to* is not acceptable as a preposition meaning "because of." *Our flight was grounded because of* [NOT *due to*] *bad weather.*

**eager, anxious** See **anxious, eager.**

**effect, affect** See **affect, effect.**

**e.g.** This is the Latin abbreviation for *exempli gratia,* meaning "for example." It is acceptable in parenthetical comments (*e.g., red, yellow, and blue*), but outside parentheses, *for example* should be spelled out.

*Our house, for example, needs a new roof.* (Both *e.g.* and *for example* are always followed by a comma.)

**emigrate from, immigrate to**  *Emigrate* means "to leave one country or area for another" and takes the preposition *from. All of my grandparents emigrated from Italy. Immigrate* means "to enter and settle permanently in another country" and takes the preposition *to. They immigrated to Canada in the 1890s.*

**eminent, immanent, imminent**  Close in pronunciation, these three words have very different meanings. *Eminent* means "outstanding, as in reputation." *John Polanyi, the Nobel laureate, is an eminent chemist. Immanent* means "existing within, inherent." *Many theologians believe that humans have immanent virtue. Imminent* means "about to happen." *A change in the structure of Canadian education is imminent.*

**enthused, enthusiastic**  *Enthused* is not widely accepted as an adjective meaning "showing enthusiasm." Use *enthusiastic* instead. *He gets enthusiastic* [NOT *enthused*] *about three things—breakfast, lunch, and dinner.*

**etc.**  *Etc. (et cetera)* is Latin for "and other things." Do not use *and etc.* because it is redundant. Also, do not use *etc.* to refer to people. Actually, it is stylistically preferable to use the expression *and so on* instead of *etc. Try varying your routine at the gym with the treadmill, stairs, rower, and so on.*

**everyone, every one**  See **anyone, any one.**

**except, accept**  See **accept, except.**

**farther, further**  Use *farther* when distance is involved. *The sailboat drifted farther away.* Use *further* to mean "more" or "to a greater extent." *The neurologist inquired further into Renee's medical history.*

**fewer, less**  *Fewer* means "amounting to a small number." *Less* is a comparative of "little." Use *fewer* with items that can be counted, and *less* with amounts. *With fewer* [NOT *less*] *tourists in town, there was less traffic congestion.*

**further**  See **farther, further.**

**goes** (for **says** or **said**)  *Goes* is non-standard for "says" or "said." *She said* [NOT *goes*], *"I want you to help me."*

**good, well**  *Good* as an adjective means "having positive or desirable qualities." *Well* as an adverb means "in a good manner, correctly." *The old Corvette not only looked good, but also ran well.* Use *well* in matters of health. *Do you feel well?*

**hanged, hung**  *Hanged* is the past tense and past participle of *hang*, meaning "to execute." *He was convicted and hanged. Hung* is the past tense and past participle of *hang,* meaning "to fasten, attach, or suspend." *Scarlet and gold banners hung from the pulpit.* See EDIT 2a.

**he/she, his/her**   See EDIT 3a for a full discussion of these pronouns and sexist language. See WORD 3 for a discussion of bias in writing.

**hisself, theirselves**   *Hisself* and *theirselves* are non-standard for *himself* and *themselves. Doug can open up the cabin by himself* [NOT *hisself*].

**hopefully**   *Hopefully* means "in a hopeful way." Do not use *hopefully* without indicating *who* is being hopeful. *The machinists look hopefully to the end of the strike.* Or, better because it is more direct, *The machinists hope the strike ends soon.* (NOT *Hopefully, the strike will be over soon.*)

**hung**   See **hanged, hung.**

**i.e.**   This Latin abbreviation for *id est* means "that is." It is used only within parentheses. *Alberta's climate in the winter is often moderated by the Chinook; that is,* [NOT *i.e.,*] *a dry, warm wind that blows from the Rockies.* (A comma is usually required after *i.e.* and after *that is.*)

**illusion, allusion**   See **allusion, illusion, delusion.**

**immanent**   See **eminent, immanent, imminent.**

**imminent**   See **eminent, immanent, imminent.**

**imply, infer**   *Imply* means "to hint" or "to express indirectly." *In her annual address the president implied she would retire soon. Infer* means "to conclude from evidence." *From what the financial officer said, students inferred it would be more difficult to get loans.*

**incredible, incredulous**   *Incredible* means "unbelievable." *Incredulous* means "disbelieving." *The judge was incredulous that the defense attorney was so incredibly unprepared.*

**individual, person**   *Individual* is a depersonalized term and should not be substituted for *person. A person* [NOT *individual*] *at high risk should get booster vaccinations.*

**infer, imply**   See **imply, infer.**

**ingenious, ingenuous**   *Ingenious* means "clever." *She offered an ingenious solution. Ingenuous* means "without sophistication." *His manner was ingenuous.*

**in regards to**   A mixture of *in regard to* and *as regards.* Use one phrase or the other. Both, however, sound very formal, if not inflated; use *about* instead. *Talk to your commanding officer about* [NOT *in regards to*] *reenlisting.*

**inside of, outside of**   Acceptable if the meaning intended is "beyond (or within) the boundaries of." *The tornado hit outside of town.* Do not use either term to mean "except" or "besides." *Except for* [NOT *outside of*] *Dr. Alvarez, the entire staff was present.*

**irregardless**   Non-standard for *regardless*. *Regardless* [NOT *irregardless*], *wear neon coloured garments if you run at night.*

**is when, is where**   Do not use *when* and *where* after *is* in definitions. *Scuttling a ship is a process by which* [NOT *is when*] *holes are cut in the hull to sink it.*

**its, it's**   *Its* is the possessive form of *it*. *It's* is the contraction of *it is*. Test whether you are using the correct spelling by inserting the words *it is*. *The spotted owl is losing more of its* [NOT *it's*] *habitat every year.*

**kind(s), sort(s), type(s)**   Use the singular forms in singular constructions. *This kind of paint gives the best results.* Use the plural with plural constructions. *These kinds of paints give the worst results.* Notice that all elements must be singular (*this, kind, paint*) or all must be plural (*these, kinds, paints*).

**kind of, sort of, type of**   Used colloquially, these expressions mean "rather" or "somewhat." They are acceptable in speech, but can add unnecessary words in writing. *I was somewhat* [NOT *kind of*] *disappointed by the low attendance.* Or, simply, *I was disappointed by the low attendance.* See WORD 4b. When you use these expressions to classify, which is acceptable in formal writing, do not use an *a*. *That kind of* [NOT *kind of a*] *potato is best for baking.*

**lay, lie**   *Lay* means "to put" or "to place" and always takes an object (principal parts: *lay, laid,* and *laid*). *Lie* means "to recline" and is an intransitive verb, meaning it does not take an object (principal parts: *lie, lay,* and *lain*). Usage errors occur because the present tense of *lay* and the past tense of *lie* are both *lay*. *Lie* [NOT *lay*] *down immediately. The minute she lay* [NOT *laid*] *down, she fell asleep. Lay the carpet carefully.*

**leave, let**   *Leave* means "to go away" or "to exit." Do not use *leave* to mean "permit." Use *let* instead. *Let* [NOT *leave*] *him do his homework.*

**less, fewer**   See **fewer, less.**

**liable, likely**   *Liable* means "legally obligated" or "responsible." *Hank was liable for his credit-card charges.* Do not use *liable* for *likely*, which means "having a high probability of occurring or being true." *The incumbent is likely* [NOT *liable*] *to win.*

**like, as, as if**   *Like* is a preposition expressing similarity. *She looks like k.d. lang.* *As* and *as if* are subordinating conjunctions and are used to introduce dependent clauses. See GRAM 4. *As* [NOT *like*] *he said, he was out of town at the time.*

**likely, liable**   See **liable, likely.**

**loose, lose**   *Loose* is an adjective meaning "not tightly." *Lose* is a verb and means "to be unable to find" or "to be defeated in a game."

Confusion between the two words comes about as much from misspelling as from misuse. *Did you lose the top button? It looked loose.*

**lots, lots of**   *Lots* and *lots of* are widely used informal substitutes for *a lot, much, a great deal,* and *many.* They should be avoided in formal writing. *Our family goes to many* [NOT *lots of*] *basketball games.* See also **a lot, alot.**

**may, can**   See **can, may.**

**may of**   Non-standard for *may have. Mother may have* [NOT *may of*] *already paid that bill.*

**media, medium**   *Media* is the plural of medium, meaning "a publication or broadcast." *Television is the medium that most influences the Canadian people.*

**might of**   Non-standard for *might have. Betsy might have* [NOT *might of*] *sent the flowers.*

**myself, himself/herself, yourself**   These are reflexive pronouns (*I saw myself reflected in the store window*) or intensive pronouns (*I myself would let bygones be bygones*). Do not use them as substitutes for *me, he/she,* or *you.* See GRAM 1c. *Packages arrived for Maria and me* [NOT *myself*].

**none**   *None* can be either singular or plural, depending on the meaning of the sentence. If the noun or pronoun that follows is plural, use a plural verb: *None of us have seen the movie.* If the noun that follows is singular, use a singular verb: *None of the fruit was eaten.* If the meaning of *none* is "not one," use *not one* to be clear. See EDIT 1f.

**nowheres**   Non-standard for *nowhere.* See **anyways, anywheres.**

**number, amount**   See **amount, number.**

**off of, off from**   The *of* and *from* are redundant. *The cans fell off* [NOT *off of* OR *off from*] *the shelf.*

**OK, O.K., okay**   In formal speech and writing use a word such as *approval* or *agreement* instead. *Our zoning board approved* [NOT *okayed*] *the new subdivision.*

**outside of, inside of**   See **inside of, outside of.**

**people, persons**   Use *people* to refer to a group of individuals who are uncounted and anonymous. *The gates opened, and the people* [NOT *persons*] *rushed in.* When referring to a countable number, you may use *people* or *persons,* though *persons* is usually preceded by a specific number. *Only three persons* [OR *people*] *asked questions.* Sometimes *persons* sounds inflated; the more commonly used word is *people.* *Not many people* [RATHER THAN *persons*] *asked questions.*

**per**   *Per* means "each." It is acceptable to use *per* in expressions such as "per person" and "per litre," but not otherwise. Use *by, a,* or *in* *accordance with* instead. *In accordance with* [NOT *per*] *Murphy's Law, if something could go wrong, it did.*

**percent, per cent, percentage**   *Percent* (the preferred spelling) or *per cent* means "out of each hundred" and is usually preceded by a specific number. *Ninety-nine percent of Canadian homes have colour televisions. Percentage* means "portion" or "part of." *A greater-than-expected percentage of Progressive Conservatives turned out to vote.*

**phenomena**   *Phenomena* means "observable facts or events" and is the plural of *phenomenon*. There is no such word as *phenomenas*. *Paul Quarrington's stories are filled with humorous phenomena.*

**plus**   *Plus* means "added to." *The bill was $90 plus tax.* Do not use *plus* to link independent clauses. *Lethal injection is cruel and unusual punishment, and* [NOT *plus*] *it does not deter murderers.*

**practical, practicable**   *Practical* means "serving a purpose, useful." *Practicable* means "capable of being done, feasible." *Walking a tightrope between the skyscrapers is practicable but hardly practical.*

**principal, principle**   As an adjective *principal* means "first or foremost, chief." *Myron is the principal cellist.* As a noun *principal* means "leader" or "a sum of money as distinguished from interest or profit." *Mr. Lyznyk is the new principal. The idea is to live off the interest and not the principal. Principle* is always a noun and means "a truth, or basic assumption." *She lives by the principle that less is more.*

**quote, quotation**   *Quote* is a verb, *quotation* a noun. In formal writing, do not use *quote* as a shortened form of *quotation*. *His term paper was a string of quotations* [NOT *quotes*].

**real, really**   In speech, *real* is used for "very" or "extremely." In formal writing, use *really*: *Jim Carrey is really* [NOT *real*] *funny.* Avoid overusing the adverb: See WORD 4b.

**reason is because, reason why**   These expressions are awkward and redundant. Simply omit them. *I'm not going away for my vacation because I don't have the money.* [NOT *The reason why I'm not going away for my vacation is because I don't have the money.*] See WORD 4a.

**sensual, sensuous**   *Sensual* pertains to bodily or sexual pleasure. *Balanchine's choreography is so sensual. Sensuous* means "appealing to the senses." *The smell of bread baking is positively sensuous.*

**set, sit**   These two verbs are often confused. *Set* means "to put something down" and takes a direct object (principal parts: *set, set, set*); *sit* means "to rest or be seated" (principal parts: *sit, sat, sat*). *Sit here, and set your popcorn on that little table.* See EDIT 2b.

**shall, will**   *Shall* was once the preferred helping verb in the first-person singular and plural, but *will* is generally acceptable. *I will* [NOT *shall*] *visit Aunt Kate when I'm in Corner Brook. Shall* is still used with polite questions. *Shall* [NOT *will*] *we eat?*

**should of**   Non-standard for *should have. We should have* [NOT *should of*] *phoned first.*

**sit, set**   See **set, sit.**

**someone, some one**   See **anyone, any one.**

**somewheres**   Non-standard for *somewhere.* See **anyways, anywheres.**

**sort of, kind of**   See **kind of, sort of, type of.**

**stationary, stationery**   *Stationary* means "not moving, fixed." *A parked car is stationary* [NOT *stationery*]. *Stationery* means "writing tools, such as paper and envelopes." Confusion about the two terms comes as much from misspelling as misuse. *Personalized stationery* [NOT *stationary*] *is less expensive than you'd think.*

**such**   Overused as an intensifier. Avoid in formal writing. *It was* [NOT *such*] *a beautiful sunset.*

**sure**   Used in speech as an adverb meaning "surely" or "certainly." In formal writing, use *surely* or *certainly. The arts in Eastern Europe will surely* [NOT *sure*] *flourish under democracy.*

**sure and**   Non-standard. Use *sure to* instead. *Be sure to* [NOT *sure and*] *proofread business letters carefully.*

**than, then**   *Than* is a conjunction used in a clause of comparison or inequality. *I would rather have ice cream than* [NOT *then*] *cake. Then* is an adverb used to indicate past or future time. *First we edited the manuscript, then* [NOT *than*] *we formatted it.*

**that, which**   *That* is always used to introduce restrictive clauses. *The pow-wow that I attended yesterday was filled with colour and movement. Which* is used to introduce non-restrictive clauses. *His morals, which are questionable, should not influence our opinion of this novel.* See PUNCT 1c.

**their, there, they're**   *Their* is a possessive pronoun. *Their sidewalk is always shovelled in winter. There* means "at or in that place." *We'll call when we get there. There* is also an expletive *(there is/are . . .). There is reason to believe that Gwen is on vacation. They're* is a contraction for *they are. They're at their house now.*

**theirself, theirselves**   See **hisself, theirselves.**

**them, them there**   Non-standard when used in place of *those. Those* [NOT *them*] *Appaloosas have beautiful markings.*

**these/those kinds, sorts, types**   See **kind(s), sort(s), type(s).**

**this here, that there, these here**   Non-standard. Simply omit the *here* and *there* in these phrases. *This* [NOT *This here*] *German shepherd is very good with children.*

**to, too, two**  Perhaps more of a spelling than a usage problem. *To* is a preposition, *too* is an adverb, and *two* is a number. *Two tickets to a rock concert are two too many for my parents.*

**toward, towards**  Both versions are acceptable. *Toward* is preferred in Canada.

**try and**  Non-standard. Use *try to* instead. *Try to* [NOT *Try and*] *be on time.*

**uninterested, disinterested**  See **disinterested, uninterested.**

**unique**  Like *perfect, straight, round,* and *complete, unique* is an absolute. There are no degrees of uniqueness; either something is one-of-a-kind or it isn't. *Very unique* is not only illogical but also an overused intensifier. *Her novel won an award for its unique* [NOT *very unique*] *portrayal of life in a Newfoundland outport.*

**use, utilize**  *Use* means "the act of employing something." *Utilize* means "to make use of." *Use* is simpler and more direct; *utilize* sounds inflated. *I used* [NOT *utilized*] *my credit card to buy the stereo.*

**use to, suppose to**  Non-standard. Be sure to use a *d* with *use* and *suppose. The Great Lakes used* [NOT *use*] *to be free of zebra mussels.*

**wait on**  *Wait on* means "to serve" and should not be used when the desired meaning is "wait for." *We waited for* [NOT *on*] *Liz, but she never showed up.*

**ways**  Colloquial; use *way* when designating a distance. *You have a way* [NOT *ways*] *to go before you get to the Trans-Canada Highway.*

**where**  Colloquial for *that. I read that* [NOT *where*] *buying imported goods leads to unemployment.*

**where . . . at**  Redundant. Omit the *at. Where are they now?* [NOT *Where are they at now?*]

**which, that**  See **that, which.**

**which, who, whose, that**  Generally use *who* or *whose* to refer to people, except in an expression such as *That's an idea whose time has come.* Use *which* or *that* to refer to things. Do not use *which* or *that* to refer to people. *It was the tall man with red hair who* [NOT *that*] *witnessed the robbery.* See EDIT 3a6.

**while**  *While* usually designates time and should not be used as a substitute for *and* or *but. He shopped for groceries while she waited in the car. Julia was convinced but* [NOT *while*] *Roberto remained skeptical.*

**who's, whose**  *Who's* is a contraction of *who is. Whose* is a possessive pronoun. *Whose* [NOT *who's*] *volleyball is this?*

**will, shall**  See **shall, will.**

**would of**  Non-standard for *would have. I would have* [NOT *would of*] *worn a tuxedo.*

**your, you're**  *Your* is a possessive pronoun. *You're* is a contraction of *you are. You're* [NOT *your*] *not going to make your plane if you don't walk faster.*

# PUNCT

## Punctuation

### *Learning Objectives*

After reading this section, you should

1. be able to use commas correctly,
2. know when to use semicolons and colons,
3. use apostrophes and quotation marks correctly,
4. use end punctuation and other punctuation marks correctly.

# PUNCT

## Punctuation

# PUNCT 1 _____
## THE COMMA

**Commas** help communicate your meaning by eliminating possible misreadings. Consider this sentence:

After telephoning Paul Lee Anne went to the library.

Depending on where you put the comma, it could be Anne or Lee Anne who goes to the library.

After telephoning Paul Lee, Anne went to the library.

After telephoning Paul, Lee Anne went to the library.

Commas are also used to mark the natural pauses of speech.

Fish, rice, and mangoes are mainstays of the diet in Thailand.

In fact, reading a sentence aloud may sometimes help you place a comma correctly, but the only reliable route to correct comma use is knowledge of basic sentence structure (see GRAM 2, 3, 4, and 5). Natural pauses in sentences are *usually* indicated by commas, but not always.

Those hooligans who spraypainted the administration building [*natural pause but no comma*] ought to be arrested.

Rules governing punctuation change over time to reflect changes in style and taste. Today writers use fewer commas than in the past without sacrificing clarity or meaning. The following comma rules reflect current practice; in some situations you may choose between two acceptable alternatives.

As you study the rules, keep in mind that the comma, of all the marks of punctuation, has the greatest variety of uses, yet in every case it functions in one of two basic ways—to *separate* or to *enclose* elements in a sentence.

## PUNCT 1a   Use a comma to separate independent clauses joined by a coordinating conjunction (*and, but, for, nor, or, so,* and *yet*).

Place a comma before a coordinating conjunction that joins two or more independent or main clauses (see GRAM 4).

> We stopped for lunch at McDonald's, and we both had salads.
>
> We knew the Robert Bateman exhibit would be popular, so we bought our tickets early.

> **EXCEPTION:**   The comma may be omitted, especially before *and* or *or,* when the main clauses in a compound sentence are short and there is no possibility of misreading.

> Elvis Stojko skated and the crowd went wild.

When main clauses linked by a coordinating conjunction already contain commas or are especially long, use a semicolon instead.

> Income tax, introduced in 1917, was intended to finance Canada's participation in World War I, and then be repealed/ ; but the Canadian public knows all too well that income tax is here to stay.

For a full discussion of the use of the semicolon, see PUNCT 2.

Be careful not to use a comma to separate compound elements that are not independent clauses (see PUNCT 1m).

> Nicolas washed the dishes/and the pots in the sink.

## PUNCT 1b   Use a comma to set off an introductory group of words.

The most common introductory word groups are adverbial clauses, prepositional phrases, verbal phrases, and absolute phrases. The comma signals the end of the introductory group of words and the beginning of the sentence proper.

### Adverbial clause

Introductory clauses that function as adverbs tell when, where, why, how, or under what terms the central action of the sentence takes place (see GRAM 4b).

> When electric power fails, hospitals rely on emergency generators.

**EXCEPTION:** If the introductory clause is short and there is no chance of misreading, the comma may be omitted.

Since George moved we haven't seen him.

In the following sentence, which also begins with a short introductory clause, the comma is needed to make clear that Shoshana was not eating the birds.

While Shoshana ate, the birds sang outside her window.

If commas are used consistently after introductory clauses, no sentence will be misread.

## Prepositional phrase

Set off a lengthy introductory prepositional phrase (four words or more) or a series of prepositional phrases with a comma to signal that the main part of the sentence is about to begin (see GRAM 3a).

After a delicious and perhaps too bountiful Thanksgiving dinner, Grandpa took a nap.

As a general rule, a short introductory prepositional phrase is not followed by a comma.

On weekends we like to sleep late.

## Verbal phrase

Set off an introductory verbal phrase, whether short or long, with a comma. **Verbals**—gerunds, participles, and infinitives—are verbs that act as nouns, adjectives, or adverbs (see GRAM 1a and 3b).

| | |
|---|---|
| GERUND | By working out every day, Maria made the team. |
| PARTICIPLE | Excited about her exam scores, Pam called her parents. |
| INFINITIVE | To get elected to public office, a candidate must have a well-managed and well-funded campaign. |

At times a single-word verbal may be used as an introductory comment. It, too, is always followed by a comma.

Huffing, Carlos arrived to see the train pull away.

[By using brackets to insert the reasons why Richler works at his craft, the writer of this statement avoids having to quote an extended passage.]

### 2. Use brackets to indicate that an error was made in the original material.

The Latin word *sic*, meaning "thus," appears within brackets in a direct quotation to indicate that you recognize an error in the original and are letting it stand.

The college handbook stated, "Students can expect to pay $100 000 [*sic*] for living expenses while in residence."

[Here *sic* indicates an error in the yearly cost of living. The quotation should have read $10 000, a typo which undoubtedly would cause concern among many students.]

### 3. Use brackets around parenthetical material already within parentheses.

The rebellions in Upper and Lower Canada (led by William Lyon Mackenzie [1795–1861] and Louis-Joseph Papineau [1786–1871]) resulted in the Act of Union.

## PUNCT 6g    The ellipsis mark

The **ellipsis mark** is three spaced periods (. . .). It indicates the writer has omitted words from quoted material.

The Minister of Transportation said that "drivers **. . .** must learn to use seat belts, because seat belts save lives."

An ellipsis mark tells the reader that you have omitted the part of a quotation that is not pertinent to your point; at the same time, it shows that you are not misrepresenting the person being quoted.

When using an ellipsis, leave a space at the beginning of the omission, a space between each of the three periods, and a space before continuing with the quotation.

### 1. Use an ellipsis mark to signal that one word or whole sentences have been omitted from a quoted passage.

If omitted words within the original passage follow some form of internal or end punctuation, retain that punctuation and then insert the ellipsis mark.

I write these words sitting outdoors in the morning sun. . . . I am supposed to be writing a Christmas piece, . . . but . . . it is only the eighth of September. . . . For a writer this is ordinarily no problem. . . . But Christmas . . . is no ordinary thing. —Gary Saunders

Do not use an ellipsis mark at the beginning of a quotation or at the end.

> EXCEPTION: If you delete words from the end of the final sentence, retain the final punctuation and then add the ellipsis.

Split families are one reason why we are buying so much for our kids. A third of Canadian marriages end in divorce, and dual households for kids demand dual toy boxes. . . . –Jennifer Hunter

## 2. Indicate the omission of a full line or more of poetry with a single typed line of spaced periods.

Hidden in wonder and snow, or sudden with summer
This land stares at the sun in a huge silence

. . . . . . . . . . . . . . . . . . . . . . . . . . . .

Not written on by history, empty as paper,
It leans away from the world with songs in its lakes
Older than love, and lost in the miles.

–F.R. Scott, "Laurentian Shield"

## 3. Use an ellipsis mark to indicate an incomplete statement or a deliberate pause when writing dialogue.

They came to the end of the furrow.
"Will we finish before supper, son?" he asked.
"Do you want to work all night, too!"
"What's wrong with you today, Dave?" he asked. "If you planned to go after partridges . . ."
"Partridges, hell!"
"Well, then, what's . . ."
David hesitated. "I'm so damned sick of this place. . . ."

# PUNCT 6h    The slash

## 1. Use a slash to indicate options or alternative words.

Every member of the band is responsible for his/her own uniform.

No space is left either before or after the slash. Although spelling out *his or her* is preferable to using *his/her* to avoid the sexist pronoun *his*, both can become awkward and repetitious in an extended piece of writing. For alternative strategies, see EDIT 3a1 and 3a3.

**2. Use a slash to mark off two or three lines of poetry when run into the text.**

> Archibald MacLeish summarizes the art of poetry in the first lines of his poem "Ars Poetica": "A poem should not mean / but be."

Leave one space both before and after the slash when quoting poetry. When quoting four or more lines of poetry, set them off from the text as a block quotation (see RESCH 4c).

**3. Use a slash to indicate a fraction that is not on your keyboard.**

> 5 3/4      4 1/2      27/64

# MECH

## Mechanics

### *Learning Objectives*

After reading this section, you should

1. be able to use capitals and abbreviations correctly,
2. understand the use of numbers, italics/underlining, and the hyphen,
3. improve your spelling.

# MECH ———————————————

## Mechanics

# MECH 1 _____
## CAPITALS

Early in English lessons we learn that **proper nouns**—the names of specific people, places, and things—are capitalized and that **common nouns**—all other nouns—are not capitalized.

| PROPER NOUNS | COMMON NOUNS |
|---|---|
| Brandon | city |
| Oscar Peterson | pianist |
| *Le Soleil* | newspaper |
| Medicare | health program |
| History 271 | course |

We also learn that the first word of an English sentence is capitalized, as are important words in a title. The rules for capitalization are quite clear-cut; even the cases involving optional capitalization are clearly defined. If you have a question about a particular word, consult your dictionary.

## MECH 1a    Capitalize proper nouns.

NAMES AND NICKNAMES OF PEOPLE

| | |
|---|---|
| Peter Pitseolak | Andrea Martin |
| Lucy Maud Montgomery | W.O. Mitchell |
| Bobby Orr | Susan Aglukark |

GEOGRAPHIC PLACE NAMES

| | | |
|---|---|---|
| Rocky Mountains | Nile River | Isle of Man |
| Beijing | Bruce Peninsula | Far East |

Used in the plural, common nouns that are part of place names are not capitalized.

Kent and Essex counties

Second and Third avenues

the North and South Atlantic oceans

Do not capitalize points of the compass unless they refer to specific geographic places.

We had seen the geese flying south for days.

Jake went East for the holidays.

Stephanie settled in Northern Ontario.

**NAMES OF CELESTIAL BODIES**

Venus      the North Star      Orion      Halley's Comet

**RACES, NATIONALITIES, AND LANGUAGES**

| | | |
|---|---|---|
| Inuit | Caucasian | Japanese |
| Pakistani | Dane | Irish Canadian |
| French | Hebrew | Slavic |

**NAMES OF REGISTERED TRADEMARKS**

| | | |
|---|---|---|
| Canadian Club | Skidoo | Pablum |
| Canada Dry | Jell-O | Kleenex |
| Vaseline | | |

Do not capitalize products used with brand names.

Nabisco cereals      Weston bakeries      Petro-Canada gasoline

**NAMES OF SHIPS, PLANES, AND SPACECRAFT (SEE MECH 4B.)**

*Bluenose*      *Dash 8*      *Alouette*

**NAMES OF HISTORICAL EVENTS, PERIODS, DOCUMENTS, AND TREATIES**

| | | |
|---|---|---|
| French Revolution | the Northwest Rebellion | World War II |
| the Sixties | the Renaissance | the Depression |
| the Canadian Constitution | the Quiet Revolution | Magna Carta |

Do not capitalize recently ascribed names of political, cultural, or scientific periods.

Trudeau years      cold war      information society

Do not capitalize centuries, as in *thirteenth century* or *twentieth century.*

**NAMES OF ORGANIZATIONS, CORPORATIONS, INSTITUTIONS, GOVERNMENT AGENCIES, AND COURTS**

| | |
|---|---|
| McGill University | Salvation Army |
| Toronto-Dominion Bank | Supreme Court of Canada |
| New Democratic Party | Department of National Revenue |
| Noranda Inc. | Alberta Wheat Pool |
| Fraser Institute | Coopers & Lybrand |
| Academy of Canadian Cinema | |

Common nouns that are part of a title are capitalized.

Taylor Field      Ellesmere Island      Canadian Pacific Railroad

Used in the plural, however, common nouns are not capitalized.

> Royal Alexandra and Elgin theatres
> Saskatchewan and Red rivers
> Canadian National and Canadian Pacific railways

Do not capitalize words such as *a, an,* or *the* when used with proper nouns.

> For the Calgary Flames, 1989 was a year of victory.

NAMES OF THE DAYS OF THE WEEK, MONTHS OF THE YEAR, HOLIDAYS

Saturday                October                Labour Day

But do not capitalize the names of the seasons.

> Saro has an internship in Ottawa this summer.

NAMES OF RELIGIONS, RELIGIOUS PRACTITIONERS, RELIGIOUS
CEREMONIES, HOLY BOOKS, HOLY DAYS, AND WORDS USED TO REFER TO
THE DEITY

Catholicism          Bar Mitzvah          Ramadan
Buddhist             Book of Mormon       God

PERSONIFICATION

> Because I could not stop for Death—
> He kindly stopped for me—
> —Emily Dickinson, "Because I could not stop for Death"

# MECH 1b    Capitalize words derived from proper nouns.

Shakespearean        Victorian            Leninism
Christian            Arabian              Torontonian

# MECH 1c    Capitalize abbreviations of organizations, government agencies, call letters for radio and television stations, and acronyms (a word formed from the initial letters of a name).

RCAF      TNT        CAAT       CBC        GST
AIDS      CFPL-TV    NHL        UIC        CIDA

## MECH 1d Capitalize titles, words denoting family relationships when they precede the name of the person, and epithets (a word or phrase used to describe a prominent characteristic).

Mayor Fisher
Reverend Jones
Grandmother Eliza
The Great One    [epithet for Wayne Gretzky]

Do not capitalize a title that follows a proper name.

Madeline Sprague, director of personnel at Holland College, is responsible for all new hirings.

When titles of world figures are used alone, capitalization is optional.

The Prime Minister [OR prime minister] spoke to the reporters.

Capitalize a word indicating a family relationship when it is substituted for a proper name.

Did Father call me?

If you are simply referring to a relative, no capitalization is required.

My mother collects stamps.

## MECH 1e Capitalize the first word of a sentence and the first word of a deliberate sentence fragment functioning as a sentence.

The cozy cabin was a welcome sight.

Superb acting.

## MECH 1f When an independent clause occurs after a colon, capitalizing the first word is optional.

The division championship is too close to call: the [OR The] Oilers and Canucks will battle until the last day of the season.

Whether you capitalize or not, however, be consistent within a composition.

## MECH 1g    Capitalize the first word of a quoted sentence.

Marshall McLuhan once wrote, "Art is anything you can get away with."

Do not capitalize the first word of a quoted sentence when it is blended into the main sentence.

Margaret Atwood states that "it's hard to explain to Americans what it feels like to be a Canadian."

If you interrupt a quoted sentence with some words of explanation, do not capitalize the first word of the quotation after the break.

"East coast fish stocks," say scientists studying the situation, "are now at just 3% of their 1990 level."

## MECH 1h    When quoting poetry, capitalize the first word of every line unless the poet does otherwise.

The light was free and easy then,
Among the maple trees,
And music drifted over
From the neighbours' balconies; . . .

—Dennis Lee, "Summer Song"

the first hours are passing when money
is made    contacts reputations
bargains promises mistakes
trains phonecalls women men
made and unmade. . . .

—Earle Birney, "January Morning/Downtown Vancouver"

## MECH 1i    Capitalize the first and last words and all other important words in the titles and subtitles of works such as books, magazine articles, films, and compact discs.

Unless they are the first or last word of a title or subtitle, do not capitalize articles (*a, an, the*), coordinating conjunctions (*and, but, or, for, nor, so, yet*), or prepositions of four or fewer letters (*in, at, with, over,* and so on).

**BOOK**
*The Writer's Brief Handbook*

| | |
|---|---|
| **BOOK/SUBTITLE** | **PAINTING OR SCULPTURE** |
| *Red China Blues: From Mao to Now* | *Leap of Faith* |
| **PLAY** | **ARTICLE** |
| *Hamlet* | "The New Nature" |
| **SHORT STORY** | **COMIC STRIP** |
| "Images of Childhood" | *For Better or for Worse* |
| **POEM** | **SONG** |
| "The End of the Journey" | "My Way" |
| **FILM** | **COMPACT DISC OR RECORD ALBUM** |
| *Birth of a Nation* | *Hits of the 1990s* |

## MECH 1j Capitalize the personal pronoun *I* and the interjection *O*.

The minute I got home, I collapsed on the couch.

"Hear, O Israel."

Do not capitalize the interjection *oh* unless it begins a sentence.

## MECH 1k Do not capitalize words unnecessarily.

Capitalize only when it is conventional to do so. Here are rules for avoiding several of the most common errors with capitalization.

### 1. Do not capitalize the names of academic subjects, except languages.

Josie is taking chemistry, math, philosophy, German, and English.

The names of specific courses, however, are capitalized.

New students are required to take Canadian Society.

### 2. Do not capitalize school terms or academic years.

fall semester     [NOT Fall Semester]

senior year     [NOT Senior year]

### 3. Capitalize only the first word in the complimentary close of a letter.

Fondly,      Sincerely yours,      All best wishes,

**4. Do not capitalize common nouns to highlight them or give them special emphasis.**

> We had fun at the company picnic.    [NOT Company]
>
> As a university student, I can use interlibrary loans.    [NOT University]

**5. Do not capitalize computer terms.**

| | |
|---|---|
| access | hard copy |
| database   [ALSO data base] | laptop |
| debug | mouse |
| e-mail | online |

Many computer terms are English words with new meanings. Brand names of hardware (IBM, Apple, Dell) and software (WordPerfect, Lotus 1-2-3, Windows 95) are capitalized. Names of commercial (America Online, MS Network) and other databases (the Internet, the World Wide Web) should also be capitalized.

# MECH 2 _____

## ABBREVIATIONS

Except for conventional usages, avoid **abbreviations** in formal writing, and that includes your college essays and exams. Spell out the names of holidays, names of days and months, addresses (street, province, country), names of academic subjects and subdivisions of books, units of measurement, names of academic departments, and parts of a business or institution's name (unless the abbreviation is part of the official name).

>        department     Christmas     December
> The shipping ~~dept.~~ is having its ~~Xmas~~ party on ~~Dec.~~ 20.

>       sociology      Mount
> Dana is a ~~soc.~~ major at ~~Mt.~~ Royal College.

>    Avenue
> Park ~~Ave.~~ is a one-way street.

>    chapter
> Read ~~ch.~~ 17 tonight.

*dozen*
Noah sent a ~~doz~~ red roses.

If you have a question about how a word is abbreviated, consult your dictionary. Most dictionaries have a separate list of abbreviations.

## MECH 2a Abbreviate academic, governmental, military, and religious titles when they are followed by a full proper name.

Rev. D.H. Shaw          Gen. A. de Chastelain
Dr. Virginia Wu         Hon. Joe Clark
Assoc. Prof. Helen Murphy          St. Joan of Arc

Do not use title abbreviations with last names alone.

*Janet*
Prof. McGinness mused, "Will we ever know?"     [OR Professor McGinness]
^

When no proper name is given, write the title.

The doctor took my grandmother's hand and smiled.

## MECH 2b Abbreviate *Jr.*, *Sr.*, and degrees such as *D.D.*, *Ph.D.*, *D.V.M.*, *M.D.*, and *LL.D.* after proper names.

Gerald R. Brown, Sr.          Michael Kaplan, D.V.M.
Eleanor T. Bates, D.D.          Elizabeth Luria, Ph.D.

It is acceptable to omit periods and spaces in some abbreviations, especially those made up of capital letters (MD, DVM, PhD, LLD).
Use a title either before or after a name, not twice.

INCORRECT     Dr. Laura Keller, M.D.

CORRECT     Dr. Laura Keller OR Laura Keller, M.D.

## MECH 2c Use the conventional abbreviations *A.D.*, *B.C.*, *a.m.*, *p.m.*, *no.*, and *$* only with specific years, times, numbers, or amounts.

32 B.C. [OR B.C.E.*]     A.D. 1812 [OR C.E.*]     10 000 B.P. (before the present)
8 a.m. [OR A.M.]     6:30 p.m. [OR P.M.]
no. 33 [OR No.]     $25

Driving straight through, Lee should be home by 7 a.m.

Always use B.C. or B.C.E. after the date and A.D. or C.E. before the date.

*Before Common Era and Common Era

# MECH 2d   Use conventional abbreviations for organizations, corporations, government agencies, provinces, states, and countries.

By convention, certain names are abbreviated with capital letters and no periods. Here are some of the most common:

| | | | |
|---|---|---|---|
| NWT | CIBC | YWCA | UK [OR U.K.] |
| GDP | CPP | NATO | TN |
| NAFTA | GATT | USA [OR U.S.A.] | AB |

If your readers may be unfamiliar with an abbreviation you wish to use, write out the complete name the first time you use it with the abbreviation immediately following in parentheses: Canadian Press (CP). Then use the abbreviation in the rest of the essay. (See PUNCT 6a2 for using periods with abbreviations, and for standard Canadian postal abbreviations.)

# MECH 2e   Use scholarly Latin abbreviations such as *c.*, *cf.*, and *et al.* in scholarly and technical writing and limit use of general Latin abbreviations in informal writing.

| ABBREVIATION | LATIN | ENGLISH |
|---|---|---|
| c. | *circa* | about |
| cf. | *confer* | compare |
| e.g. | *exempli gratia* | for example |
| et al. | *et alii* | and others |
| etc. | *et cetera* | and so forth |
| i.e. | *id est* | that is |
| vs. [OR v.] | *versus* | versus |
| N.B. | *nota bene* | note well |

Because not everyone is familiar with Latin abbreviations, keep them to a minimum and present them parenthetically. If you cannot present them parenthetically, write out the English equivalent.

Basic spices (e.g., basil, dill, oregano) come with the deluxe cabinet.

*that is,*
Kimiko calls herself a "Jeopard"; ~~i.e.~~ someone who never misses *Jeopardy*.

Do not use the ampersand (&) in formal or academic writing. (See WORD 7 for further information about *e.g.*, *etc.*, and *i.e.*)

# MECH 3 _____
## NUMBERS

## MECH 3a    Spell out numbers of one or two words; use figures for all other numbers and amounts.

*thirty-five*
Petar found that mirror for ~~35~~ dollars at a garage sale.    [OR $35]

*$1.99*
Raspberries are on sale for ~~a dollar ninety nine~~ a quart.

However, when you use more than one number in a sentence or paragraph and at least one of those numbers is expressed by figures, then all numbers that refer to the same thing should be expressed by figures, regardless of other rules.

*96*                                                       *98*
Of the 3779 seniors, ~~ninety-six~~ were from Alberta, ~~ninety-eight~~ from Manitoba, and 428 from Saskatchewan.

If your paper uses numbers very frequently, you can spell out numbers from one to nine, and use figures for 10 and up (check with your instructor). In business and technical writing, numbers are sometimes preferred to words for brevity and clarity.

## MECH 3b   When numbers appear in combination, spell out one and use figures for the other for clarity.

*6*
In our literature class we wrote ~~six~~ five-page papers.

# MECH 3c   Follow convention in using figures.

**DATES**
July 19, 1994          32 B.C.   [OR 32 B.C.E.]        A.D. 60   [OR C.E. 60]

the nineteenth century   [NOT the 19th century]

1970s   [ALSO the seventies or '70s]

When the year is not given in a date, the forms *1st, 2nd, 3rd, 4th,* and so on can be used.

Our anniversary is October 25th.

**TIME**
5:30 a.m.   [OR half-past five in the morning]

3 p.m.   [OR three o'clock in the afternoon]

**ADDRESSES**
16 Third Avenue   [NOT Sixteen Third Avenue]

328 West 128th Street

**PAGE AND DIVISION NUMBERS IN BOOKS AND PLAYS**
page 67     chapter 2     volume 1
Act 4, scene 2   [OR Act IV, scene ii]

**FRACTIONS, DECIMALS, AND PERCENTAGES**
33 1/3                3.26 kilometres               75 percent [OR 75%]

However, fractions of less than one are normally written out: *one-third, three-eighths.*

**NUMBERS IN SCORES AND STATISTICS**

The score was Canucks 8, Maple Leafs 3.   [OR 8 to 3, OR 8–3]

The union membership voted 173–25 against accepting the new contract.

The survey shows that 7 players out of 10 prefer Nike.

**EXACT MEASUREMENTS OR COUNTS**

6.32 kilometres

1.87 litres

32 753 people in attendance

EXACT AMOUNTS OF MONEY

$19.99

$20    [OR twenty dollars]

$56 007.68

LARGE ROUND NUMBERS

263 000 000    [OR 263 million]

35 billion    [NOT 35 000 000 000]

IDENTIFICATION NUMBERS

channel 3          Highway 401          room 27          #10772683

## MECH 3d    Spell out a number at the beginning of a sentence.

One hundred fifty-seven

~~157~~ passengers were stranded at the airport.

If you think the sentence is awkward, revise so that the number does not appear at the beginning.

There were 157 passengers stranded at the airport.

It is acceptable to begin a sentence with a date.

1995 was a good year for Niagara ice wine.

# MECH 4 _____

## ITALICS/UNDERLINING

*Italics* is a typestyle in which the letters slant to the right and are more scriptlike than the letters of standard typefaces. Italics are used, by convention, to indicate certain types of works and, because of their visual contrast, to give emphasis. In a handwritten or typed paper, <u>continuous underlining</u> is used to indicate italics.

C-Tip
*Italic typeface (underlining)*

On your computer use the command for italic typeface if your printer is capable of producing it. If your word-processing program does not have a command for italic typeface, use the command for underlining.

## MECH 4a  Italicize or underline the titles of works issued separately; that is, those that are not a part of a larger work.

**BOOK**  *Barometer Rising*

**PLAY**  *Executive Decision*

**FILM**  *Antony and Cleopatra*

**RADIO OR TELEVISION SERIES**  *Canada A.M.*

**COMIC STRIP**  *Chubb and Chauncey*

**MAGAZINE**  *Canadian Living*

**JOURNAL**  *The Journal of Canadian Studies*

**NEWSPAPER**  *The Hamilton Spectator*

**LONG MUSICAL COMPOSITION**  *The Phantom of the Opera*

**PAINTING OR SCULPTURE**  *Horse and Train*

**COMPUTER SOFTWARE**  *WordPerfect*

**COMPACT DISC OR RECORD ALBUM**  *Abbey Road*

The titles of shorter works published as part of a longer work (e.g., poems, essays, and newspaper articles) are enclosed in quotation marks (see PUNCT 5c).

The Bible, books of the Bible, and titles of legal documents are neither italicized nor put in quotation marks.

Bible  [NOT *Bible*]

Ecclesiastes  [NOT *Ecclesiastes*]

Charter of Rights  [NOT *Charter of Rights*]

Do not italicize or put in quotation marks the titles of academic, business, or other types of papers and reports.

> Personification in Atwood's "The Landlady"
>
> Annual Marketing Plan for 1999

## MECH 4b  Italicize or underline the names of ships, planes, trains, and spacecraft.

> *Trillium*  　　*The Canadian*  　　*Empress of Canada*  　　*Anik A-1*

## MECH 4c  Italicize or underline numbers, letters, and words referred to as such or used as illustrations.

> A large gold *10* was painted on the door.
>
> The letter *e* is the most frequently used letter in the English language.
>
> Did you know the word *fan* is a shortened form of *fanatic*?

Although italicizing is preferred, quotation marks are sometimes used (see PUNCT 5d).

## MECH 4d  Italicize or underline foreign words and phrases that have not been Anglicized.

Whether a foreign word should be italicized depends on how widely it is used by speakers of English. Many foreign words have become part of the English language and are not, therefore, underlined. Consult your dictionary if you are unsure.

> *maitre-d'hotel*  [French: "headwaiter"]
> *ab initio*  [Latin, legal term: "from the beginning"]
> *chérie*  [French: "dear one, darling"]
> café au lait  [NOT *café au lait*]
> bon voyage  [NOT *bon voyage*]
> du jour  [NOT *du jour*]

## MECH 4e  Underline (italicize) a word or words for emphasis, but do so sparingly.

Writers sometimes underline (italicize) the key word in their argument.

The time to save an endangered species is *before* it becomes endangered.

Underlining for emphasis can be effective, but only when it is not overused. If too many words in a sentence or paragraph are underlined, none will stand out as more important. Every time you underline a word, ask yourself if there is another way of achieving the emphasis you desire. Can you reorder the ideas in your sentence (see SENT 6a) or add telling details instead?

technically    and stylistically innovative
Glenn Gould was a *brilliant* pianist.
                  ^          ^

# MECH 5 _____
## THE HYPHEN

The **hyphen** is a versatile mark; it is used to form compound words, to add certain prefixes, suffixes, and letters to words, and to divide words. Do not confuse the hyphen (-) with the dash (—) (see PUNCT 6d). And do not overuse the hyphen; learn the following rules to use it correctly.

## MECH 5a    Use a hyphen to form certain compound words.

A **compound word** is made up of two or more words that function as a single word or expression. A compound may be two separate words (*half brother*), one word (*stepmother*), or hyphenated words (*father-in-law*). Sometimes the only way to be sure which form is correct is to consult your dictionary. If you cannot find an entry in your dictionary, treat the compound as two words.

Police blamed the incident on two or three rabble-rousers.
                                                ^

Mr. Rodriguez is strictly interested in the bottom/line.

## MECH 5b    Use a hyphen to join two or more words serving as a single adjective before a noun.

When two or more words function together as an adjective before a noun they are hyphenated, but not when they follow a noun.

| HYPHENATED FORM | NONHYPHENATED FORM |
|---|---|
| brand-new car | The car is brand new. |
| nineteenth-century literature | The literature of the nineteenth century |
| 18-year-old woman | The woman is 18 years old. |
| all-but-indestructible toy | The toy is all but indestructible. |

When a descriptive phrase functions as a noun, it is hyphenated.

I drink instant coffee, but fresh-perked is better.

Do not hyphenate when the first word of a descriptive phrase is an adverb ending in -*ly*.

frequently used dictionary      widely known fact

Use suspended hyphens with a series of single-hyphenated modifiers before a noun.

At Canada's Wonderland visitors can buy one-, two-, or three-day passes.

## MECH 5c   Use a hyphen with compound numbers from twenty-one through ninety-nine and with written fractions.

twenty-five         three-fourths

## MECH 5d   Use a hyphen to avoid ambiguity and awkward combinations or repetitions of letters.

Hyphens prevent confusion between words otherwise spelled the same.

resign   [to relinquish]

re-sign   [to sign again]

recount   [to narrate the facts]

re-count   [to count again]

Hyphens prevent mispronunciation from similar letter combinations and from doubled or tripled letters.

co-worker   [NOT coworker]

anti-inflammatory   [NOT antiinflammatory]

pre-existing   [NOT preexisting]

ball-like   [NOT balllike]

## MECH 5e   Use a hyphen with the prefixes *all-*, *ex-*, *great-*, and *self-*, and with the suffix *-elect*.

all-city                    ex-fighter              great-grandfather

self-appointed              premier-elect

Also use a hyphen between a prefix and a proper noun.

anti-Semitic                post-World War II       pre-Columbian

And, use a hyphen to join a single letter to a word.

T-square                    L-shaped                U-turn

## MECH 5f   Use a hyphen to signal that a word is divided and continued on the next line.

Politicians who want the respect of voters should take firm positions on such important and relevant issues as the deficit, unemployment, and taxes.

 C-Tip

### *Hyphenating words at the end of lines*

Most word-processing programs have the capacity to hyphenate words
at the end of lines. Before you use this feature, check that the hyphenation pattern of your word-processing program hyphenates only between syllables; some programs break at the margin however the word
falls. Also, watch for proper names (which should not be hyphenated)
because a program cannot identify them as such and will therefore hyphenate them.

In general avoid hyphenating at the end of a line, but when there is
not enough space for the full word without violating the right-hand
margin, refer to the following seven rules for correct hyphenation.

## 1. Divide words between syllables.

mem-
Mary Ellen could not remember whether her golf club ~~memb-~~
bership
~~ership~~ had expired or not.

If you are uncertain about the syllabification of a particular word, consult your dictionary.

## 2. Divide a word that is already hyphenated at the point of hyphenation or carry it entirely to the next line.

budget-
When the economy is slow more Canadians become ~~bud-~~
conscious
~~get conscious~~.

## 3. If a consonant has been doubled in adding *ing* to a word, divide between the doubled consonant.

bet-
The provincial legislature voted to allow ~~bett-~~
ting
~~ing~~ in casinos on a trial basis.

But if the word already ends in a double consonant, divide at the suffix:

fill-
Cut the dough into small squares, put a little ~~fil-~~
ing
~~ling~~ in the middle of each, and pinch the corners together.

## 4. Do not divide one-syllable words.

With 200 students in the band and over 300 in other choral ~~grou-~~
groups
~~ps~~, it isn't easy to schedule practice times.

## 5. Do not divide a word so that one letter is left at the end of a line or fewer than three letters at the beginning of a line; carry it entirely to the next line.

I'll have some turkey and mashed potatoes, but I don't want ~~a-~~
any
~~ny~~ dressing or gravy.

6. **Do not divide proper names or the first name and middle initial.**

Thousands of people turned out to hear Billy ~~Gra-~~
*Graham*
~~ham~~ preach in Toronto.

7. **Do not separate a contraction.**

After a long and heated discussion, the trustees decided they ~~should-~~
*shouldn't*
~~n't~~ invest in environmentally unfriendly companies.

# MECH 6 _____
## SPELLING

Although there is little correlation, if any, between spelling and intelligence, many people consider poor spelling symptomatic of some greater deficiency. At the least, poor spelling distracts the reader from the content of your writing and gives a general impression of carelessness. There is no reason, however, why someone has to remain a poor speller.

There are several things you can do to improve your spelling. First, keep your dictionary handy when writing, and check the spelling of any words about which you feel uncertain. Second, proofread: you will be surprised by the number of obvious, minor errors you catch. Finally, because spelling problems differ from one writer to the next, keep a list of the words you continually misspell at the front of your dictionary. By practising correct spelling, you will shorten your list.

## MECH 6a    Distinguish between words that sound alike but have different meanings and spellings.

Words such as *cereal* and *serial* or *symbol* and *cymbal* that sound alike but have different spellings and meanings are called **homophones.** These and other frequently confused words are listed here.

 C-Tip

## *Spell-checker*

Many computer programs have a spell-checker. This feature is useful, but it can give a false sense of security. While a spell-checker catches spelling errors, it often does not catch a lot of other problems: for example, homophones (words that sound alike but are not the same: *to, two, too*), omitted words, part of a word that you typed inadvertently (*bout* for *about*), or a correctly spelled word but one that you did not intend (*worm* when *word* was intended).

| | |
|---|---|
| accept | *v.,* to receive |
| except | *prep.,* to exclude |
| advice | *n.,* recommendation |
| advise | *v.,* to give information |
| affect | *v.,* to influence |
| effect | *n.,* the result |
| all ready | everyone is prepared |
| already | *adv.,* by this time |
| all together | as a group |
| altogether | entirely, completely |
| altar | *n.,* place of worship |
| alter | *v.,* to change |
| ascent | *n.,* movement up |
| assent | *n.,* agreement; *v.,* to agree |
| breath | *n.,* air drawn into lungs |
| breathe | *v.,* to take a breath |
| capital | *n.,* official seat of government; accumulated wealth |
| capitol | the building in which the legislature meets |
| choose | to select |
| chose | past tense of *choose* |
| cite | to quote or use as example |
| site | location |
| sight | vision; to see |
| coarse | *adj.,* rough; crude |
| course | *n.,* a route; a program of instruction |

| | |
|---|---|
| complement | that which completes |
| compliment | praise |
| council | *n.,* an assembly |
| counsel | *n.,* a lawyer; *v.,* to advise |
| decent | respectable |
| descent | the act of going down; ancestry |
| dissent | disagreement |
| desert | *n.,* arid region; *v.,* abandon |
| dessert | final course of meal |
| dual | twofold |
| duel | *n.,* a fight; *v.,* to fight |
| dying | ceasing to live |
| dyeing | process of colouring fabrics or hair |
| eminent | distinguished |
| immanent | remaining within |
| imminent | about to happen |
| foreword | *n.,* a note about an author's work |
| forward | *adv.,* ahead |
| formally | in a formal manner |
| formerly | in time past |
| forth | forward |
| fourth | referring to the number 4 |
| implicit | implied |
| explicit | distinctly stated |
| incredible | unbelievable |
| incredulous | unwilling to believe |
| its | possessive form of *it* |
| it's | contraction of *it is* |
| lie | *v.,* to be at rest; *n.,* an untrue statement |
| lye | a strong alkaline solution |
| loose | *adj.,* not fastened |
| lose | *v.,* to mislay; to fail to win |
| pair | two of something that go together |
| pare | to trim or shave off |
| pear | fruit |
| past | *n.,* time gone by |
| passed | *v.,* past tense of *pass*, to go by |
| peace | not war |
| piece | a portion |

| personal | pertaining to a particular individual |
| personnel | body of persons employed in the same place |
| principal | *n.*, a school official; in finance, a capital sum; *adj.*, most important |
| principle | *n.*, a basic law or rule of conduct |
| stationary | not movable |
| stationery | writing paper |
| steal | *v.*, to take without permission |
| steel | *n., adj.*, referring to metal |
| than | *conj.*, used in comparisons |
| then | *adv.*, at that time |
| their | possessive form of *they* |
| they're | contraction of *they are* |
| there | adverb of place |
| to | toward |
| too | also, excessively |
| two | the number 2 |
| vain | futile; excessively proud |
| vane | object that indicates wind direction |
| vein | blood vessel |
| whose | possessive form of *who* |
| who's | contraction of *who is* |
| your | possessive form of *you* |
| you're | contraction of *you are* |

## MECH 6b    Learn the basic spelling rules.

Learn the basic rules of spelling that apply to large groups of words. Investing a little time now will pay off many times over in your university or college career and later in life.

### 1.  Use the traditional rhyme for *ie* and *ei* spellings.

Write *i* before *e*
Except after *c*
Or when sounded like *a*
As in *neighbour* or *weigh*.

| IE | EI AFTER C | EI PRONOUNCED AS A |
|---|---|---|
| believe | ceiling | neighbour |
| chief | deceit | reign |
| grieve | perceive | veil |
| siege | receive | vein |
| yield | | |

| EXCEPTIONS | EXCEPTION |
|---|---|
| either | financier |
| forfeit | |
| leisure | |
| neither | |
| seize | |
| sovereign | |
| weird | |

## 2. Drop a final *e* before adding a suffix beginning with a vowel, but not before a suffix beginning with a consonant.

| SUFFIX BEGINNING WITH A VOWEL | SUFFIX BEGINNING WITH A CONSONANT |
|---|---|
| fame + ous = famous | achieve + ment = achievement |
| desire + able = desirable | hope + ful = hopeful |
| hope + ing = hoping | love + ly = lovely |

| EXCEPTIONS | EXCEPTIONS |
|---|---|
| dyeing | argument |
| gluey | awful |
| hoeing | duly |
| | ninth |
| | truly |
| | wholly |

Retain the final *e* after a soft *c* or *g*:

    courage + ous = courageous
    exchange + able = exchangeable
    notice + able = noticeable

## 3. Double a final consonant before a suffix beginning with a vowel if the word is one syllable and ends in a consonant preceded by a single vowel.

    swim + ing = swimming
    fit + ed = fitted
    set + ing = setting

*But:*

> feed + ing = feeding
>
> [Here the word is one syllable and ends in a consonant, but there is a double vowel, *ee*.]

## 4. Double a final consonant before a suffix beginning with a vowel if the word ends in an accented syllable and a consonant preceded by a single vowel.

> commit + ing = committing
> occur + ed = occurred
> abhor + ent = abhorrent

*But:*

> benefit + ed = benefited
>
> [The word ends in a consonant that is preceded by a single vowel, but it does not end in an accented syllable.]

NOTE: This rule does not apply to the Canadian spelling of words ending in the consonant "l":

> travel + er = traveller
> label + ing = labelling

## 5. Change a final *y* preceded by a consonant to *i* before adding a suffix. Keep the final *y* when it is preceded by a vowel.

| FINAL Y PRECEDED BY A CONSONANT | FINAL Y PRECEDED BY A VOWEL |
|---|---|
| beauty + ful = beautiful | array + ed = arrayed |
| embody + ment = embodiment | buy + er = buyer |
| modify + er = modifier | obey + ing = obeying |
| lonely + ness = loneliness | sway + ed = swayed |

| EXCEPTIONS | EXCEPTIONS |
|---|---|
| essay + ist = essayist | day + ly = daily |
| study + ing = studying | gay + ety = gaiety |
| | lay + ed = laid |
| | pay + ed = paid |
| | say + ed = said |

## 6. Most nouns form the plural by adding *-s* or *-es* to the singular.

Add *-s* to most nouns.

stick + s = sticks
pattern + s = patterns
elephant + s = elephants

Add -es if the noun ends in -s, -sh, -ch, -x, or -z.

pass + es = passes                tax + es = taxes
brush + es = brushes              buzz + es = buzzes
peach + es = peaches

If the noun ends in *y* preceded by a consonant, change the *y* to *i* and add -es.

spy + es = spies
inventory + es = inventories
penny + es = pennies

### 7. Follow convention in forming the plurals for nouns that do not follow the -s or -es pattern.

For nouns ending in *o* preceded by a consonant, add -es.

tomato + es = tomatoes           embargo + es = embargoes
echo + es = echoes

Some nouns ending in *f* or *fe* form the plural by adding -s, while others change the *f* to *v* and add -es.

| -S | -ES |
|---|---|
| roof + s = roofs | wharf + es = wharves |
| safe + s = safes | wife + es = wives |
| chief + s = chiefs | hoof + es = hooves |

Some nouns form their plurals by changing internal vowels.

| SINGULAR | PLURAL |
|---|---|
| foot | feet |
| mouse | mice |
| woman | women |

Plural forms of foreign borrowings usually retain the plural of the original language.

| SINGULAR | PLURAL |
|---|---|
| datum | data |
| phenomenon | phenomena |

Some foreign borrowings, however, have an Anglicized plural in addition to the plural of the original language; both forms are acceptable.

| SINGULAR | PLURAL | |
|----------|--------|--|
| formula | formulae | formulas |
| index | indices | indexes |
| syllabus | syllabi | syllabuses |
| appendix | appendices | appendixes |

Some nouns make no changes to form the plural.

| SINGULAR | PLURAL |
|----------|--------|
| deer | deer |
| fish | fish [OR fishes] |
| swine | swine |

**8. Form the plurals of compound words by adding -s to the end of the word except when the first word is more important.**

| SINGULAR | PLURAL |
|----------|--------|
| mastermind | masterminds |
| passer-by | passers-by |
| editor-in-chief | editors-in-chief |

## MECH 6c   Watch for commonly misspelled words in your writing.

Following is a list of 300 words that students frequently use and commonly misspell.

COMMONLY MISSPELLED WORDS

| | | | |
|--|--|--|--|
| abbreviate | accustom | altogether | appropriate |
| absence | achievement | always | argument |
| absorption | acknowledge | amateur | arising |
| absurd | acquaint | among | arouse |
| abundance | acquire | analysis | arrange |
| academic | acquittal | analyze | article |
| accede | across | annual | ascend |
| acceptable | additionally | answer | associate |
| accessible | address | apartment | athletic |
| accidental | aggravate | apologies | attendance |
| accommodate | allotted | apparatus | audience |
| accompany | all right | apparently | authority |
| accomplishment | almost | appearance | auxiliary |
| accumulation | a lot | appreciate | awkward |

bachelor
balance
barbarous
bargain
basis
becoming
beginning
behaviour
belief
beneficial
boundary
brilliance
bulletin
bureau
burial
business

cafeteria
calendar
candidate
capitalism
carburetor
career
category
certain
changeable
character
choose
chosen
commission
commit
committee
comparative
competitive
completely
compulsory
concede
conceivable
concentrate
conference
conqueror
conscience
conscientious
courteous
criticism
criticize

curiosity
curriculum
cylindrical

decision
definitely
dependent
describe
description
despair
desperate
diction
difference
dilemma
disagree
disappear
disappointment
disastrous
discipline
dissatisfied
dissipate
dominant
dormitory

efficient
eighth
eligible
elimination
embarrassment
eminent
enthusiastic
entrance
environment
equipped
equivalency
erroneous
escape
exaggerate
exceed
excellent
exceptionally
exercise
existence
experience
explanation
extraordinary

extremely
fallacy
familiar
fascinate
fictitious
foreign
frantically
friend
fundamental
further

generally
grammar
guarantee
guard
guidance

harass
height
heroine
hindrance
humorous
hungrily
hypocrisy

idea
illiterate
imaginary
imagination
imitation
immediately
impromptu
incident
incredible
indefinite
indispensable
inevitable
infinite
ingenious
initiation
intellectual
intelligence
interesting
interpretation
involve
irrelevant

irresistible

jealousy

knowledge

laboratory
legitimate
lightning
literature
liveliest
loneliness
luxury

magazine
maintenance
manoeuvre
marriage
mathematics
meant
medieval
miniature
mortgage
mysterious

necessary
nevertheless
ninety
noticeable

obligation
obstacle
occasion
occurrence
omission
operate
opinion
opportunity
optimistic
original
outrageous

pamphlets
parallel
paralyze
particular

| | | | |
|---|---|---|---|
| peer | propaganda | sacrifice | temperament |
| permanent | prove | sandwich | tendency |
| permissible | psychology | schedule | thorough |
| perseverance | | secretary | tragedy |
| physical | quantity | separate | tries |
| politics | quizzes | severely | Tuesday |
| practical | | similar | typical |
| precedence | recede | simultaneous | tyranny |
| predominant | recognize | soliloquy | |
| preference | recommend | sophomore | unanimous |
| prejudice | reference | special | until |
| preparation | referred | species | |
| prevalent | regard | strictly | vengeance |
| privilege | religious | succeed | villain |
| probably | repetition | supercede | |
| proceed | representation | surprise | whether |
| profession | restaurant | syllable | written |
| prominent | rhythm | | |
| pronunciation | ridiculous | | |

# FORMAT

## Essentials of Formatting

### *Learning Objectives*

After reading this section, you should

1. be able to format your papers on computer and prepare visuals,
2. know how to distinguish between MLA and APA styles of formatting,
3. be able to format business letters, résumés, and memos.

# FORMAT
## Essentials of Formatting

$\text{T}$he arrival of the Information Age has brought with it a flood of written material. It is not surprising, therefore, that increased attention is being paid to the presentation of written materials. Formatting—improving readability through good page design—helps the reader understand your message by highlighting content and organization. Today's word-processing software makes it easy to format your written work. You can use different type sizes or styles for emphasis and even insert tables and graphs to help your reader visualize information. The same word-processing software also simplifies writing that must appear in conventional formats, such as academic manuscripts, business letters, résumés, and memos.

# FORMAT 1

## BASIC COMPUTER FORMATTING OPTIONS

With all the formatting capabilities available on even the most basic computer software, how do you decide what to do? The answer lies in the piece of writing itself. What is the subject matter? A research paper in the humanities, for example, must follow MLA guidelines (see FORMAT 2). How long is the paper? Would headings (and subheadings) make it more readable? What is your purpose, and who is your audience? Is your topic very complicated? Would a list instead of an extended narrative paragraph help your reader understand a particular point better? Aside from these questions, there are, of course, such fundamental matters as setting margins and choosing a text typeface.

### FORMAT 1a    Basic page design

Formatting of any kind of writing begins with four basic decisions: margins, spacing, type style, and type size.

#### Margins and line spacing

Unless your instructor tells you otherwise, leave a 2.5 cm (1 inch) margin at the top and bottom of the page and on the right and left sides. (Some instructors prefer a 3.8 cm [1 1/2 inch] margin on the left.) Leave a ragged (uneven) margin on the right, because a justified (even) margin causes odd spacing between words and too many hyphenated words at the end of lines.

Most academic writing is double-spaced. Long research papers or reports may be spaced a line and a half so that they are readable but not any longer than necessary. Memos are usually single-spaced to fit on a single page, the preferred length in the business world.

 C-Tip

## Use templates

Many word-processing programs provide templates—model formats—for letters, memos, and reports. You can customize a template by changing the margins, for example, or the type style. (So as not to destroy the original template, save your template under a different name.)

Using a template allows you to be consistent in formatting written work, and saves you time.

### Type styles and sizes

Use familiar styles (Courier, Times Roman, Helvetica, Geneva) in a standard size (10 or 12 point). Do not use a script typeface, all italics, or all capitals for your main text; they are too difficult to read. If you have heads and subheads (headings and subheadings), use the same type style, though you may slightly increase the point size.

When you have made your basic page-design choices, you may want to print out a sample page. Adequate margins and a type style and size that do not call attention to themselves will transmit your message most effectively.

## FORMAT 1b    Improving readability

Use the formatting capabilities of your computer to improve the readability of long and complex pieces of writing.

## Heads and subheads

There is no substitute for good organization in a piece of writing, but in long or complex research papers and reports, the use of heads and sometimes even subheads can enhance readability. Heads and subheads break an extended piece of writing into visibly distinct chunks, allowing the reader to follow your train of thought, to stand back and see what has gone before and what is to come. Heads serve as a road map for reading.

Consistency is very important in using heads. First, you must be consistent in how you phrase headings. Most heads are a single word, usually a noun (*Stress*) or phrase (*Types of Stress*). Often they are gerund phrases (*Relieving Stress*). Heads may also be questions, which are then answered in that section (*How Can You Relieve Stress?*). Whichever type of head you start with, however, you must continue using that type throughout your paper. If you are using both heads and subheads, you can make all your main heads one type (say, single-word nouns) and all your subheads another type (perhaps gerund phrases).

You must also be consistent in the type style and size of your heads. Suppose your text type is 10 point Helvetica. All your heads should also be Helvetica, but you might put your main heads in 14 point and your subheads in 12 point. You have some options in how you present your heads: boldface (heavier type), underlining, italics or bold italics, all capitals, and capitals and lower case.

| | |
|---|---|
| **Types of Stress** | *Types of Stress* |
| <u>Types of Stress</u> | TYPES OF STRESS |
| *Types of Stress* | Types of Stress |

As with phrasing, you may choose one style for heads and another for subheads. Again, though, you must be consistent in whichever you choose.

Finally, you must be consistent in the placement of heads. By convention, main heads are usually centred and subheads are flush to the left margin.

## Main Head

### Subhead

Heads can improve the readability of a long or complex piece of writing, but they must be used judiciously. Too many heads and levels of subheads can be distracting or annoying. Every head should introduce a key concept, not a major point.

Lists

Breaking an extended piece of writing into sections makes it more manageable for your reader. Within sections, you may further help your reader by pulling material out of the text narrative and presenting it as a more visually accessible list. Some types of material lend themselves to listmaking more than others, of course. Steps in a process, categories, and how-to instructions naturally fit into a list.

Set off a list by indenting from the left margin. You can draw attention to the individual items in your list with graphic symbols, such as bullets (large, solid dots •), squares (■), or dashes (—). Graphic symbols are a good idea if the items in your list run over one line; in this case, it is also a good idea to indent the second line. See how indentation and graphics work in this example:

> Experts say there are four major ways to relieve stress:
> - consider whether you are accurately appraising the situation,
> - use your problem-solving skills to take action,
> - seek the support of family and friends, and
> - pay attention to your health by eating properly, getting enough exercise, and going to bed at a regular time.

If the list is introduced by an independent clause, as here, end the clause with a colon (see PUNCT 3b). Put a comma (or semicolon) after each item, and end with a period. Note, too, that the phrasing should be parallel (see SENT 1a). In this list, every item begins with a verb: *consider, use, seek, pay.* Do not overuse lists. As with heads, they are only effective if used judiciously.

## FORMAT 1c   Using visuals

Visuals—charts and graphics, tables, and diagrams—can add a new dimension to your writing. They allow the reader to visualize as well as read the information you are presenting.

Types of visuals

Different types of visuals serve different purposes. **Charts** and **graphs** show relationships among numerical data. A **pie chart** is a circular graph; it shows a whole and the percentages that make up the whole. A **bar graph** uses bars, usually vertical, to indicate frequency or quantity; it is useful for showing large-scale size or mass comparisons. A **line graph** shows finely delineated data in a continuum, such as age, speed, or temperature. Overlaid lines in a line graph highlight points of intersection and deviation. Examples of these visuals follow.

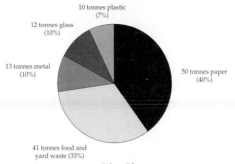

**Annual Landfill Deposits**

10 tonnes plastic (7%)

12 tonnes glass (10%)

13 tonnes metal (10%)

50 tonnes paper (40%)

41 tonnes food and yard waste (33%)

**Pie Chart**

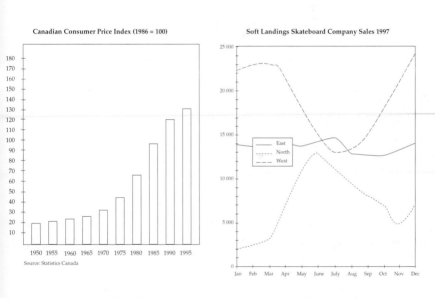

Canadian Consumer Price Index (1986 = 100)

Source: Statistics Canada

Soft Landings Skateboard Company Sales 1997

East
North
West

**Bar Graph**                    **Line Graph**

A **table** is useful for summarizing large amounts of information, either numerical data or text narrative. Because tables are columnar, they are also useful for making comparisons.

A **diagram**, or drawing, is a concise visual representation of an object or idea that would take many words to convey. The diagram of clustering on page 10, for example, allows the reader to see quickly how ideas and information can be generated using this strategy.

Incorporating visuals

You can create your own visuals with computer graphic software, or you can use visuals you find in your research sources. If you use visuals someone else created, you must give proper credit. The acknowledgment should be placed directly beneath the visual and should include the name of the creator of the visual, and the place and date of publication. The acknowledgment should also be included in your list of Works Cited.

Be sure that your visuals are properly sized (neither too large to fit within your margins nor too small to be legible), placed as close after (never before) the text to which they refer, and that the quality of your reproduction does not defeat the purpose of the visual aids. Better not to use a visual at all than to use one that confuses rather than enhances your message.

# FORMAT 2

## FORMATTING ACADEMIC MANUSCRIPTS FOLLOWING MLA AND APA GUIDELINES

The standard formatting guide for written work in English and the humanities is the Modern Language Association's *MLA Handbook for Writers of Research Papers,* 4th ed. (New York: MLA, 1995). For a model paper written according to MLA format, see RESCH 5. The standard guide for the social sciences is the *Publication Manual of the American Psychological Association,* 4th ed. (Washington, D.C.: APA, 1994). For a model paper written in the APA style, see OTHER DOCU 3.

The following guidelines are for formatting a manuscript according to MLA style. Wherever APA formatting style differs from MLA guidelines, information is provided.

General instructions

1. For academic purposes use letter-size 20-pound white paper.
2. Leave a 2.5 cm (1″) margin at the top and bottom of the page and on the right and left sides.

3. Double-space the text of the paper including set-off quotations, information notes, and the entries on the Works Cited page (see RESCH 5).
4. Do not justify (make even) the right-hand margin.
5. Use a letter-quality or near-letter-quality printer to produce your final copy. Dot-matrix printing is acceptable for working drafts, but the type is too light and certain letters are too hard to distinguish from others for final copy.
6. Make sure that your printer has a fresh cartridge or ribbon.
7. If you use continuous feed paper, remove the perforated strips from the sides of the paper, separate the pages, and use a paper clip (do not staple) to secure the pages.
8. Finally, be sure you keep a copy of your paper.

## Title and title page

Do not underline, put quotation marks around, or put a period at the end of the title of your paper. Capitalize the first letter of all words in the title except articles (*a, an, the*), coordinating conjunctions (*and, but, for, nor, or, so, yet*), and prepositions of four or fewer letters (*in, till, over*), unless your title begins with an article or preposition, in which case the word should be capitalized.

If your instructor does not require a separate title page, centre your title on the first page of the paper. Double-space between the title and the first sentence. In addition, papers without a title page should display the writer's name, course information, and the date in the upper-left corner of the first page (see page 265).

If your instructor requires a title page, place the title 15 lines from the top and centre it. Approximately six double-spaced lines below the title, centre the word *by*, skip two or more lines, and centre your name. About 20 lines below your name, place the course title, professor's name, and date, all centred and double-spaced. Do not number the title page. For a sample MLA title page, see page 340.

APA formatting requires a title page that is numbered. The page number should be placed 1 cm from the top of the page and 2.5 cm from the right edge of the page. Before the page number, and separated from it by five spaces, type a shortened title (usually the first three words of the title). Centre the title on the page about 15 lines from the top. Double-space and type your name and the course information directly under the title. For a sample title page in APA format, see p. 385.

## Outline or abstract

An outline is not required by either MLA or APA formats. If your instructor requires an outline, see the MLA model in the student essay on pages 334–35 for style suggestions. The outline should be presented after the title page.

Some instructors who follow APA formatting require an abstract, or brief summary (not exceeding 100 words) of your paper. Your abstract should state your thesis, the major points of your argument, and the conclusions you draw. The abstract should be placed after the title page and numbered as page 2.

## Heads and subheads

MLA format has no specific style requirements for heads. APA, however, has set forth requirements. The most important requirement is that heads are to be upper- and lower-case, and centred. Subheads are to be placed at the left-hand margin and underlined; they should also be upper- and lower-case. Do not number heads.

## Indentation

Indent the first line of each paragraph five spaces. For prose or poetry set off from the text, follow these MLA guidelines:

1. If you quote more than four typed lines of prose, indent 10 spaces from the left margin and double-space. (The right margin remains 2.5 cm.) Do not use quotation marks. See page 348 for an example.
2. If you quote four or more lines of poetry, indent 10 spaces from the left margin. (The right margin remains 2.5 cm.) Do not double-space, and present poetry exactly as it is in the original (see MECH 1h).

APA style requires that quotations of more than 40 words be indented five to seven spaces from the left margin and double-spaced. Do not use quotation marks.

## Paging

Use arabic numerals for page numbers together with your last name. Place your last name and the page number in the upper-right corner of each page, approximately 1.25 cm (1/2″) from the top and 2.5 cm (1″) from the right edge of the page (for example, *Smith 1*). Do not use the word *page* or its abbreviations *p., pp.* or use a period or any other mark of punctuation. Number all pages of your paper.

APA style requires a header, or a shortened title (usually the first three words), on each manuscript page. The header and the page number should be separated by five spaces. The page number should be 2.5 cm from the right edge of the paper (see OTHER DOCU 3).

**SAMPLE PAGE FORMAT**

2.5 cm

1.25 cm

Wright 1

Allison Wright

Professor M. Dickson

English 001, Section A

April 23, 1998

Capital Punishment: In Pursuit of Revenge    Centre title

Indent
5
spaces

Beginning in early childhood, most people have
been taught that it is not always in their best interest to act
on their feelings. And, while it is perfectly natural to feel
overwhelmed with anger or sorrow, they have learned not
to channel those emotions into actions that are offensive or
harmful to themselves or others. Then there is the old
saying: "Two wrongs don't make a right." Most people
have learned that lesson by the time they leave high
school. How, then, is it that some people who set such

2.5 cm

standards for themselves condone and even encourage    2.5 cm
capital punishment?

In our society individuals considered to be well
balanced and civilized must be able to differentiate
between their most basic emotions and what is
intellectually correct or acceptable. Canada as a nation has
elected a government and set up a legal system with
punishments to protect citizens from those who are unable
to behave in what is considered a civilized fashion. Modern
society has no place for punishment as medieval and
barbaric as the death penalty. Many people believe

2.5 cm

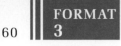

 C-Tip
## *Using the header option*

Use the header option on your word-processing program to create a heading of your last name and page number (for MLA format) or shortened title and page number (for APA format) that will automatically appear on each page of your essay. Remember to activate the consecutive numbering function if it is a separate option.

### Spacing for punctuation

Observe the conventions for spacing after punctuation marks: two spaces after punctuation at the end of a sentence; one space after a comma, colon, and semicolon, and between the periods in an ellipsis. Type dashes by using two hyphens with no space before or after.

APA style differs significantly here. It calls for one space after all marks of punctuation, including end punctuation.

# FORMAT 3 _____
## FORMATTING BUSINESS DOCUMENTS

### FORMAT 3a    Business letters

In the past, **business letters** were formal and stiff, with standardized phrasings and exaggerated courtesy. Today, courtesy is just as important, but modern business practice allows for a relaxed tone. Clarity is imperative; there should be no confusion over the message you are sending, and your writing should be grammatically correct and free of clichés, jargon, and other inappropriate language (see WORD 2 and 3). Finally, business letters follow the conventional formats outlined here.

### Format

Three patterns are used to format business letters today: **full block**, **modified block**, and **indented** (see next page). Select the format appropriate for your purpose: full block is the most formal, whereas indented

## BUSINESS LETTER FORMATS

### Full block

| 6–12 spaces |
| 2–4 spaces |
| 2–4 spaces |
| 2–4 spaces |
| 2 spaces |
| 2–4 spaces |
| 2–4 spaces |

### Indented

| 6–12 spaces |
| 2–4 spaces |
| 2–4 spaces |
| 2–4 spaces |
| 2 spaces |
| 2–4 spaces |
| 2–4 spaces |

### Modified block

| 6–12 spaces |
| 2–4 spaces |
| 2–4 spaces |
| 2–4 spaces |
| 2 spaces |
| 2–4 spaces |
| 2–4 spaces |

is the least formal. A job application letter, for example, is best presented in the full block pattern.

All business letters should be typed on unlined white paper and on one side of the page only. Use 2.5 cm (1 inch) margins on the left and right sides. Single-space the letter except where indicated in the sample layouts. A sample letter of application in the full block pattern is shown on page 264.

## Return address

Unless you are using stationery on which your name or your company's name and address are imprinted, include your return address and the date. Their placement depends on the format you have chosen (see the model layouts).

## Date

Always include the full date on which your letter is being written. Include the day, month, and year. It is always better to write the date out in full (February 28, 1998) rather than using abbreviations. The date should be placed between the letterhead or return address, and the inside address.

## Inside address

At the left margin, type the name, title, and address of the person to whom you are writing. The placement is the same for all formats.

## Salutation

The salutation is a word or phrase of greeting that conventionally comes before the body of a letter (such as *Dear Mr. Sampson*). If you do not know the name of the person you are addressing use *Dear Sir or Madam*, the person's position (*Dear Manager* or *Dear Director of Personnel*), or the name of the company (*Dear Klein Refrigeration*). If you are addressing a woman and do not know the way she prefers to be addressed, use *Ms.* If a title is necessary, put it after the person's name, separated by a comma (not on a separate line); capitalize the title (Dear Ms. Wong, Vice-President). A colon follows the salutation.

## Subject line

A subject line may be used to emphasize the topic of your letter or to make a reference, such as

Subject: Request for Information

Re: Competition #345

Subject lines are often underlined for emphasis.

## Body

The body of a business letter begins at the left margin in the full block and modified block formats. If you are using the indented pattern, indent each paragraph five spaces.

## Close

The first word (and *only* the first word) of the close begins with a capital letter. Customary closes include *Sincerely, Sincerely yours,* and *Yours truly.* Put a comma after the close. The placement of the close depends on the format you have chosen (see the sample layouts).

## Name and signature

Four spaces beneath the close, type your name (and your title, if you have one, on a separate line) and then sign your letter above the typed name (see the sample letter of application).

## Special notations

Other information may follow the signature, and should be abbreviated as follows:

| NOTATION | MEANING |
|---|---|
| JMN: as<br>JMN/as | The writer's initials are given in capital letters and the typist's in lowercase letters for reference. |
| CC Stephen Smith<br>cc: Stephen Smith | A copy of the letter is being sent to Stephen Smith. |
| Enclosure<br>Encl. | The recipient is alerted that something besides the letter is enclosed in the envelope. |

## Postal abbreviations

Use the standard postal abbreviations in your return address and the inside address.

## SAMPLE LETTER OF APPLICATION, FULL BLOCK, OPEN PUNCTUATION

316 Rymal Road
Hamilton, Ontario
L2R 8T6

April 1, 1998

Mr. Brian Westwood
Director of Personnel
Mohawk College
Fennell & West 5th Streets
Hamilton, ON L8N 3T2

Dear Mr. Westwood:

Re: Competition A345–1996

Through the placement office at Mohawk College, I have learned that the college has an opening for a trainee accountant in the payroll office. Since my training and career interests lie in the field of accounting, I wish to apply for the position.

At the May convocation I will graduate from the Business Program at Mohawk College with a three-year diploma in business administration, majoring in accounting.

In addition to my course work, I have worked summers at the accounting firm of Roberts and Mann in Burlington as a junior clerk. I feel, therefore, that I have both practical and theoretical experience upon which to base my choice of a career in the accounting field.

My résumé is enclosed. I can also provide you with the names of people who are prepared to provide references.

I can be reached through the business administration office or I can be contacted at home at (905) 575-1212.

Sincerely yours,

*Marie Garvey*
Marie Garvey

Encl. Résumé
cc: Placement office

| AB | Alberta | NS | Nova Scotia |
|----|---------|-----|-------------|
| BC | British Columbia | ON | Ontario |
| MB | Manitoba | PE | Prince Edward Island |
| NB | New Brunswick | QC or PQ | Quebec |
| NF | Newfoundland | SK | Saskatchewan |
| NT | Northwest Territories | YT | Yukon Territory |

The following are American postal system abbreviations:

| | | | | | |
|----|-----|----|-----|----|-----|
| Alabama | AL | Kentucky | KY | Oklahoma | OK |
| Alaska | AK | Louisiana | LA | Oregon | OR |
| Arizona | AZ | Maine | ME | Pennsylvania | PA |
| Arkansas | AR | Maryland | MD | Puerto Rico | PR |
| California | CA | Massachusetts | MA | Rhode Island | RI |
| Colorado | CO | Michigan | MI | South Carolina | SC |
| Connecticut | CT | Minnesota | MN | South Dakota | SD |
| Delaware | DE | Mississippi | MS | Tennessee | TN |
| District of | | Missouri | MO | Texas | TX |
| Columbia | DC | Montana | MT | Utah | UT |
| Florida | FL | Nebraska | NB | Vermont | VT |
| Georgia | GA | Nevada | NV | Virgin Islands | VI |
| Guam | GU | New Hampshire | NH | Virginia | VA |
| Hawaii | HI | New Jersey | NJ | Washington | WA |
| Idaho | ID | New Mexico | NM | West Virginia | WV |
| Illinois | IL | New York | NY | Wisconsin | WI |
| Indiana | IN | North Carolina | NC | Wyoming | WY |
| Iowa | IA | North Dakota | ND | | |
| Kansas | KS | Ohio | OH | | |

## FORMAT 3b  Résumés

A **résumé** tells a prospective employer of your qualifications for a particular position. Because your chances of getting a job interview—the first step in getting a job—rest, in large part, on how well your résumé communicates your training and experience, your skills and abilities, think carefully about what information to include and how to present it. Your résumé should reveal why you are the ideal candidate for the position.

There are many good books in school libraries or career centres that will assist you in preparing your résumé and getting ready for a job search.

There are two types of résumés that you can prepare, depending upon your situation. A functional résumé emphasizes your skills and training, and a chronological résumé emphasizes your education and experience. It starts with your present situation and then sets out information on your past years. A chronological résumé, shown on page 267, contains the following information:

## Name, address, phone number

Centre your name at the top of the résumé. If appropriate, give both your present address and your permanent home address, with phone numbers for both, including area codes.

## Job objective, position sought

As concisely as possible, describe the position you are seeking.

## Education

Give the name of the institution from which you graduated, the year you received your degree or diploma, the type of degree, your major and minor, and, if you like, your grade average. Include other educational experiences if they are pertinent to the position you are seeking.

## Awards and honours

Include awards and honours that reveal you are a superior student or have special talents or leadership abilities.

## Employment

List the jobs you have held, starting with the most recent. If your responsibilities are not clear from your job titles, briefly outline what they were. Include the name of your supervisor.

## Activities

List the campus organizations, volunteer groups, and collegiate sports in which you participated and name or describe the positions of responsibility you held.

## Skills

List the computer operating systems and programs with which you are familiar. If you have desktop publishing experience or have worked with graphics or cameras, add that information. Other skills might include sales, telemarketing, academic research, laboratory research, political campaigning, data collection and entry, programming, and science or social science fieldwork.

## SAMPLE CHRONOLOGICAL RÉSUMÉ

Marie Garvey
1342 New Street
Burlington, Ontario
L6P 1L3
(905) 575-1212

**Career Objective**
A progressive position in an accounting firm with the goal of obtaining professional certification.

**Education**
Three-year diploma in business administration, May 1999, Mohawk College of Applied Arts and Technology

Major: Accounting

Minor: Marketing

**Awards**
Dean's list for last four semesters.

Recipient of McDonald Fine Paper Company award for excellence in the accounting program.

**Employment**

1997–98
Part-time employment during the academic year: Receptionist and clerk, Roberts and Mann, Inc., Burlington, Ontario. Supervisor: Mr. Roger Mann.

1998
Summer: Office assistant for Roberts and Mann, Inc., Burlington, Ontario. Supervisor: Mr. Roger Mann.

**Activities**
Business Club, Mohawk College (1997, 1998), intramural basketball (1998), peer tutor (1997, 1998).

**Skills**
MS-DOS, WordPerfect, Lotus 1-2-3, Microsoft Word, Pagemaker, Q&A.

**References**
Supplied upon request.

### References

You can either indicate where your references are on file (if your institution provides this service) or list the names, addresses, and phone numbers of your references.

## FORMAT 3c    Memos

A **memo** is a brief, usually one-page, written communication between workers within the same office or company. Memos are used for a wide variety of communications: queries and answers, reminders, calls for meetings, and announcements affecting products, services, and personnel, for example. It is a good idea to cover only one topic in a memo. Your receiver can then take action on it if necessary, and then file it in the proper file. Memos follow a conventional format. A company or organization may even supply special printed stationery for memos, with the company logo at the top and conventional headings:

To:

From:

Date:

Subject:

You can add a *CC:* (copy) to send the memo to someone other than the person to whom the message is addressed. It can follow the *To:* or be placed at the very end of the memo.

 C-Tip

### *Memo templates*

Many word-processing programs include templates for memos. These can be customized for different purposes, and some will also automatically insert the date and your name.

In writing a memo, use your own voice. Be natural but to the point. Courtesy is also important; use "please" and "thanks." Sign your name or initials next to your name or at the end of the memo.

## SAMPLE MEMORANDUM

Mohawk
College

**TO:**       Law and Security Students

**FROM:**   L. Morton, Professor          *L. M.*

**DATE:**    April 27, 1998

**SUBJECT:**  Florida Trip

The annual first-year law and security trip to Dade County
Community College in Miami, Florida, has been approved.
Those students who have paid a deposit for the trip should
be aware of the following:

1. We will leave the college Saturday, May 6, at 8:30 a.m.
   and be back in Hamilton in the early evening of Sunday,
   May 14.
2. The trip will be by KAO bus charter.
3. The bus trip will last approximately 22 hours, with three
   rest stops along the way.
4. No alcohol will be allowed on the bus.
5. Accommodation has been booked at the Ramada Inn
   Downtown, Miami.

Students who have paid deposits are expected to pay the
remainder of the $700 cost (covering all meals and
accommodation) by April 30. Anyone who has not paid in
full by this date will not be considered for the trip. I will be in
my office (411E Carr Building) from noon until 3 p.m. on the
30th to accept payment and to answer questions about the
trip.

## FORMAT 3d    Reports

A **report** is an objective presentation of factual data. It is prepared to present the facts of a situation either inside or outside a business or organization. The report is primarily a study of a particular topic written for people who are most interested in the subject.

There are many different types of reports, but most can be classified as either informal or formal.

### Informal reports

The **informal report** is brief (often no more than three or four pages in length) and conveys information or instructions. Informal reports can be written as either memorandum reports (see FORMAT 3c) or letter reports (see FORMAT 3a), depending on the needs of the writer. Some of the most common informal reports include the following:

1. Occurrence reports—on events that have happened.
2. Progress reports—on progress on specific projects, either periodically or occasionally.
3. Field trip reports—on results of field trips.
4. Investigation reports—on results of investigations.
5. Lab reports—on results of lab experiments.

Essentially, the writing strategy for the informal report involves the following elements:

| | |
|---|---|
| SYNOPSIS | a brief statement containing parts of the following three elements |
| PROPOSAL | the reasons for writing the report |
| FINDINGS | the subject of the report |
| RECOMMENDATIONS | the results; what more needs to be done |

### Formal reports

The **formal report** is a more complex document than the informal report. The formal report is used for a variety of purposes, such as annual reports, shareholders' reports, and longer technical reports. The formal report is often 10 pages or longer, is usually intended to reach an audience outside the business or organization, contains graphics and headings (see FORMAT 1), and often contains supplementary material. Other elements of the formal report include the following:

## SAMPLE MEMORANDUM REPORT

**TO:**      Members of the Office Lotto 6/49 Pool

**FROM:**    S. Bantoft      *S.B.*

**DATE:**    May 31, 1998

**SUBJECT**: Progress of Investment

On January 1 of this year, we invested in a weekly group purchase of Lotto 6/49 tickets. So far, we've had very little luck. More money will be needed to keep the pool going.

On January 1 of this year, 15 of us from the office decided to form a lottery pool. Each member contributed $20, which I invested in weekly Quick Pick numbers, and I returned our winnings to the pool.

Although we have won a number of $10 prizes, we have never been lucky enough to win any significant amount. The entire pool of $300, along with another $90 that we won, has been used up. There is no money to invest in Saturday's lottery.

To keep the pool alive, I'm asking each of you for another $20, which should carry us through to the end of the year. If you're interested in playing the lottery again as a group, please see me by noon Friday in my office.

1. Letter or memo of transmittal
2. Title page
3. Summary or abstract page
4. Contents page
5. Body of the report
6. Recommendations

A format report may also include these elements:

7. Acknowledgments
8. Preface
9. Glossary of terms
10. Bibliography or works cited
11. Appendices

# ARGUE/LIT

# Writing an Argumentative Essay and Writing About Literature

## Learning Objectives

After reading this section, you should

1. understand how writing an argument is different from other writing,
2. know some techniques for providing evidence, making appeals, and refuting the opposition,
3. understand the importance of establishing credibility,
4. know some basic questions to ask in analyzing a piece of literature,
5. be able to use quotations and observe basic conventions in writing about literature.

# ARGUE/LIT ─────────

## Writing an Argumentative Essay and
## Writing About Literature

### Writing an Argumentative Essay

### Writing About Literature

# WRITING AN ARGUMENTATIVE ESSAY

A written argument tries to convince the reader to agree with the writer's particular point of view or take a particular course of action. The writer takes a stand on an issue, provides supporting evidence, appeals logically, emotionally, and ethically to the reader, and carefully uses language to move the reader to agree.

In many ways, writing an argument is like writing any other kind of composition. To start, you must choose a subject and generate ideas. You may sketch an outline to organize your ideas. After writing a draft, you need to revise and finally to edit (see COMP 2, 3, 4, and 5). At the same time, an argument has a slightly different kind of thesis statement, provides some special kinds of evidence, answers the opposition's arguments, and pays special attention to establishing the writer's *credibility*, the belief that the writer is worth hearing.

# ARGUE 1 _____

## DEVELOPING A THESIS

The thesis statement of an argumentative essay is an *assertion*—a claim made about a debatable issue that can be supported with evidence. An assertion cannot be a statement of fact because a fact is provable or verifiable. A fact is either true or false.

FACT      Sir Wilfrid Laurier was Canada's seventh prime minister. [You can check an encyclopedia to find out whether or not this is correct.]

ASSERTION   Sir Wilfrid Laurier was a great prime minister. [This statement can never be proven true or false; it remains an opinion. If you provide enough good evidence, you can convince your reader that the statement is *valid*—that it logically follows from the evidence.]

The assertion in an argumentative essay is not just any opinion. It is an assertion on which there is a legitimate and recognized difference of opinion. For example, few people would dispute that true love is a rare and intense experience, that crime rates should be reduced, or that computers are changing the world. These assertions are not, therefore, generally arguable. But not everyone would agree that women experience love more intensely than men, that imprisonment deters crime, or that computers are changing the world for the better. There are differences of opinion on these assertions, and that makes them arguable. These last assertions would make good argumentative thesis statements. Each would, of course, have to be supported with ample and solid evidence.

# ARGUE 2 _____
## PROVIDING EVIDENCE

*Evidence* is information used to support an assertion. There are various kinds of evidence.

### FORMS OF EVIDENCE

FACTS:  statements that can be verified (*Surinam is located on the northeast coast of South America.*)

STATISTICS:  facts expressed in numerical form (*The Halifax explosion occurred at 8:45 a.m. on December 6, 1917.*)

EXAMPLES:  specific cases in point (*Some students, Jaime and Kris for example, could not attend the meeting.*)

EXPERT TESTIMONY:  judgment of an authority (*The Minister of Health has stated that smoking causes cancer.*)

RESEARCH FINDING:  result of a scientific study (*Child psychologist Karen Wynn has shown that five-month-old babies know simple arithmetic.*)

The amount and quality of the evidence you use to support your assertions will determine your success in convincing your readers. Your evidence should be

- accurate (reliable, correctly interpreted and honestly communicated, current)
- complete (full and presented in the proper context)
- meaningful (specific and pertinent)
- representative (reflects the larger body of information from which it is drawn)
- appropriate (neither too sophisticated nor too simple for your subject and audience)

# ARGUE 3 _____
## MAKING APPEALS

An effective argument can appeal to the reader through logic, emotion, and ethics.

## ARGUE 3a  Use logical appeals.

Being able to reason is the most important requirement of argumentative writing. Nothing is more convincing to a reader than a good, clear, logical approach to an issue. Two ways we reason are **induction** and **deduction**, patterns of thinking we use so naturally that we are virtually unaware of them.

When you reason inductively, you generalize from specific pieces of information. Let's say you want to buy a camera but don't know which one is best for you. You would probably learn all you could about the different kinds of cameras on the market—their cost, features, available options. You would talk to friends who own cameras to find out which are easy to use and dependable. You might visit camera shops and read photography magazines. Finally, from all the specific evidence you gather, you would make a generalization—called an *inductive leap*—about which camera is right for you.

Deductive reasoning is more formal and complex than inductive reasoning. It moves in the opposite direction—from the general to the specific. Deductive logic follows the pattern of the **syllogism**, a simple three-part argument consisting of a major premise, a minor premise, and a conclusion. If the premises are true and the reasoning is valid, the syllogism is said to be *sound*.

1. All human beings are mortal. (*major premise*)
2. Alessandro is a human being. (*minor premise*)
3. Therefore, Alessandro is mortal. (*conclusion*)

A syllogism will fail to work if either premise is untrue:

1. All living creatures are mammals. (*major premise*)
2. A lobster is a living creature. (*minor premise*)
3. A lobster is a mammal. (*conclusion*)

The problem is immediately apparent. The major premise is false: many living creatures are not mammals, and a lobster is one of them. Consequently, the conclusion is false and the syllogism is invalid.

A syllogism can also fail to work even if both premises are true, but the reasoning is not valid:

1. All college students read books. (*major premise*)
2. Liz reads books. (*minor premise*)
3. Liz is a college student. (*conclusion*)

Both premises in the syllogism are true, but the syllogism is invalid because it does not take into account that not all people who read books

## Logical Fallacies

A logical fallacy is an error in reasoning that renders an argument invalid and untrue. Here are some of the more common fallacies:

**Oversimplification:** Offering simple solutions to complex problems: "If mothers would stay home to raise their children, we'd have fewer juvenile delinquents." There are many reasons for juvenile delinquency, and what evidence is there that working mothers is even one of them?

**Non sequitur** ("It does not follow"): A conclusion that does not follow from the premises: "If we can put a man on the moon, we ought to be able to find a cure for AIDS." Success in space doesn't guarantee success in medical science or any other field.

*Post hoc, ergo propter hoc* ("After this, therefore because of this"): Confusing coincidence with causation. Because one event follows another, it does not mean the first event caused the second. "Every time I wear my orange sweater to the game, we win." Does one fan's clothing really determine whether or not the team wins?

**Begging the question:** Assuming what needs to be proven. "If you value your health, you'll take an aspirin every morning." How do you know that your physical health will be improved by aspirin? In fact, once that question is answered, it may be that your health will be harmed by taking an aspirin every day.

**False analogy:** Making a connection between two logically unrelated ideas. "Eating crackers in bed is like driving with your foot on the clutch." Both may be bad habits, but how are they connected?

**Either/or thinking:** Seeing an issue as having only two sides. "If I can't make the starting team, there's no use trying out at all." Not everyone can be a starter, and there's value in just being on the team. Besides, practice and being a good team player might lead to a starting position.

are in college. If the minor premise were "Liz is a college student," then the conclusion "Liz reads books" would logically follow, and the syllogism would be sound, that is, both valid and true.

It is fairly easy to see the problem in a deductive argument when its premises and conclusion are presented in the simple form of a syllogism. It is more difficult to see errors in logic when the argument is presented in essay form. But if you can reduce an argument, whether made by you or an opponent, to its major and minor premises, and then test the truth of each premise, as well as the validity of the form of the syllogism, you can determine the soundness of that argument.

## ARGUE 3b    Use emotional appeals.

While some experts think there is no place in an argument for emotional appeals, others believe that as humans we are not merely logical machines. Our emotional responses to issues are very important to us and sway our thinking on issues. When an editorial writer argues for stricter community leash laws by telling about a child bitten by a dog, she appeals to our fears for our own safety. Such fears can change minds. When a student writer argues for greater participation in campus volunteer activities by describing the satisfaction she gets from preparing meals for residents at the local Ronald McDonald House, she appeals to our sense of caring and, as a result, she may change our minds about volunteering. Emotional appeals are not a substitute for sound reasoning, but an effective addition.

## ARGUE 3c    Use ethical appeals.

Ethical appeals are based on the credibility and, to some extent, the morals of the writer. This idea comes from Aristotle and Cicero, two classical theorists, who believed that speakers must be credible and that they should argue only for worthwhile causes. Using argumentative skills in the service of a questionable cause was unacceptable.

But how do you establish credibility? There are three ways: First, know your subject. Knowledge can either be first-hand (you're the person to explain how to change the oil in a car because you have been doing it for years), or it can be second-hand (it comes from someone else who has first-hand knowledge). For example, if you want to argue that a good day-care centre has a low ratio of children to day-care workers, but you aren't an expert in day-care, you can cite research studies and quote experts.

Second, consider the opposition. You do not have to agree with the opposition (see ARGUE 4). Rather, by acknowledging that there are arguments for both sides, you establish yourself as a reasonable person.

Third, maintain a fair and even tone. Back up your assertions with solid evidence instead of spouting generalities. Use language sincerely and carefully: be aware of connotative meanings and avoid pretentious words and doublespeak (see WORD 1b and 2c). At all times, show respect for the intelligence and interest of your readers.

# ARGUE 4
## REFUTING THE OPPOSITION'S ARGUMENTS

You won't have much trouble convincing readers who already agree with your assertions. But what about those who are sceptical or think differently from you? You need to discover who they are and what they believe. Talk to them and read what they have written. Once you understand the other side's position, you can refute it. You can present evidence to counter the opposing argument, show why you think its evidence is incomplete or distorted, why its reasoning is faulty, or why the conclusions drawn don't fit the evidence. Again, do your research, be reasonable, and agree where you can, but take issue where you must.

# ARGUE 5
## CONSIDERING YOUR AUDIENCE

When you consider your audience, first ask yourself the basic audience questions you ask for any kind of writing (see COMP 2g). But then remind yourself that you are arguing a point and that not everyone will agree with you. In fact, your readers will likely range from extremely sympathetic and accepting to extremely hostile and resistant—with many responses in between. It is therefore important in writing an argument that you try to anticipate different responses (especially your opponents' responses) and shape your argument accordingly (see ARGUE 6).

# ARGUE 6 _____
## ORGANIZING THE ESSAY

**Checklist for writing, organizing, and revising an Argumentative Essay**

1. Have I properly introduced the issue that is the focus of my paper? Do I provide necessary background information for my readers and explain why my issue is important?
2. What is my assertion and where have I placed it? Would it be more effective if placed elsewhere?
3. Have I used enough evidence? Is the evidence accurate, reliable, and up to date? Does the evidence support my assertion?
4. Have I made appropriate appeals to my readers? Have I established my credibility?
5. Is my reasoning sound? Have I checked for logical fallacies?
6. Are the points in my argument arranged in the most effective organizational pattern (simplest to most complex, least important to most important, most familiar to least familiar, and so on)?
7. Have I taken into account the opposition's arguments? Have I done this at the best possible point in my paper? Am I thorough and fair in my refutation?
8. Is my conclusion strong, and does it grow naturally out of my assertion, evidence, and reasoning?

# ARGUE 7 _____
## ANNOTATED STUDENT ESSAY

In the following student essay, Sherry Turple argues for abandoning fad diets and diet pills in favour of more sensible ways of losing weight.

Turple 1

Sherry Turple

English 1

Mr. Rosa

October 20, 1998

Author's surname and page number of essay (upper right corner).

Course information (see FORMAT 2).

Dying to Look Good

North Americans are obsessed with thinness—even at the risk of dying. In the 1930s, people took dinitrophenol, an industrial poison, to lose weight. It boosted metabolism, but caused blindness and some deaths. Since then, dieters have used thyroid hormone injections, amphetamines, and liquid protein diets—all of which were directly traced to some deaths (Kolata, "Fearful Price" 3). Most recently, U.S. dieters embraced fen-phen, a combination of fenfluramine or dexfenfluramine, which suppresses appetite, and phentermine, an amphetamine-like drug. In September 1997, however, the makers took the two "fen" drugs off the market because fen-phen was linked to heart valve damage and death (Kolata, "Companies Recall"[1]).

Wouldn't you think we North Americans would have learned our lesson by now? Apparently not. When fen-phen was withdrawn, one woman said, "If the treatment killed me, at least I would fit in my coffin" (Cowley and Springen 46). But there is no magic way to lose weight—no pill, no crash diet plan. The only way to permanent weight loss is sensible eating and exercise.

Title centred.

Introduction states problem.

In-text citations to two works by the same author use abbreviated titles (see MLA DOCU 1).

Transition to argumentative thesis.

Thesis statement is an assertion on which opinions differ.

Turple 2

Pills and crash diets don't work for several reasons. First, the body can't tell the difference between dieting and starving during a famine. So when it doesn't get enough food, metabolism slows down to conserve energy. At the first increase in calories, weight gain is rapid because the body is still functioning at a lower metabolism.

Then there is the psychological effect of dieting. According to University of Toronto psychologist Janet Polivy, "If you're told you can't have something, then that's what you want. You want it so much, in fact, that you become preoccupied with food at the expense of emotional stability" (Fraser 56).

Polivy and a colleague, Peter Herman, also did research to show that people on diets binge-eat more often than people not on diets (Fraser 56). In one study, they gave dieters and non-dieters milk shakes and then offered them a snack. Dieters ate much more of the snack than non-dieters. Polivy and Herman say this is because dieters were not eating according to whether they were full or not, but whether they were being "good" or "bad" on their diets. If they'd gone off their diets with a fattening milk shake, they seemed to reason, why not just keep eating?

The best way to lose weight is to eat sensibly and exercise. Choose a well-balanced, low-fat diet and watch calories, but don't become obsessive. You should also exercise regularly. Walking for 30 to 45 minutes three to

Writer provides expert testimony as one logical appeal.

Writer provides research findings as another logical appeal.

Writer establishes credibility with a fair and even tone.

Turple 3

five times a week, for example, will raise your metabolism and help you lose weight faster. If you want to exercise more vigorously, it's a good idea to assess your fitness level to be sure you don't do yourself more harm than good (Koop).

Writer states the opposition's argument and refutes it with an example.

Easy to say, but it takes so long to lose weight by eating sensibly, and there are so many temptations to go off a diet. Besides, it's hard to fit exercising into an already busy schedule. Isn't it easier to just get a pill? Sure, if you don't mind risking your life, and if you think you'll be the one who really will keep off the weight. The fact is that pills and crash diets simply do not work. The television talk show host, Oprah Winfrey, is a perfect example. In 1988, she lost 76 pounds on a liquid diet. Within two years, she was back to 200. Over the last few years, though, Oprah has stabilized her weight at 150—not ultra-thin—by eating sensibly and exercising (Fraser 58).

Conclusion grows naturally out of assertion and evidence.

The problem with losing weight is that we may know what is best for us, but we want instant results. With some of the recent "fad" drugs and diets either no longer available or not seen as effective, how many North Americans will take a sensible approach to losing weight? And how many will just wait for the next diet pill? New diet drugs seem to become available on a regular basis. Unfortunately, there will probably be a lot of people just dying to use them.

## Works Cited

Cowley, Geoffrey, and Karen Springen. "After Fen-Phen."

Newsweek 29 Sept. 1997: 46–48.

Fraser, Laura. "Say Good-Bye to Dieting." Health April, 1997: 56+

Kolata, Gina. "Companies Recall 2 Top Diet Drugs at F.D.A.'s

Urging." Globe and Mail 16 Sept. 1997: A1+.

———. "The Fearful Price of Getting Thin." Globe and Mail

13 July 1997: E3.

Koop, C. Everett. "Assess Your Fitness Level." Healthy Weight for

Life: Shape Up America. Online. Internet. 10 Oct. 1997.

Available: http://www2.shapeup.org/sua/health-

fitness/assess.htm

The heading
*Works Cited* is
centred at the
top of the
page.

Turple uses
MLA style for
her list of
works cited.
She begins the
list on a new
page.

The correct
forms for vari-
ous kinds of
sources are
given in MLA
DOCU 2.

# WRITING ABOUT LITERATURE

In some of your courses, your instructor will ask you to read a piece of literature—a short story, poem, play, or novel—and respond to it in writing. Your first step in completing the assignment will be to read the work carefully. As you interact with the text, you will begin to make connections, see patterns, and finally generate possible meanings. Ultimately, of course, whatever interpretations you make will have to be supported by examples from the text.

On one level, writing about literature gives you the opportunity to demonstrate your understanding and appreciation of the work. On a deeper level, such an assignment allows you to learn something about art and human experience.

# LIT 1

## READING AND ANALYZING A LITERARY TEXT

Very few pieces of literature yield their full meaning on a first reading, and their full meaning is what you want to extract. You should, therefore, allow yourself enough time to read the text *at least* twice. Sometimes, however, as in the case of a novel, this is not always possible. It is a good idea, if the book is your own, to annotate as you read. Jot down questions ("Why would she do that?"—about a character) or reactions ("Why does this author write such long sentences?") in the margin. Underline or highlight what seem to be important lines or passages.

Your goal in the first reading is to get an overall feel for the text. You want to find out what the text is about, where it is going, and how it gets there. Along the way, you'll form some first impressions of what it all means. Your second reading will be quite different. You're now ready to dig deeper—to analyze the various parts and relate the parts to the whole. You'll want to carefully examine passages that were puzzling on your first reading. You'll want to test your first impressions against the words on the page, developing and deepening your understanding of what the text means—or changing your mind about it.

As you analyze the text, you'll want to examine its basic elements. Here is a list of basic literary elements and some questions to get you thinking logically and creatively about what you read and what it means.

**GENRE:** the type of work—novel, novella, short story, play, poem, essay, or film.

- What kind of work is it—a science fiction novel, an autobiography, a sonnet, or a one-act play, for example?
- What conventions—established techniques, practices, or devices —characterize this type of work?

**PLOT:** the pattern or sequence of events in a literary work.

- What happens in the story? Does the action occur in chronological order or in flashbacks?
- Is there a central conflict? What other conflicts occur?
- How are the events related to one another?
- Are there any subplots?

**CHARACTERS:** the people the writer creates.

- Who are the central people in the story, play, or poem, and what seems to motivate them?
- How do the characters interact? How are their conflicts resolved?
- What do the characters reveal about themselves and others in what they do, say, and think?
- Do any of the characters change? What, if anything, have they learned about themselves from their experiences?

**SETTING:** the time (historical period or season) and place (locale) against which the action takes place.

- What does the setting contribute to the writer's meaning?
- What is the social/cultural context for the work?
- What is the importance of scene changes when they occur?

**POINT OF VIEW:** the perspective from which the story is told.

- Who is the narrator? Is the story being told by a character—in the first person (*I, we*), third person (*he, she, it, they*), or omniscient voice?
- Is the narrator trustworthy? How do you know? If the narrator is not trustworthy, how does that affect the story?
- What is the significance of the writer's choice of a narrator and point of view?
- In a poem, who is the speaker and to whom is this person speaking?

**THEME:** the main idea or meaning of the work.

- What does the work tell you about life or people?
- How do the other literary elements in this list work together to develop this meaning for you?

TONE: the feelings presented, the predominant mood conveyed through the writer's choice of words.
- What attitude do you hear in the words of the story, play, or poem?
- Is the narrator reliable, or is the writer being ironic?
- Is the tone appropriate for the theme of the work? For the audience?

IMAGES: descriptive details and figurative language appealing to the five senses.
- To which of your senses do the writer's images appeal?
- What patterns, if any, do you find in the images? Do recurring images seem symbolic to you?
- What metaphors, similes, and personification does the writer use? How do these figures contribute to the meaning of the work?

# LIT 2

## OBSERVING THE CONVENTIONS

As you work on your essay, observe the **conventions**—or widely accepted practices—for writing about a literary text. Adhering to these conventions focuses your readers on the content of your paper and not on the details of your presentation.

- Avoid unnecessary and extended plot summaries. You can assume that your readers have read the piece of literature you are discussing. Your paper should therefore analyze and interpret the work and present any conclusions you wish to draw, not retell the story.
- Use literary terms accurately. Remember, for example, that an *essay* is not a *story*, the *speaker* or *narrator* is not necessarily the *author*, and that a group of lines in a poem is a *stanza* and not a *paragraph*. If you have questions about the use of a particular term, ask your instructor or consult one of the many dictionaries of literary terms available in libraries.
- Use *suggests* or *implies*. When attributing a particular meaning to a writer, be careful not to claim absolute knowledge about a writer's intentions or meaning.
- Support your points with specific references to the text about which you are writing—summarize an important scene, describe the atmosphere/setting, or paraphrase (or quote) what a character says. Be sparing, however, in your use of quotations (see LIT 3). For specific advice about using quotations, paraphrasing, and summarizing, see RESCH 2c.
- Give the page number parenthetically when citing a passage from a work of fiction or non-fiction; the line number(s) for a poem; the act, scene, and line numbers for a play; and book, chapter, and verse for the

Bible (see MLA DOCU 1, pp. 359–60). In all cases, be sure to integrate evidence smoothly into your paper (see LIT 3).

- Use the present tense when discussing works of literature (see EDIT 2c).
- Use the past tense when talking about historical events, presenting biographical material about the writer, or referring to events that occurred prior to the time of the story's central action.
- Use a writer's or critic's full name the first time you mention it. Thereafter, use only the last name.
- Underline or use italics for the titles of novels, novellas, plays, and films (see MECH 4a). Enclose the titles of short stories, poems, essays, and songs in quotation marks (see PUNCT 5c).
- If you use the work of others to support your analysis, you must acknowledge the source. Introduce each quotation, paraphrase, or summary by referring to the source in a signal phrase, and follow the borrowed material with parenthetical documentation (see RESCH 4b).
- Use the MLA documentation style, including in-text parenthetical citations (see MLA DOCU 1), and include a list of Works Cited (see MLA DOCU 2).

# LIT 3 _____

## USING QUOTATIONS

Using quotations purposefully means using only those that truly support your interpretation. Using quotations effectively means reserving direct quotation for important ideas stated in vivid, imaginative, and memorable language or for revealing statements made by characters themselves. When you are considering using a quotation, ask yourself these questions:

- How well does the quotation illustrate or support my analysis?
- Is this quotation the best evidence of the point I am making?
- Why am I quoting the text instead of saying this in my own words?

Resist the temptation to use quotations simply because they sound good or because you think you don't have "enough" of them in your paper. Finally, remember that good use of quotations gives your paper authority.

Whenever you quote, you need to relate the quotation to your point. Don't leave it to your readers to guess your intent. Introduce each quotation and draw a conclusion from it. Smoothly integrate quotations into your paper so that they are not stylistically jarring. Consider the following uses of quotations in a student paper on Brian Moore's *The Luck of Ginger Coffey.*

**WEAK**

Moore often uses specific details from the settings of his novel to suggest the psychological state of his character. For example, in describing the office buildings as being "the colour of a dead man's skin" (97), he prefigures Coffey's imminent failure.

**EFFECTIVE**

Moore often uses specific details from the settings of his novel to suggest the psychological state of his main character, Ginger Coffey, an Irish immigrant to Canada. For example, as Coffey treks across Montreal looking for a job, the office buildings along Rue Notre Dame are described as "the colour of a dead man's skin" (97), prefiguring Coffey's imminent inability to deal with life in Canada.

Stating the fact that the main character is an immigrant to Canada, and that he is looking for a job, places the quotation in context and heightens the comparison between the setting and the psychological state of the character. For additional examples of integrating quotations from literary texts, see RESCH 4c and MLA DOCU 1.

Finally, use quotation marks around all passages borrowed word-for-word (see PUNCT 5a).

# LIT 4
## ANNOTATED STUDENT ESSAY

The following student essay was written by Catherine Fraser, a student at Mohawk College, in response to Jan Bell's essay "Return to the Land." The student supports her interpretation of the essay by paraphrasing and quoting from Bell's text. She also draws upon secondary sources to lend the additional support to her ideas. The student essay follows the manuscript format guidelines of the MLA (see FORMAT 2) and illustrates correct MLA documentation style (see MLA DOCU).

Fraser 1

Catherine Fraser

English 11

Dr. Roberts

March 15, 1998

### The Untamed

When asked to comment on the purpose of "Return
to the Land," Jan Bell said, "The person described in this
essay was someone I encountered on a single occasion
when I was about nine years old. In writing the essay, I
discovered that an early childhood experience had made
more of an impression upon me than I had ever thought"
(Hookey and Pilz, 23). In "Return to the Land," an old
farmer is remembered from the author's past, a man who
has worked with the land all of his life, and now seems to
be defeated by the land—at least until he decides not to
give up but to return to the struggle. The old farmer's
despair with his situation is all too evident. "All that
remained of the man sat before me, beaten by the very
land he had nurtured" (Bell, 23). Bell's essay not only
conveys the hopelessness of the farmer's situation—to
attempt to farm the land amidst drought, insects, and
plague—but also mirrors the Canadian experience of
taming the great Canadian West. She accomplishes this
through the use of description.

Author's
surname and
page number
of essay.

Course
information
presented in
upper left
corner (see
FORMAT 2).

Title centred.

In-text
citation with
authors'
names and
page number
in parenthe-
ses (see MLA
DOCU 1).

Writer uses
present tense
to discuss
story.

Writer
quotes text
but doesn't
overquote.

Writer
presents
thesis.

Fraser 2

Bell begins her description by comparing the farmer's posture to that of a famous statue, Rodin's <u>The Thinker</u>. This is, on one hand, a particularly effective comparison in that the pose of the statue places the old farmer into a classical context, lending dignity to his appearance and to his struggle with the land. It also gives the reader a visual reference to the setting of the essay, in which the entire scene is focused entirely on the farmer, with no distracting external description. On the other hand, if the reader has never seen Rodin's statue, Bell's comparison becomes ineffective.

The author is attempting to create a portrait in this essay through the use of descriptive language, language that paints a picture for a particular purpose. Bell's picture of the farmer as he smokes cigarette after cigarette is intended to convey the sense of time passing in an endless stream of cigarettes, with wasted shreds of tobacco dropping to the ground in the same manner that wasted minutes fall along the wayside of life and are forgotten. The farmer feels a sense of loss in his life; he feels that his calloused, gnarled hands have produced nothing but ashes, despite his hope for the future and for the land, and the tear that runs down his unshaven, weatherbeaten face is symbolic of all who have failed in their quest to tame the land.

Fraser 3

It is not difficult to picture the farmer as an early pioneer on the Canadian prairies, bringing his family, as George Brenner describes it, "to the vast open spaces of Manitoba or Saskatchewan to start life anew amid the ashes of the failed dreams of the Old World" (337). But hard work was never enough to bring "civilization" to the West. The vagaries of weather and fortune were always the deciding factors.

In the last paragraph of "Return to the Land," Bell makes her most important point, that despite his failures, the farmer will return to the land, and the land will receive him, possibly as the man who nurtured the land, or possibly as an old man coming home to die. The reader feels, despite the overwhelming sense of failure conveyed in the essay, that the farmer, or those who follow him to the land, will win in the end. The farmer's spirit, although battered, will not be broken. It is this unconquerable spirit that tamed the West and allowed the farmer to hold his head high and take from the land the fruit of his labours.

*In-text citation with the author's full name given in a signal phrase and the page number in parentheses. Writer uses secondary source.*

*Conclusion presents the central idea the writer wants to leave with the reader.*

### Works Cited

Brenner, George A. <u>The Opening of the West</u>. Hamilton: Grant, 1996.

Hookey, Robert, and Joan Pilz. <u>Contest Essays by Canadian Students</u>. Toronto: Holt, 1991.

# LIB/RESCH

# The Library
# and
# The Research Paper

## *Learning Objectives*

After reading this section, you should

1. know the kinds of reference books and periodical indexes available in the library,
2. be able to use computerized periodical indexes,
3. be able to use card and computer catalogues,
4. know what's available for online research,
5. understand researching well enough to set a realistic completion schedule,
6. know how to use the library's print and online resources for research,
7. understand the importance of correct note-card form and when to summarize, paraphrase, and quote directly,
8. know how to integrate quotations into your paper,
9. understand the importance of crediting others' ideas.

# LIB/RESCH _____

The Library

and

The Research Paper

## The Library

## The Research Paper

## THE LIBRARY

The college library is a storehouse of information, and learning how to retrieve information from it is a basic part of your education.

If your college library provides guided tours, take one; if not, obtain a map showing the location of the library's various holdings. In either case, learn to ask for help. Reference librarians are trained specialists in information retrieval, and will soon have you feeling at home in your college's library. If you learn early in your college career how to use the library efficiently, you will save yourself time and frustration and greatly enhance the quality of your education.

Generally, most libraries contain four types of resources: (1) reference books, (2) periodicals, (3) books in the general collection, and (4) computer databases and the Internet.

# LIB 1 _____

## REFERENCE BOOKS

The **reference section** of a library houses encyclopedias, dictionaries, abstracts, atlases, yearbooks, handbooks, almanacs, catalogues, bibliographies, indexes, biographical guides, and other types of reference works. As you begin your research project, use one or more of these reference books to get an overview of your subject. Books and other reference materials published in Canada contain Canadian Cataloguing in Publication information on the copyright page of the publication, which could assist you in your overview of the information available. An annotated sample is provided on the next page.

For a comprehensive descriptive guide to all reference books published in the world, see Eugene P. Sheehy's *Guide to Reference Books*.

If you cannot locate a particular reference book or if you are simply looking for general assistance, do not hesitate to talk about your research project with the reference librarian. Finally, be aware that reference books are usually not allowed to circulate, so plan your library time accordingly.

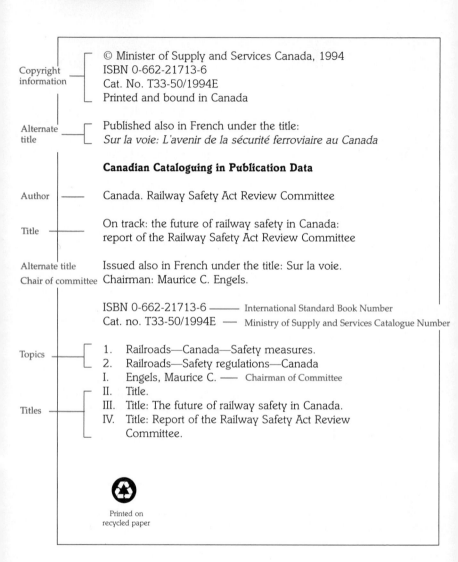

Copyright information
© Minister of Supply and Services Canada, 1994
ISBN 0-662-21713-6
Cat. No. T33-50/1994E
Printed and bound in Canada

Alternate title
Published also in French under the title:
*Sur la voie: L'avenir de la sécurité ferroviaire au Canada*

**Canadian Cataloguing in Publication Data**

Author
Canada. Railway Safety Act Review Committee

Title
On track: the future of railway safety in Canada:
report of the Railway Safety Act Review Committee

Alternate title
Issued also in French under the title: Sur la voie.

Chair of committee
Chairman: Maurice C. Engels.

ISBN 0-662-21713-6 —— International Standard Book Number
Cat. no. T33-50/1994E —— Ministry of Supply and Services Catalogue Number

Topics
1. Railroads—Canada—Safety measures.
2. Railroads—Safety regulations—Canada
I. Engels, Maurice C. —— Chairman of Committee

Titles
II. Title.
III. Title: The future of railway safety in Canada.
IV. Title: Report of the Railway Safety Act Review Committee.

Printed on recycled paper

# LIB 2

## PERIODICALS

The term **periodicals** refers to magazines, journals, and newspapers; that is, materials published on a regular basis (daily, weekly, monthly, yearly, or at some other time interval).

## LIB 2a   Periodical indexes

To locate articles in periodicals, use a **periodical index**, which is usually found in the reference section of the library. Unless you are trying to locate a particular article by a particular author or know of an author who generally writes on a particular subject, start your search under subject headings

The most widely used index to periodicals is *The Readers' Guide to Periodical Literature* (1900–present). *The Readers' Guide* annually indexes nearly 200 periodicals of popular interest, such as *Newsweek, Maclean's, Sports Illustrated,* and *Scientific American.* Monthly paperback supplements keep *The Readers' Guide* current throughout the year. *The Readers' Guide* lists articles both by subject and by author in alphabetical order with cross-references to related subject headings.

On the next page are shown the subject and author entries from *The Readers' Guide* for two articles consulted by Patricia LaRose, the student who wrote the sample paper on recycling (in RESCH 5). As you can see, all the information needed to locate an article is provided.

Articles from major newspapers can be located in the following newspaper indexes: [London] *Times Index, National Newspaper Index, NewsBank, New York Times Index, Wall Street Journal Index,* [Toronto] *Globe and Mail Index, Vancouver Sun Index, Halifax Gazette Index.*

Specialized periodical indexes list articles that have appeared in technical and scholarly journals or government publications. They are organized in much the same way as the *Readers' Guide.* Remember that the reference librarian is always available to help you locate specialized periodical indexes for your particular subject.

**SUBJECT ENTRY FROM** *THE READERS' GUIDE*

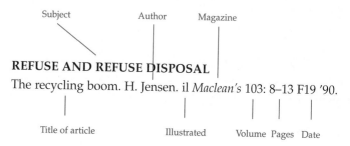

Subject      Author      Magazine

**REFUSE AND REFUSE DISPOSAL**
The recycling boom. H. Jensen. il *Maclean's* 103: 8–13 F19 '90.

Title of article      Illustrated      Volume  Pages  Date

**AUTHOR ENTRY FROM** *THE READERS' GUIDE*

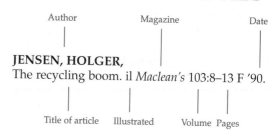

Author      Magazine      Date

**JENSEN, HOLGER,**
The recycling boom. il *Maclean's* 103:8–13 F '90.

Title of article    Illustrated    Volume  Pages

## LIB 2b    Computerized periodical indexes

Most libraries offer online and CD-ROM (compact disc—read only memory) computer database versions of periodical indexes. Computer searches can save you valuable time in locating articles—time that you can use in reading what you find.

To use a computerized periodical index, type in the access codes explained in the opening menu on the terminal screen. You can begin your search for articles by author, title, or subject key words. At any time, if you have a problem, ask a reference librarian for help.

Bibliographic records of potentially useful articles will appear on the screen. In some cases you can access an abstract or even the full text of an article. Here is a sample of a full-record display:

**FULL RECORD DISPLAY SCREEN**

. . . . . . . . . . . . . . . . Full Record Display . . . . . . . . . . . . . . . .

tabase
entified DATABASE: ReadGuideAbs          LIMITED TO:

SEARCH: su:recycling

Record 64 of 961__YOUR LIBRARY (VTU) MAY OWN THIS
ITEM__ (Page 1 of 3)

| | |
|---|---|
| AUTHOR: | Grove, Noel. |
| TITLE: | Recycling. |
| SOURCE: | National Geographic v. 186 (July '94) pp. 92-115 il. |
| STANDARD NO: | 0027-9358 |
| DATE: | 1994 |
| RECORD TYPE: | art |
| CONTENTS: | feature article |

ABSTRACT:   Not since World War II have Americans been so
fervent about recycling. The renewed interest in
recycling stems from a number of concerns,
including loss of landfill space, contamination of
groundwater by landfills, dwindling natural
resources and, possibly, a growing compre-
hension of America's unmatched waste
production—300 million tons a year. The
rapidly evolving recycling industry nonetheless
struggles with acceptance and financing.
Economic arguments against it point to the
expense of implementing recycling programs
and the difficulty of selling recycled materials,
which often pile up unused. Supporters of
recycling contend, however, that it just takes
time for regional markets to evolve and close
the loop from manufacturer to consumer and
back to manufacturer again. Various recycling
programs around the country are discussed.

SUBJECT:   Recycling (Waste, etc.).

Subject
being
searched

Publication
information
for item #64

Summary
of article

# LIB 3
## BOOKS

Subject being searched

Summary of search

**SEARCH RESULT SCREEN**

Search Request: S=GARBAGE          UVM Online Catalog
Search Results: 12 Entries Found    Subject Index
----------------------------------------------------- T261

GARBAGE
*Search Under:
1 ORGANIC WASTES
2 REFUSE AND REFUSE DISPOSAL

GARBAGE AS FEED–LAW AND LEGISLATION–
UNITED STATES
3 ACT TO REGULATE THE FEEDING OF GARBAGE
TO SW (1980)                                    (BH)

Library of Congress subject headings

4 SWINE HEALTH PROTECTION ACT
HEARING BEFORE T (1980)                         (BH)
5 SWINE HEALTH PROTECTION ACT REPORT
TO ACCOMP (1980)                                (BH)

Alternative search options

GARBAGE AS FUEL
6 *Search Under: REFUSE AS FUEL

GARBAGE AS MODELS OF DECISION MAKING –
CONGRESSES
7 AMBIGUITY AND COMMAND ORGANIZATIONAL
PERSPEC (1986)                                  (BH)

GARBAGE COLLECTION
8 *Search Under: REFUSE COLLECTION

Books located in search

GARBAGE COLLECTION COMPUTER SCIENCE
9 PERFORMANCE ANALYSIS OF GARBAGE
COLLECTION A (1991) (microfiche)               (BH)

GARBAGE PROJECT UNIVERSITY OF ARIZONA
10 RUBBISH: THE ARCHAEOLOGY OF GARBAGE (1992)  (BH)

GARBAGE TRUCKS
11 *Search Under: REFUSE COLLECTION VEHICLES

GARBAGEMEN
12 *Search Under: REFUSE COLLECTORS

-----------------------------------------------------------------
STARt over    Type number to display record    (F7) BACk page

Directions for continuing search

HELp
OTHer options
NEXT COMMAND:

## LIB 3a    The computer catalogue

If your college library has computerized its holdings, it no longer uses the traditional card catalogue. The **computer catalogue** gives the same immediate three-way access to the library's holdings—by subject, author, and title—and, in many cases, provides access by keywords or combinations of keywords.

The "keyword" option greatly increases the scope and possibilities of your search. Patricia LaRose started her search by entering the subject *garbage*. Within moments, her search had netted 12 entries (see the opposite page).

LaRose quickly reviewed these entries and noted that "Refuse and Refuse Disposal" and "Refuse Collection" were subject headings she should search later. She also wanted to take a closer look at item #10, so she typed in the number *10* and pressed *Enter*. The printout was as follows:

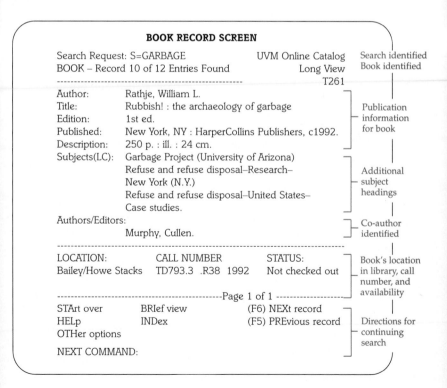

The information that appears on the terminal screen is almost exactly the same as that on a subject card in a card catalogue. Most computer catalogues also tell you if a book is available or, if it is checked out, they can tell you when it is due back. Some terminals also have printers so you can get a printout of a title's complete bibliographic information.

## LIB 3b  The *Library of Congress Subject Headings (LCSH)*

The National Library of Canada in Ottawa was established to collect, preserve, and promote the printed heritage of Canada. The library houses Canadian and foreign books, maintains a central file of the principal collections held by Canadian libraries, develops and promotes bibliographic standards, and publishes bibliographies, checklists, surveys, and catalogues.

Your college or university probably uses the Library of Congress system of classification for its books. Based on this system, the library uses standardized headings to catalogue its holdings, just as a telephone book lists *pharmacies* (not *drug stores*) and *service stations* (not *gas stations*). Sometimes these headings are not immediately obvious. For example, if you are looking for books about test-tube babies, you might not know that they are listed under *fertilization in vitro, human,* and not under *test-tube babies.*

If your subject headings are not yielding much information, try the *Library of Congress Subject Headings (LCSH)*, a four-volume reference work that lists the subject headings libraries use to catalogue their holdings. Even if you are not having trouble finding what you are looking for, it is still a good idea to check the *LCSH*. The main entry there might help you limit or focus your subject or suggest a new and more interesting aspect of that subject.

If your research subject were *recovery of waste materials* or *waste reuse,* you would soon discover that there is nothing in the computer catalogue under these headings. A quick check of the *LCSH* under these headings, however, would cross-reference you to *recycling,* for which there is almost a half-column of related terms and subheadings. Abbreviations are fully explained at the beginning of each *LCSH* volume. Many computer catalogues have had the *LCSH* incorporated into the search systems for subject searches (see the "Search Result Screen" on page 298).

# LIB 4

## THE INTERNET

Research today is both easier and more difficult than it was when print sources in the library were your only choices. Now, with the Internet, you can access resources anywhere in the world 24 hours a day. Finding the materials you want, however, can be a challenge. Because there are no librarians in cyberspace, you need to know how the Internet works—where the information is stored and how to retrieve it. Most experts agree that the Internet should not supplant, but complement, traditional print sources. First, a great deal of scholarship is not available. Second, because anyone can publish on the Internet, reliability and bias can be real problems (see RESCH 2b for evaluating online sources).

## LIB 4a   Access the World Wide Web.

The **World Wide Web** (WWW) was originally accessed through a program known as a "gopher," which was text-based (no graphics) and menu-based, making it tedious to use. Today, however, Netscape and Mosaic, two widely used "browser" programs, make it possible to move around the WWW easily with the aid of a mouse, to view colour graphics, and to jump easily from one web site or location to another by clicking on highlighted hypertext links. Each web site has a unique address known as a Uniform Resource Locator (URL). Here, for example, is the URL for the *Librarians' Index to the Internet*:

   http://www.sunsite.berkley.edu/InternetIndex/

## LIB 4b   Plan an Internet search strategy.

To do an Internet search, you need to know about search engines and Internet guides. A search engine is a program that enables you to locate web sites through a web crawler. An Internet guide enables you to locate web sites that reside in its directory. When you type in a keyword, the search engine or Internet guide looks for web sites that match your term. The problem with keyword searches is that they can sometimes produce tens of thousands of matches, making it very difficult to find those of immediate value. An alternative, and sometimes more efficient, approach is to use the subject directory provided by most Internet guides and some search engines. Once you choose a subject in the directory, you can click your mouse to narrow the subdirectories and eventually arrive at a list of sites closely related to your topic. At that point, you can do a keyword search.

Suppose you are researching the development of women's hockey, and you are using the Internet guide called Yahoo! Canada (**http://www.yahoo.ca/**). This is the subject directory that would appear on your screen:

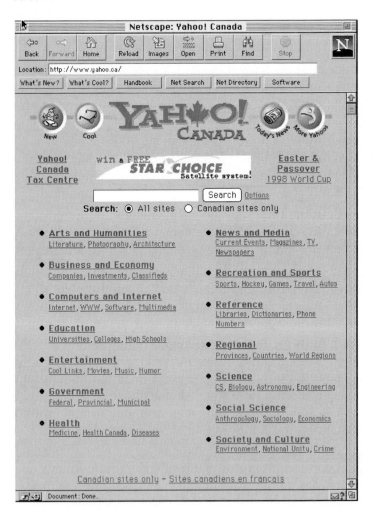

You would then click on "Recreation and Sports." When that screen appears, click on "Sports." (Note that directories in Internet guides are updated frequently. If you repeat this search yourself, you will probably find minor changes and additions made since this example was written.) This takes you to a screen that lists over 120 individual sports. For hockey alone there are more than 3200 web sites. When you click on "Hockey," you see this list:

Broomball (12)
Companies
Field Hockey (108)
Floorball (34)
Ice Hockey (2873)
Lesbian, Gay and Bisexual
Ringette (7)
Roller Hockey (185)
Sledge Hockey (3)
Underwater Hockey (15)
Unicycle Hockey (5)
Wheelchair Hockey (5)
Women (5)

The last entry in this list indicates that there are five web sites that deal with women's hockey. Click on "Women," which gives you this screen:

Top: Recreation:Sports:Hockey:Women
    Canada Only
    Ice Hockey
    Roller Hockey
Women's Ringette
Women's Hockey Magazine

Click on "Ice Hockey." One of the options available is "Women's Hockey Information." Click on this option, which gives you a number of other options. Click on, for instance, "Women's Hockey FAQ," which will produce a long list of topics related to Women's hockey (URL: **http://www.cs.utoronto.edu/~andria/womens-hockey.html**). These topics, or some of those listed on the previous screen, should provide you with a wealth of information for your research.

The subject directories on the home pages of search engines also make it easy to browse various subjects and topics, a big help if you are undecided about a research topic or simply want to see if there is enough material to supplement your other library research.

## LIB 4c    Use search engines to find Internet sources.

It is advisable to try more than one search engine in your research, because each one yields slightly different results. You can get to search engines easily by using the Net Search at the bottom of your browser.

 C-Tip

### *Search engines*

You will get the most out of your favourite search engines if you click on the Help button and spend a few minutes learning how search engines work. For example, what kind of search tip (use of logical connectors such as AND, OR, and NOT, quotation marks, and other specialized symbols) does the engine use? How does the engine search the WWW, and in what order does it present the results? Knowing how to get the most out of your search engine makes you a more efficient and thorough researcher.

The following is a list of popular search engines:

*All-in-One.*    **http://www.albany.net/allinone/**
A search engine that searches all other search engines for web sites. A fill-in search form is provided for your requests.

*AltaVista.*    **http://www.altavista.digital.com**
Fast and comprehensive, this search engine indexes millions of sites and is, therefore, most useful for retrieving well-narrowed or hard-to-find topics.

*InfoSeek.*    **http://guide.infoseek.com**
A reliable search engine using keyword, concept, and related terms. Recommended for Usenet Newsgroups searches.

*Lycos.*    **http://www.lycos.com**
Indexing over 90 percent of web sites, Lycos allows you to search file transfer protocol (FTP) and Gopher sites but not Usenet Newsgroups.

*WebCrawler.*    **http://wc3.webcrawler.com**
One of the fastest search engines because it is selective. Search results are ranked by frequency of occurrence of keyword.

*Netscape's Net Search.*    **http://home.netscape.com/home/internet-search.html**
Easily accessed on Netscape's task bar, Net Search is a jump station to WWW search engines and very useful in beginning a search.

## LIB 4d   Use subject directories to focus your Internet search.

In addition to the subject directories provided on the homepages of most search engines, there are a number of web sites containing more comprehensive and sophisticated subject directories. The following "stand alone" directories can be very helpful to your research. They can be reached at their WWW addresses.

*The Argus Clearinghouse.*   **http://www.clearinghouse.net/**
A directory of detailed subject guides, each containing links that have been compiled by experts in their fields. An excellent place to begin your research.

*Galaxy.*   **http://www.einet.net/**
An extensive database of subject-classified links with descriptive titles in lieu of annotations.

*INFOMINE: Scholarly Internet Resource Collections.*   **http://libwww.ucr.edu/**
Nearly 10 000 subject-classified links to Internet sites, helpful to both students and scholars.

*The Internet Public Library Reference Center.*   **http://www.ipl.org/ref/**
Librarians have annotated this list of subject-classified links provided by the School of Information at the University of Michigan.

*Liszt.*   **http://www.liszt.com/**
A well-managed database of discussion lists that also provides useful information on how to select and subscribe. Searchable by category and topic.

*Scholarly Journals Distributed by the World Wide Web.* By Robert C. Spragg.
   **http://info.lib.uh.edu/wj/webjour.html**
An alphabetical listing of links to scholarly journals on the Internet.

*The World Wide Web Virtual Library Subject Catalog.*
   **http://www.w3.org/pub/DataSources/bySubject/Overview.html**
A large directory of guides to subject-classified links with limited annotations.

*Yahoo.*   **http://www.yahoo.ca/**
A huge, regularly updated database of subject-classified sites with informative annotations. Searchable by keywords in URLs, titles, or descriptions.

The following web sites are useful for improving your writing and researching skills:

## Writing essays: an overview

Writers on the Net—Classes, Tutoring and Mentoring, Writers' Groups
**http://www.writers.com**

Inkspot: Writer's Resources on the Web—good, extensive range of links
**http://www.inkspot.com**

Resources for Writers and Writing Instructors—another good range of links
**http://www.english.upenn.edu/~jlynch/writing.html**

Rensselaer Writing Centre: Handouts
**http://www.rpi.edu/dept/llc/writecenter/web/handouts.html**

University of Victoria's Hypertext Writer's Guide
**http://webserver.maclab.comp.uvic.ca/writersguide/welcome.html**

Ryerson Polytechnic University—The Writing Centre Guide #3: Writing a University Essay
**http://gopher.ryerson.ca:70/0.services/.write/.essay**

## Essay topics

York University Computer Assisted Writing Centre—Strategies—Techniques for Generating Ideas for Your Essay
**http://www.yorku.ca/admin/cawc/strategies/contents.html**

Handout on brainstorming by consultants at the Undergraduate Writing Center at UT Austin
**gopher://gopher.utexas.edu:3003/00/pub/uwc/Handouts/brainsto.txt**

## Special types of essays

Writing Tips for Specific Essay Forms
**http://lc.byuh.edu/R_WCTR/handout.html**

## Grammar and style

The classic *Elements of Style* by Strunk and White
**http://www.columbia.edu/acis/bartleby/strunk**

An On-line English Grammar Resource
**http://www.edunet.com/english/grammar/toc.html**

*Hypergrammar*—an online grammar handbook from the University of Ottawa
**http://www.uottawa.ca/academic/arts/writcent/hypergrammar/grammar.html**

*Grammar Hotline Directory 1995*, from Tidewater Community College—a list of phone numbers or e-mail addresses that you can contact for information on grammar
**http://www.tc.cc.va.us/vabeach/writcent/hotline.html**

Punctuation Guide, from NASA's *A Handbook for Technical Writers and Editors*
**http://sti.larc.nasa.gov/html/Chapt3/Chapt3-TOC.html**

Capitalization Guide, from NASA's *A Handbook for Technical Writers and Editors*
**http://sti.larc.nasa.gov/html/Chapt4/Chapt4-TOC.html**

Online English Grammar, from St. John's Wood School of English, London
**http://www.edunet.com/english/grammar/index.html**

*Word Processing Style Guide*
**http://ourworld.compuserve.com/homepages/timg/**

Gender-Free Pronoun Frequently Asked Questions (GFP FAQ)
**http://www.lumina.net/OLD/gfp/**

## Dictionaries and thesauri

*Webster's Dictionary*
**http://work.ucsd.edu:5141/cgi-bin/http_webster**

*The Oxford English Dictionary* Online
**http://www.oed.com/index.htm**

*Roget's Thesaurus*
**http://humanities.uchicago.edu/forms_unrest/ROGET.html**

Research Institute of the Humanities of the Chinese University of Hong Kong: extensive listing of dictionaries and thesauri
**http://www.arts.cuhk.edu.hk/Ref.html#dt**

Carnegie-Mellon Online Reference Works
**http://www.cs.cmu.edu/references.html**

## Documentation

*Bibliography Styles Handbook*: summarizes and illustrates APA and MLA styles
**http://www.english.uiuc.edu/cws/wworkshop/bibliostyles.htm**

APA Frequently Asked Questions about the *Publication Manual of the American Psychological Association* (4th ed.)
**http://www.apa.org/journals/faq.html**

Citing Electronic Materials with the New MLA Guidelines
  **http://www-dept.usm.edu/~engdept/mla/rules.html**

Guides for Citing Internet Sources: links
  **http://acm.ewu.edu/cscourse/cs315/cite.htm**

# LIB 4e   Use newsgroups, listservs, and synchronous sources.

A **newsgroup** is a group of people interested in a particular topic who read and post messages on an electronic bulletin board. The board is open to the general public.

A **listserv** is similar to a newsgroup but restricted to people who subscribe to it. Members of a listserv routinely receive all the postings of the list as e-mail messages. Members usually have more than passing interest in the topic and stand ready to answer research queries and discuss the finer points of the listserv topic.

A **synchronous source** is one in which information is being exchanged in "real time," or simultaneously. Two popular synchronous communications are Internet Relay Chat groups (IRCs) and Multi-user domain, object oriented groups (MOOs). The Daedalus Group's Educational Information Moo Site is available at: **http://www.daedalus.com/net/border.html**

These forms of electronic communication allow you to pursue very specific questions about your topic when you are well into the research process. You also receive information rapidly or, in the case of synchronous communication, in real time, much as you would in a telephone conversation. To find out if there's a newsgroup or listserv in the area of your research, consult Tile.Net's web site: **http://www.tile.net**

## THE RESEARCH PAPER

The **library research paper** is an essential part of a college or university education and for good reason: in writing a library paper, you acquire a number of indispensable research skills that you can adapt to other assignments and to situations in life after graduation.

The real value of a library paper, however, goes beyond acquiring basic research skills; it is a unique hands-on learning experience. The purpose of a research paper is not to present a collection of quotations that show you have been in the library and can report what others have said about your topic. Rather, your goal is to analyze, evaluate, and synthesize the materials you research—in other words, to take ownership of your topic, and thereby learn how to do so with any topic. You learn how to view the results of research from your own perspective and arrive at an informed opinion of a topic. That, after all, is the mark of an educated person.

# RESCH 1 _____

## PLANNING

In writing a library research paper, you draw heavily on what you learned about writing short essays (see COMP). You decide on a purpose, develop a thesis, consider your audience, marshal your evidence, write a first draft, revise and edit the paper, prepare the final copy, and proofread. The only new ingredient here is research. In addition to all the stages of writing a composition, a library research paper involves locating sources, evaluating these sources, reading to gather information, taking notes, and documenting your sources. A research project easily spans several weeks. So, to avoid facing an impossible deadline at the last moment, establish a realistic deadline for each key task, and stick to your schedule.

## RESCH 1a    Set a schedule and follow it.

A library research project can be broken down into eight key tasks or stages. By thinking of the research paper as a multistaged process, you avoid becoming overwhelmed by the size of the undertaking. If your instructor has given you five weeks to complete your project, consider the following time allotments:

1. Choose a suitable research topic or question (2 days).
2. Prepare a working bibliography (4 days).
3. Develop a preliminary thesis and make a working outline (2 days).
4. Take complete and accurate notes (5-6 days).
5. Arrive at a final thesis and modify your outline (2 days).
6. Write a first draft, citing sources (8-9 days).
7. Revise your paper and proof citations, including the list of works cited (7 days).
8. Prepare your final copy, in correct form, and proofread (2 days).

Your schedule, like the preceding one, should allow at least a few days to accommodate unforeseen delays.

The research process is by nature recursive. No matter how carefully you plan and carry out each step, you may find yourself returning to one or more of the earlier steps. For example, while writing a first draft, you may discover that you need certain statistics to support a point you want to make. You return to the library. That means time spent locating the right source before you can finish drafting your paper. Such delays can be annoying, but do not dwell on them or let them interfere with your overall schedule.

## RESCH 1b   Choose a suitable research topic or question.

The first step in the research process—**selecting a suitable topic**—may be the most important task in the entire research paper project. A clearly focused topic makes researching and writing the paper manageable and the likelihood of sound—even exciting—results possible.

Sometimes your instructor will assign a topic or give you a list of topics from which to choose. Be sure that you understand what your instructor is asking for and that the topic you select from the list really interests you. But what happens when you are allowed to choose your own topic and nothing comes to mind immediately? Relax. Spend a day or two brainstorming (see COMP 2d) and observing what interests you. Jot down the names of interesting contemporary or historical persons, important social issues, intriguing political happenings, noteworthy medical and scientific discoveries, environmental crises, artistic movements and achievements, controversies in sports, economic issues in a global setting, puzzling moral and ethical issues—in short, anything that interests you or that you want to know more about.

In compiling your list of possible research subjects, you will find that one or two subjects interest you more than the others. These are the ones worth pursuing further. However, avoid subjects for which there are insufficient research materials in your college library. That is, avoid subjects so recent or so obscure that very little has been published about them anywhere (e.g., Is laser surgery a safe method to correct vision loss?), subjects based almost exclusively on your own experiences (What are my personal religious beliefs, and why?), subjects that are highly speculative (Would Canada be better off if the Meech Lake Accord had passed?), and subjects that are too technical for your general audience (How is technology used in medicine?).

Having settled on a general subject (see COMP 2b), you now need to limit that subject to a manageable topic. It cannot be emphasized enough that your topic should feel right to you from the very start. Do not select a topic because you think it will be easy to write about—too often seemingly easy topics turn out to be the most difficult to write on. Also do not select a topic just because it is popular. Rather, choose a topic that genuinely interests you and that is manageable given your time and resources. Finally, if you have any doubts about your topic, consult with your instructor about its suitability for the assignment.

One effective way of focusing on a topic is to brainstorm by asking some specific questions about your subject (see COMP 2c and 2d). At the start of her research project, Patricia LaRose, the student who wrote the sample research paper in RESCH 5, chose *recycling paper waste in North America* as her subject and brainstormed the following list of possible **research questions** on her computer.

How serious is our paper waste problem?

How much of our paper waste is currently being recycled?

Is recycling paper waste an economic or an environmental issue?

Should North Americans be required to recycle household paper waste?

What are the problems of collecting waste paper?

What is currently being done with old newspapers and telephone books?

What is made from recycled paper?

Do newspapers use recycled newsprint?

If we don't recycle old newspapers, what will be the impact on our environment?

Should we concentrate on recycling non-biodegradable wastes first?

Each question narrows the general subject area, suggesting a more manageable research project. Also, simply phrasing your topic as a question gives you a starting point; that is, thinking in terms of a *research question* gives your work focus and direction from the outset. A one- or two-sentence answer to your research question often provides you with a preliminary thesis statement (see COMP 2e). Finally, when you are ready to begin planning your paper, you can approach the task by exploring and answering your research question.

LaRose reviewed her list and found she kept returning to the question about what North Americans do with their old newspapers and telephone books. At this point LaRose was ready to head to the library and start her research.

# RESCH 2 _____
## CONDUCTING LIBRARY RESEARCH

Your library research will involve working with both print sources and online electronic sources. In both cases, though, the process is essentially the same: you're reducing your list of sources to the best few. For a discussion of the resources available in most college and university libraries, see LIB.

### RESCH 2a    Use the library's print sources.

Although you want to be thorough in your research, you will soon realize that you do not have the time to read every source. Rather, you must preview your sources to decide which you will read, which you will skim, and which you will simply eliminate.

One last piece of advice: at this early stage of research, it is better to list too many sources rather than later having to find the ones you discarded or did not list at all.

Developing a working bibliography

For each work that you think might be helpful, make a separate bibliography card, using a 7.5 x 13 cm (3 x 5 inch) index card. As your collection of bibliography cards grows, alphabetize the cards by the authors' last names. Using separate cards for each book or article allows

## Guidelines for Previewing Print Sources

1. Although a book or article may be about your subject, eliminate it if it isn't directly related to your research question.
2. Do not spend time with material that is obviously outdated (e.g., a 1960s source on nuclear energy).
3. Check tables of contents and indexes in books to locate relevant material quickly.
4. Read the opening paragraph or two of an article to see if it is what you are looking for; if you are still unsure, quickly skim the piece.

you to continually edit your working bibliography, dropping sources that you decide are not helpful and adding new ones.

Make sure you record *all* the necessary information about each source for which you make a bibliography card. You will use the cards to compile the **final bibliography**, or the **list of Works Cited**, for your paper (see MLA DOCU 2 and OTHER DOCU 2 and 4).

For books, record the following information:

All authors; any editors or translators
Title and subtitle
Edition (if not the first)
Publication data: city, publishing company, and date
Call number

For periodical articles, record the following information:

All authors
Title and subtitle
Title of journal, magazine, or newspaper
Volume and issue numbers
Date and page numbers

Using correct bibliographic form ensures that your entries are complete, reduces careless errors, and saves time when you are preparing your final bibliography. For specific directions on writing bibliographic entries for various other types of sources, consult MLA DOCU 2 and OTHER DOCU 2 and 4.

## BIBLIOGRAPHY CARD: BOOK

Authors ——— Blumberg, Louis, and Robert Gottlieb. <u>War</u>
Title and
subtitle ——— <u>on Waste: Can America Win Its Battle</u>
<u>with Garbage?</u> Washington: Island ——— Complete
publishing
Press, 1998. data

TD788
Call ——————————————————————— B58
number 1989

## BIBLIOGRAPHY CARD: ARTICLE

Jensen, Holger. "The Recycling Boom:
Author Successful Programs Have Produced
Gluts." <u>Maclean's</u> 19 Feb. 1998, Title
Day, month
Magazine 42–44. and year of
publication

Pages

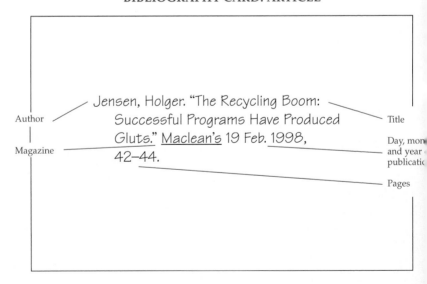

Evaluating print sources

Before beginning to take notes, evaluate your sources for their relevance and reliability in helping you answer your research question. Look for the writers' main ideas (don't read material just because it's interesting). Also look for information about the authors themselves, information that will indicate their authority and perspective on the issue.

### Questions for Evaluating Print Sources

1. Does your source clearly relate to your research question?
2. Is your source too abstract, general, or technical for your needs?
3. Does your source reflect current thinking and research in the field?
4. Does your source promote a particular view, or is it meant to inform?
5. What biases, if any, does your source exhibit?
6. Is the author of your source an authority on the issue? Do other writers mention the author of your source in their work?

## RESCH 2b   Use the library's online sources.

The abundance of print sources available in the library does not even approach the number of online sources available to you. Your library is local, but the Internet is a *global* network of computers and computer users. You can access information stored on computers anywhere in the world, and communicate with people worldwide who might have information on your research topic.

Given the abundance of Internet sources, the key to successful online research is identifying the web sites and other online sources that will help you the most (see LIB 4). Use the following questions to weed out sources that hold no promise (we focus on web sites here because you will find yourself using them most often).

### Questions for Reviewing Web Sites

1. Scan the homepage of the site. Do the contents and links appear to be related to your research topic?
2. Can you identify the site's author? Are the author's credentials available?
3. Has the site been updated within the last six months? (This information is usually given at the bottom of the homepage.)

C-Tip

## *Using bookmarks*

Take a few minutes to learn how to use your web browser's bookmark or hotlist feature. This feature allows you to electronically capture web site addresses of potentially useful sources. By merely clicking on an address in your bookmarks, you can revisit a site quickly and as often as you need. Later, as the number of sites you collect increases, you may want to categorize the bookmarks by subtopics of your research question.

Remember, too, that the copy and paste feature of your web browser enables you to accurately capture and position web site addresses in your working bibliography, thus eliminating the possibility of error.

### Developing a working bibliography

Just as for print sources, you must maintain accurate records for the online sources you use. You can record each online source on a bibliography or index card, or you can set up a separate file where you maintain an ongoing research log. Either way, this is the information you need for each source:

All authors and sponsoring agents
Title and subtitle of the document
Title of longer work to which the document belongs (if applicable)
Document date (or date last modified)
Date you accessed the site
Publishing data (place: publisher, date) for print version (if available)
Address of the site, URL, or network path (see LIB 4)

### Evaluating your online sources

The quality of Internet sources varies tremendously. You will, therefore, want to carefully evaluate the sites in your working bibliography.

### Downloading web files to disk

When you find a useful web site for your paper, you may want to download the entire file to disk so that you can refer to it later offline. If you are working in the library, downloading reduces your time online and allows other students to access online materials. Downloading is also insurance against a source's being removed from the Internet.

If you are more comfortable working with hard copy, you can print documents directly from the online web site or from your downloaded

## Questions for Evaluating Web Sites

### Type of Web Page

Who hosts the web site? Often the URL domain name suffix indicates the source of information provided. These are the most common suffixes:

- com    Business/commercial
- edu    Educational institution
- gov    Government
- mil    Military
- net    Various types of networks
- org    Nonprofit organization
- ca     Canadian site (although some Canadian sites use other suffixes)

### Authority/Author

Is it clear what individual or company is responsible for the site?

Can you verify if the site is officially sanctioned by an organization or company?

What are the author's or company's qualifications for writing on this subject?

Is there a way to verify the legitimacy of this individual or company (e.g., are there links to a homepage or résumé?)

### Purpose and Audience

What appears to be the author's or sponsor's purpose in publishing this web site?

Who is the intended audience?

### Objectivity

Are advertising, opinion, and factual information clearly distinguished?

What biases, if any, can you detect?

### Accuracy

Is important information documented through links so that it can be verified in other sources?

Is the text well written and free of errors in spelling and grammar?

### Coverage and Currency

Is there any indication that the site is still under construction?

For sources with print equivalents, is the web version more or less extensive?

**Questions for Evaluating Web Sites (continued)**

How detailed is the treatment of the topic?
Is there any indication of the currency of the information (date of last update or statement regarding frequency of updates)?

Graphics
Are the graphics helpful?
Are the graphics simply window dressing?

 C-Tip

## *Downloading a web site file*

To download a web site using Netscape, for example, go into the **File** menu and use the **Save As** option, and then save the file by using its URL name or renaming it. Be sure to use an **.htm/.html** extension if you rename the file. You can then access the file in Netscape by clicking on the **File** menu and choosing the **Open file** option.

file. Hard copy is easier to read than a computer screen, and you can mark it up as you analyze it. If the printout does not include the title of the site, the URL, and the date you accessed it, make a handwritten notation of this information on the printout because you will need it later when you compile your list of Works Cited.

## RESCH 2c    Systematically take complete and accurate notes of your reading.

Having collected a number of print and online sources that look helpful for researching your topic, you're ready to begin taking notes. As you work through your sources, look for pertinent facts, opinions, statistics, and examples, of course. But look especially for connections among ideas and recurring themes. Keep in mind that you are not merely collecting information, but analyzing and synthesizing what you find.

Jot down the patterns you see—and the pieces that do not fit. By looking at evidence on both sides, you'll refine your topic and begin to see possible organizational plans. If you find yourself thinking about the paper's main units or general movement and direction, make a rough outline. Having some sense of your paper's shape can, in turn, direct further research efforts. And remember, you are always free to modify your thinking as you conduct your research.

Now for some practical advice on **taking notes**: first and most important, be systematic. As a rule, write one note on a card, and use cards of uniform size (preferably index cards that are large enough to accommodate a long note on a single card and small enough to be easily handled and conveniently carried). When you get to planning and writing your paper, you will be able to organize your notes according to your organizational plan. Furthermore, should you alter your outline, you can easily reorder your cards to reflect the changes.

The quality of your research paper will be determined by the quality—and not the quantity—of your notes. In fact, try not to take too many notes. Novice researchers often write down anything and everything that looks remotely usable, only to discover later that most of their notes are irrelevant. Besides being a waste of valuable research time, too many note cards make it difficult to distinguish what is important from what is not. Before taking a note, ask yourself, "How exactly does this material help prove or disprove my thesis?" You might even try envisioning where you could use the information in your paper.

A useful note card has three essential parts and one optional part.

## Elements of a note card

1. **Topic heading**   In the upper-left corner of the note card, write a topic heading—a key word or phrase that describes the contents of the note—and underline it for easy identification. Thoughtful topic headings make it easy to organize your notes and then outline your paper.
2. **Note**   Take the note as a summary, a paraphrase, or a direct quotation (explained on the following pages).
3. **Source**   Record the author's last name and the page number on which you found the information; this is enough information because you have the full reference in your preliminary bibliography.
4. **Comment** (*optional*)   Record any thoughts you have on the source or on how the material might be used. Do not trust ideas like these to your memory. Be sure to separate these comments or in some other way indicate that your commentary is not part of your actual note.

Whether to summarize, paraphrase, or quote directly largely depends upon the nature of the item and the way you envision using it.

Summary

When you **summarize** material from a source, you capture in your own words the essential idea of a passage or of an entire chapter or article in highly condensed form. Summaries are particularly useful when you are working with lengthy, detailed arguments or long passages of descriptive background information. You can distill a chapter or more into a paragraph or several paragraphs into a sentence or two.

Following are two paragraphs from a book source that LaRose used in researching her paper and the summary note she took (see opposite).

> The *Titanic* sank twenty minutes after hitting an iceberg. The ship's reckless captain failed to appreciate that over 90 percent of an iceberg is hidden from view; even though the iceberg looked far away to the ship's stunned passengers, its submerged base had poked a fatal hole through the *Titanic*'s hull.
>
> Waste is like an iceberg. Ninety-five percent of it is hidden from view; the 1.8 kg of discards we put in our garbage cans each day represent only a fraction of our total waste. And, like icebergs, our wastepiles pose major obstacles to our path of resource conservation. They can sink us if we don't reduce their threat. We can't melt icebergs, but we can trim waste.
>
> —Arthur H. Purcell, *The Waste Watchers*
> (Garden City, NY: Anchor Books, 1980), 14–15.

**SUMMARY NOTE CARD**

<u>Waste problem</u>
Purcell likens waste to an iceberg.
Because we are not aware of the
size/amount of our waste, the danger
is greater than we think.

Purcell, pp. 14–15

Paraphrase

When you **paraphrase** a source, you restate the information in your own words instead of quoting the source directly. Unlike a summary, which is a short version of the essential information in the original, a paraphrase presents the information in the original in approximately the same number of words, but the wording is your own. That is, a paraphrase should closely parallel the presentation of ideas in the original but not use the same words or sentence structure as the original. To do so would be to plagiarize (see RESCH 4d).

Here are the original source and LaRose's paraphrase note card.

> Two million more households had access to recycling programs in 1994 than in 1991. In 1994, 69.6% of households had access to the most widely available program, paper recycling, compared to 52.6% in 1991. As in 1991, paper recycling was the most widely available program. Paper makes up the largest component of residential waste. The increase in accessibility also varied by the type of dwelling. Access to paper recycling grew fastest among apartments, rising from 37.0% in 1991 to 57.6% in 1994, as communities with existing recycling programs extended them to a wide variety of housing types.
> —Canada. Statistics Canada. "Paper Recycling by Province 1994."
> *Households and the Environment 1994.* Catalogue 11-526 Occasional.
> Ottawa: Queen's Printer, 1994: 7–8.

**PARAPHRASE NOTE CARD**

<u>Paper recycling statistics—households</u>

The number of households in Canada having access to paper recycling programs in 1994 increased significantly over 1991. In the former year, 69.6% of households had access to paper recycling, one of the most available types of recycling programs in the country, compared to 52.6% in 1991. Paper is the most significant component of household waste. The variety of types of dwellings that have access to paper recycling has increased as well. Between 1991 and 1994, paper recycling programs available to apartments rose from 37.0% to 57.6%.

"Paper Recycling," pp. 7–8

In most cases it is better to summarize or paraphrase source materials—restating them in your own words—than it is to quote them verbatim (word-for-word). In the paraphrase note card, for example, LaRose says, "The variety of types of dwellings that have access to paper recycling has increased as well. Between 1991 and 1994, paper recycling programs available to apartments rose from 37.0% to 57.6%," paraphrasing Statistics Canada's wording: "Access to paper recycling grew fastest among apartments, rising from 37.0% in 1991 to 57.6% in 1994, as communities with existing recycling programs extended them to a wide variety of housing types." LaRose's reconceptualizing of the figures shows that she has captured the idea in her own words. Paraphrasing requires that you think about an idea and understand it.

## Direct quotation

When you **directly quote** your source, you copy the words of your source *exactly,* putting all quoted material in quotation marks. When you take a direct quotation note, carefully check for accuracy, including punctuation and capitalization (see PUNCT 5). Be selective about what you choose to quote. Reserve direct quotation for important ideas stated memorably, for especially clear explanations by authorities, and for proponents' arguments conveyed in their own words.

Following are a source LaRose quoted directly because of its startling specificity and the quotation note card she wrote.

> In those eight tons [7.2 tonnes] of garbage and dirt cover there were fewer than sixteen pounds [7.2 kg] of fast-food packaging; in other words, only about a tenth of one percent of the landfills' contents by weight consisted of fast-food packaging. Less than one percent of the contents by weight was disposable diapers. The entire category of things made from plastic accounted for less than 5 percent of the landfills' contents by weight, and only 12 percent by volume. The real culprit in every landfill is plain old paper—non-fast-food paper, and mostly paper that isn't for packaging. Paper accounts for 40 to 50 percent of everything we throw away, both by weight and by volume.
> —William L. Rathje, "Rubbish!" *The Atlantic Monthly* Dec. 1989: 102.

What if LaRose had chosen to use only part of the statement as a direct quotation? She could combine summary or paraphrase with quotation as in the following note card. Notice that LaRose is careful to put quotation marks around all words that are quoted directly.

## QUOTATION NOTE CARD

<u>Paper waste</u>

"In those eight tons [7.2 tonnes] of garbage and dirt cover there were fewer than sixteen pounds [7.2 kg] of fast-food packaging; in other words, only about a tenth of one percent of the landfills' contents by weight consisted of fast-food packaging. Less than one percent of the contents by weight was disposable diapers. The entire category of things made from plastic accounted for less than 5 percent of the landfills' contents by weight, and only 12 percent by volume. The real culprit in every landfill is plain old paper — non-fast-food paper, and mostly paper that isn't for packaging. Paper accounts for 40 to 50 percent of everything we throw away, both by weight and by volume."

Rathje, p. 102

## QUOTATION AND SUMMARY NOTE CARD

<u>Paper waste</u>

A team of landfill archeologists made some surprising discoveries when they analyzed eight tons [7.2 tonnes] of garbage taken from several sites. Fast-food packaging, disposable diapers, and plastic items were not as plentiful as some environmentalists suspected.

"The real culprit in every landfill is plain old paper—non-fast-food paper, and mostly paper that isn't for packaging. Paper accounts for 40 to 50 percent of everything we throw away, both by weight and by volume."

Rathje, p. 102

 C-Tip

## *Notetaking on the Internet*

You can easily and accurately capture passages of text from the Internet by copying them into a separate computer file on your hard drive or diskette. In Netscape, for example, use your mouse to highlight the part of the text you want to save, and then use the copy and paste features to add it to your file of research notes. You can use the same commands to capture bibliographic information (see RESCH 2b).

In taking notes, you must be absolutely accurate. Check all direct quotations against the wording of the original source, and double-check your paraphrases to be sure you have not inadvertently used the writer's wording or sentence structure. If you are careful at the notetaking stage, you greatly reduce your chances of committing *plagiarism*— the unacknowledged use of someone else's ideas or wording. Plagiarism is discussed in depth in RESCH 4d, but it is important in notetaking because inadvertent plagiarism often begins at this stage. The writer is always held responsible for plagiarism, no matter how inadvertent.

## RESCH 2d   Use interviews, questionnaires, and other community sources to supplement your library research.

Some topics lend themselves to another type of research—community-based resources. Often we become so involved with looking for materials in the library that we forget about the rich research possibilities in our communities.

As LaRose was learning more and more about recycling efforts at the national level, she wondered what was happening at the local levels. She identified several local authorities and interviewed them, gathering information she could use in her paper (see RESCH 5). Another student writing a research paper on the nature of friendship came up with the idea of finding out what other students thought. He constructed a brief six-item questionnaire and administered it to everyone in his dormitory. He was able to use the results of this questionnaire to support several key points in his research paper. Finally, a third student who was researching the Ronald McDonald House Foundation visited the local Ronald McDonald House. There she not only spoke with staff and families staying in the facility, she also received an assortment of publications about the foundation that gave her a great deal of up-to-date information. So, as you are working your way through your library resources, be thinking about research opportunities in your community.

# RESCH 3

## ORGANIZING THE RESEARCH PAPER

Having taken notes on the connections, patterns, and recurring or opposing ideas, opinions, and facts in your sources, you are ready to develop an organizational plan for your paper.

### RESCH 3a    Formulate a final thesis.

The first step in developing an overall plan for your paper is re-evaluating your preliminary thesis. Do you want to commit to it? Or, in the course of doing research and notetaking, has your thesis evolved? This is what happened to LaRose. She found in the course of doing research that her preliminary thesis—*North Americans are currently collecting more old newsprint than they can recycle*—had shifted focus. From wanting to find out what is being done with old newspapers and telephone books, LaRose found herself more specifically interested in the uses of old newsprint. This shift in focus was, of course, reflected in her notetaking: she had many notes under the topic headings *uses for recycled newsprint, the recycling process, the enormous amount of waste, collection efforts,* and *future uses.*

True to the recursive nature of research (see RESCH 1a), then, LaRose reformulated her thesis. She decided to take a much stronger, more argumentative position in her final thesis: *To stem the tide of the tremendous newspaper waste problem, North Americans must find long-term uses for old newsprint that are environmentally and economically sustainable.*

At this time, too, LaRose thought about her purpose—whether her paper would be largely informative or persuasive (see COMP 2f). Initially, she intended to write an informative report on the status of newsprint recycling efforts. Now, though, based on her research, she decided to add a persuasive edge to her paper; she thought it important to urge her readers to make recycling part of their lifestyle.

### RESCH 3b    Develop a working outline.

With a final thesis in mind, you are ready to sort your note cards by topic headings and develop a **working outline**. You may want to take this working outline in steps, starting with a brief list of what you will cover and in what order. It is a quick way of concretizing your thinking. You can start with your scratch outline if you made one while taking notes. This is the list LaRose created:

1. Newsprint as a major problem—the enormous amount of waste

2. Efforts to collect and recycle old newsprint

3. The process of recycling old newsprint

4. Uses for recycled newsprint—what's currently being done

5. What needs to be done—future uses of recycled newsprint

From your list, create an informal outline (see COMP 2h). Use the examples, quotations, figures and statistics, and other facts and ideas you collected in your research to flesh out your main ideas. This working outline will serve as your plan for writing the initial draft of your paper. As the name implies, the working outline can itself change as you write. The outline you submit with your paper is a final, cleaned-up version of your working outline—the one that reflects all the changes you made while drafting and revising. LaRose's final outline is included with her research paper in RESCH 5.

# RESCH 4 _____

## WRITING THE RESEARCH PAPER

Writing and revising a research paper are like writing and revising an essay or a composition (see COMP), with one difference—you are relying more heavily on information collected from various sources. You will want to learn, then, how to integrate your research findings into your paper without plagiarizing and how to document your sources correctly.

## RESCH 4a  Document your sources using the MLA style or APA style.

Whenever you use information from a note card, you must cite your source in your paper. Your citations must consistently follow an established system of documentation, such as that of the Modern Language Association (MLA style) or the American Psychological Association (APA style). Your instructor will tell you which to use.

But before we discuss the *do's* of correct documentation, keep one *don't* in mind: do not clutter your paper with citations for facts or common knowledge. For example, everyone knows Marc Garneau was the first Canadian in space, and that Newfoundland was the last province to enter Confederation. Look for *repeated* facts. LaRose, for example, quickly discovered in her research that most of her sources pointed to the 1980s as the decade that conservationists first pushed for recycling newsprint. Because this was a fact that could be objectively verified, and because many sources mentioned the fact as baseline knowledge, LaRose decided it was common knowledge and thus did not document it in her paper.

There are two main elements of documentation in a research paper. The **in-text citation** is placed within the body of the paper (see MLA DOCU 1 and OTHER DOCU 1). The **list of works cited**, which provides complete publication data on your sources, is placed at the end of the paper (see MLA DOCU 2 and OTHER DOCU 2).

In-text citations usually consist of the author's last name and a page reference. Often the author's name is given in an introductory or signal phrase at the beginning of the borrowed material and only the page reference is given in parentheses at the end. If the author's name is not given at the beginning, put it in the parentheses together with the page number. The parenthetical reference signals the end of the borrowed material and directs readers to the list of works cited should they want to pursue a source.

IN-TEXT CITATION (MLA STYLE)

According to Leslie Pardue, Earth Care Paper Company sells a variety of recycled paper products, as well as educational materials on recycling for classroom use (56).

WORKS CITED ENTRY (MLA STYLE)

Pardue, Leslie. "What Goes Around Comes Around: A Look at Paper Recycling." *E Magazine* Mar.-Apr. 1990: 54–56.

For a complete discussion of MLA-style in-text citations, see MLA DOCU 1. If your instructor asks you to use the *Chicago Manual of Style* documentation style, see OTHER DOCU 4; if your instructor prefers APA style, consult OTHER DOCU 1 and 2.

## RESCH 4b   Integrate quotations smoothly.

When you refer to borrowed material in your research paper, whether by summary, paraphrase, or direct quotation, it is best to introduce the material with a **signal phrase**, which alerts the reader that the borrowed information is about to be stated. Signal phrases (such as, *according to Leslie Pardue*) help the reader follow your train of thought. They also tell the reader who is speaking and, in the case of summaries and paraphrases, signal phrases indicate exactly where your ideas end and someone else's begin. Without a signal phrase to integrate a quotation into the flow of your paper, the quotation seems to come from nowhere and jars the reader. Consider the following examples:

UNANNOUNCED QUOTATION

Most North Americans think that we are producing more trash per person than ever, that plastic is a huge problem, and that paper biodegrades quickly in landfills. "The biggest challenge we will face is to recognize that the conventional wisdom about garbage is often wrong" (Rathje 99).

INTEGRATED QUOTATION

Most North Americans think that we are producing more trash per person than ever, that plastic is a huge problem, and that paper biodegrades quickly in landfills. William L. Rathje, director of the Garbage Project at the University of Arizona, views the issue differently; he believes that "the biggest challenge we will face is to recognize that the conventional wisdom about garbage is often wrong" (99).

The quotation in the second example is integrated into the text not only by means of a signal phrase but also in two other ways. By mentioning the speaker's authority and that he "views the issue differently," LaRose provides even more of a context for the reader to understand how the quotation fits into the discussion.

How well you integrate a quotation, paraphrase, or summary into your paper depends partly on your choice of signal phrase; and, in particular, on the verb in the signal phrase. It is the verb that conveys the tone and intent of the writer being cited. If a source is arguing, use the verb *argues* (or *asserts, claims,* or *contends*); if a source contests a particular position or fact, use *disagrees* (or *denies, disputes, refutes,* or *rejects*); if a source agrees with a particular position, use *concurs* (or *admits, concedes,* or *grants*). By using verbs that are specific to the situation in your paper, you help the reader process and organize the information you are presenting and thereby better understand your use of the quotation. Also, by choosing verbs carefully, you avoid the monotony of repeating the overworked *notes, says, states,* or *writes.* For advice on integrating quotations from literary texts, see LIT 3, RESCH 4c, and MLA DOCU 1.

## RESCH 4c   Set off long quotations.

Set off or block prose quotations that are longer than four lines to help the reader more clearly see the quotation as a whole. Verse quotations are set off when longer than three lines. Set-off quotations are indented 10 spaces from the left margin and double-spaced; quotation marks are unnecessary because the format itself indicates the passage is a quotation. When quoting two or more paragraphs from the same source, indent the first line of each paragraph three additional spaces.

Patricia LaRose quotes a lengthy passage from Purcell in her research paper because his vivid description and concrete facts capture the drama and proportions of recycling efforts (see RESCH 5, pages 348–49). The impact on the reader is much greater than if LaRose had summarized or paraphrased instead.

The following example is taken from student Rob Bradford's library research paper on Margaret Laurence's novel *The Stone Angel.* Here Bradford is discussing the story's main character, Hagar Shipley, who looks back on her life from the perspective of an old woman during her last days:

> Margaret Atwood has described Hagar Shipley as "the most extended portrait of a frozen old woman," a woman who inherited her father's self-control and pride. So great is this self-control and pride, in fact, that Hagar refused to weep at the death of her beloved son, John. Pride is the controlling factor in her life, her "wilderness," her "demon." William H. New, in his introduction to the New Canadian Library version of the novel, discusses Hagar's "shackles" of pride:

> She will not bend to play a role, for example, even when role-
> playing would bring relief to another person. When her brother
> Dan is dying, it is not Hagar but another brother, Matt, who
> pretends to be their mother in order to give Dan some comfort.
> Hagar refuses to play the role because her mother had been
> weak and frail. Similarly she refuses, early in the book, ever to be
> a housekeeper like Auntie Doll. (vii)

The colon following Bradford's sentence introducing the quotation indicates that the quotation is closely related to what precedes it. Note that, unlike an integrated quotation in which the parenthetical citation is inside the end punctuation, with a long quotation the parenthetical citation is outside the final punctuation, according to the MLA style.

On occasion, long quotations contain more information than you need. In such situations you can use an ellipsis mark to show that you omitted material from the original text. In this way you keep the quotation to the point and as short as possible. For a complete discussion of the use of the ellipsis, see PUNCT 6g.

Another mark of punctuation that is useful when working with quotations is brackets (see PUNCT 6f). These squared parentheses allow you to insert your own words into a quotation to explain a pronoun reference, for example, or to change a verb tense to fit your text.

> According to Rathje, "There are no ways of dealing with [garbage] that
> haven't been known for many thousands of years" (100).

## RESCH 4d    Credit other people's ideas to avoid plagiarism.

The importance of honesty and accuracy cannot be stressed enough. Any material borrowed word-for-word must be placed within quotation marks and properly cited; any idea, explanation, or argument you borrow in a summary or paraphrase must be documented, and it must be clear where the borrowed material begins and ends. In short, to use someone else's ideas in their original form or in an altered form without proper acknowledgment is **plagiarism**. And plagiarism is a serious offence whether it occurs intentionally or accidentally.

RESCH
4d

A little attention and effort at certain stages in the research process can go a long way in eliminating inadvertent plagiarism. At the notetaking stage, check what you record on your note card against the original, paying particular attention to word choice and word order, especially if you are paraphrasing. It is not enough simply to use a synonym here or there and think it is a paraphrase; you must restate the idea in your own words, using your own style. At the drafting stage, check whenever you incorporate a source into your paper, be careful to put quotation marks around material taken verbatim, and double-check your text against your note card—or better yet, against the original source if you have it on hand.

Lifting material from the Internet without adequate documentation is also considered plagiarism, and it is treated just as seriously as plagiarism from printed materials. Keep in mind that much of the material on the Internet credits neither an author nor an origin. Students must pay attention to the correct citation of sources on the Internet and give the reader full and exact information on how to access the source. See OTHER DOCU 2, Electronic Sources, for the proper method of citing sources from the Internet.

The following example illustrates how plagiarism can occur when care is not taken in the wording or sentence structure of a paraphrase. An acceptable paraphrase of the original source is also shown.

### ORIGINAL SOURCE

In theory, recycled paper should be cheaper, since it turns garbage that someone would otherwise have to pay to dispose of into a marketable commodity.

—Leslie Pardue, "What Goes Around Comes Around,"
*E Magazine* Mar.-Apr. 1990: 56.

### UNACCEPTABLY CLOSE WORDING

Turning someone's garbage into a marketable product while avoiding the costs of disposal would seem in theory to make recycled paper less expensive (Pardue 56).

### UNACCEPTABLY CLOSE SENTENCE STRUCTURE

It seems only reasonable that recycled paper would be less expensive because it turns someone's waste that would have to be landfilled into a new product (Pardue 56).

ACCEPTABLE PARAPHRASE

By eliminating landfill costs, recycling, according to Pardue, should enable people to produce paper that is less expensive than paper made from virgin pulp (56).

If at any time while you are taking notes or writing your paper you have a question about plagiarism, it is your responsibility to consult your instructor for clarification and guidance before proceeding.

# RESCH 5

## ANNOTATED STUDENT RESEARCH PAPER

Patricia LaRose wrote the research paper that appears on the following pages. Her paper is the product of a sustained research and writing effort that stretched over a period of five weeks. Beginning with her choice of a research question, LaRose stayed on task as she prepared a working bibliography, took notes, reformulated her thesis, made a working outline, and wrote an initial draft. She took her rough draft through several revisions before arriving at the final copy presented here.

LaRose used the MLA guidelines for manuscript preparation presented in FORMAT 2. She also used the MLA style of in-text citations (MLA DOCU 1), informational endnotes (MLA DOCU 4), and list of works cited (MLA DOCU 2) to document her research paper. LaRose was required to include a title page (FORMAT 2) and a final outline (COMP 2h) with her paper (some instructors, as well as the MLA guidelines, do not require these items).

Recycling Used Newsprint:
Coming to Terms with an Environmental Problem

Title is centred
and placed about
a third of the way
down the page.

by

Patricia LaRose

Six doublespaced
lines below the title,
centre *by*; double-
space and centre
your name.

English 001, Section G
Professor P. Eschholz
April 1, 1998

Course information
is centred and
doublespaced

LaRose ii

Outline

Title piques readers' interest and announces the writer's topic (see COMP 3a).

Title: Recycling Used Newsprint: Coming to Terms with an Environmental Problem

Thesis answers the research question (see RESCH 1b).

Thesis: To stem the tide of newspaper waste, North Americans will have to find long-term uses for old newsprint that are environmentally and economically sustainable.

Purpose is to inform and urge reform (see COMP 2f and RESCH 3a).

Purpose: To show there is a serious problem with newspaper waste in North America and to explore some environmentally and economically sound solutions.

Introduction conveys the writer's strategy for developing the thesis.

Introduction: Trash disposal, especially of old newsprint, is one of North America's most pressing environmental problems. It is not enough simply to recognize the problem and start recycling programs; long-term uses for old newsprint must be identified and developed.

Topic outline. For an example of a sentence outline, see COMP 2h.

I. Recycling old newspapers in the 1980s
   A. Success of early collection efforts
   B. Low demand for old newsprint
   C. Programs needed to meet projected supply

II. Current uses for old newsprint
   A. Egg cartons
   B. Paper board
   C. Kitty litter
   D. Cellulose flower pots
   E. Cereal boxes
   F. Corrugated cardboard boxes
   G. Books

LaRose iii

    H. Home insulation

    I. Wallboard

    J. Animal bedding

III. Problems of recycling newsprint as newsprint

IV. Using recycled newsprint as newsprint

    A. Newspapers currently using recycled newsprint

    B. Prospects for the future

Conclusion: In a world of shrinking resources, we must increase pressure on the newspaper industry to recycle old newsprint for use as newsprint and to save our limited supply of virgin pulp for more critical uses.

LaRose 1

RECYCLING USED NEWSPRINT:

COMING TO TERMS WITH AN ENVIRONMENTAL

PROBLEM

Title is centred.

Several years ago, the City of Toronto negotiated a $1.5 million deal with the Notre Development Corporation to haul the city's garbage 600 km north to an abandoned mine site near Kirkland Lake, Ontario. Toronto had been looking for a "willing host" for its garbage, because the city no longer had room for the tonnes of waste collected each day. The dumps were almost full, the city was expanding, and alternate solutions had to be found for the city's burgeoning trash heaps (Rushowsky A2).

Anecdotal introductory paragraph grabs readers' attention and involves them in the issue.

Without a signal phrase, the author's surname and a page reference are necessary.

Toronto is no different from other major centres in Canada and the United States. Many Canadians and Americans are finally coming face to face, through increasing media exposure to the problem and increasingly higher costs of waste disposal, with the fact that garbage is one of our most pressing problems. This problem was created because North Americans are a "throw-away society." According to Jim Hightower, commissioner of agriculture in Florida, every year Americans toss out "41 million tons [36.9 million tonnes] of food and yard waste, 13 million tons [11.7 million tonnes] of metal, 12 million tons [10.8 million tonnes] of glass, and 10 million tons [9 million tonnes] of plastic" (xv–xvi).

In-text citation with the author's name given in a signal phrase and the page number given in parentheses. LaRose uses MLA-style documentation.

LaRose 2

Canadians are no slouches in the waste department either. Environment Canada reported that in 1992 Canadians produced almost one tonne of municipal waste per capita, including all residential, industrial, commercial, and institutional waste. One-third of this, or nearly 350 kg, was generated on a per capita basis as household waste. When all types of garbage are taken into account, Canadians are the most waste-producing people on earth. At this rate, more than half of the landfill sites serving Canada's residents will be full by the year 2000 (Rushowsky A2).

For a long time North Americans identified plastic and Styrofoam as the chief culprits, and perhaps justifiably so because they are not biodegradable. But with all the attention we have paid to them, we have ignored a problem that is even worse. Noel Grove reports that paper waste in the United States accounts for more than 63 million tonnes annually—approximately 37 percent of the nation's waste—and that 45 million tonnes end up in landfills (112). This is enough to fill 2.5 million trailer trucks to the brim. The problem is not expected to lessen. The Environmental Protection Agency in the United States calculates that paper waste will reach nearly 60 million tonnes by the year 2000 (Carra 223). By most estimates, Americans consume about 265 kg of paper per person, more than any other nation in the world, and only about 25 percent of it is recycled.

Paraphrase of a source with the author's name in a signal phrase and page number in parentheses.

LaRose 3

As this paper blitz fills dumps, it is also emptying forests. Each Christmas North Americans consume more than 15 million trees just for paper to wrap presents, and this gift wrap in turn results in 77 000 tonnes of waste (Eller). William L. Rathje, director of the Garbage Project at the University of Arizona, reports that telephone books from the city of Phoenix alone accounted for 5 400 tonnes of waste in 1989 (102). The real culprit, however, is old newsprint (ONP). According to Rathje, newspapers account for the greatest amount of paper waste, using up 10–18 percent of the area of the typical landfill by volume. If all the Sunday newspapers in North America were recycled, some 500 000 trees a year would be saved. To stem the tide of the tremendous newspaper waste problem, North Americans must find long-term uses for old newsprint that are economically and environmentally sustainable.

In the early 1980s conservationists called for the recycling of newspapers along with other solid wastes. At first, there was reason to be optimistic. The Blue Box program in many Canadian cities was an outstanding success, so much so that there became a glut of newsprint on the recycling market. The results also surpassed expectations in the United States. Elizabeth A. Brown reports that in 1988 almost one-third of the 12.5 million tonnes of newsprint used in the United States was collected after use from consumers (12) . That figure was

---

Citation of a one-page article needs only the author's name in parentheses.

To establish Rathje's authority on the subject, LaRose gives his title in the signal phrase.

By establishing the immensity of the problem, LaRose has prepared readers for her thesis: long-term solutions are needed.

LaRose 4

even higher in Canada. According to Statistics Canada, in one area of paper use alone, that of packaging, 43.4 percent of all packaging used was recycled (64). In both countries, collection efforts proved so successful that by the early 1990s the supply of ONP exceeded the demand for it.

Information about the conservation movement is common knowledge, and therefore is not documented (see RESCH 4a).

Instead of entering the recycling loop—the cycle that takes a product from the consumer to the recycling bin to a manufacturer and back again to the consumer to use[1]— much of the ONP eventually ended up in landfills. Even today, only about 35 percent of it is recycled in the United States.

LaRose defines "recycling loop" for her general audience (see COMP 2g).

Raised note number 1 indicates there is an informational note at the end of the paper.

Newsprint is, however, seen as a major money earner for municipalities in both Canada and the United States. Four American states—Florida, California, Connecticut, and New York—have enacted laws requiring from 25 to 40 percent recycled content in all newspapers sold in their jurisdictions (Jensen 43). That should increase the demand for waste newsprint in the United States and relieve the pressure on landfills. Canada is already the world's leading importer of waste paper and cardboard fibre because there isn't enough at home to meet the needs of the energy industry, which incinerates paper to create energy ("Paper People" B5). In fact, Canada's environment industry has been growing at the rate of 87 percent yearly and is now the fifth largest in the country, with 150 000 employees and 4 500 companies across the country ("Green Business Group" B5).

LaRose 5

There has always been a market for ONP for the manufacture of such recycled paper products as egg cartons and paperboard. But while people are looking for new ways to use the growing supply of ONP, they cannot let up on collection efforts. In fact, to make recycling easier for citizens, many American towns have instituted curbside sorting. According to environmental reporter Gregg Easterbrook, some 3 700 U.S. curbside collection programs existed in 1993 and the prospect is for more ("Good News" 5). Other American cities and towns, Louis Blumberg and Robert Gottlieb note, have already passed bylaws making it an offence punishable by fine to throw ONP out with the garbage (208).

William McGrath of the Vermont Agency of Natural Resources mentioned in a personal interview several possible uses of newsprint that are being actively explored. Manufacturers are experimenting with using ONP in the production of kitty litter. Another use is the manufacture of flower pots from cellulose—a wood by-product—rather than plastic. Both Canadian sources and the American Forest and Paper Association report that recovered newsprint is now being used to make "cereal boxes, corrugated cardboard boxes, books, and insulating materials."[2] An upswing in the construction of new homes and commercial buildings would also increase the use of ONP for such needed products as wallboard (Lipschutzhe).

In citing one of two works by the same author, LaRose gives a shortened title in the parenthetical citation.

In citing a work by multiple authors, LaRose gives both names in the signal phrase.

Using personal interviews to supplement print sources is good research.

LaRose 6

Most experts agree, however, that for sheer volume and reliability of use—and to save our forests—newsprint is the best use of recycled newsprint (Lipschutzhe). And because newspaper publishers create the bulk of the problem, many environmentalists and economists believe that it makes sense that the newspapers themselves take the lead in solving it. Using one tonne of 100 percent post-consumer recycled paper saves 17 trees, 2.5 cubic metres of landfill space, 4 100 kilowatt-hours of electricity, 26 600 litres of water, and approximately 27 kilograms of air-polluting effluents (Shaw 6).

After cataloguing the uses and potential uses of ONP, LaRose describes its best use in the most emphatic position, last (see SENT 6a).

LaRose wisely uses several sources to justify what she claims is the best use of recycled newsprint.

As obvious as the solution appears, it will not be easy to implement. Recycling newsprint for use as newsprint presents myriad problems: it is expensive, it pollutes, and markets for recycled newsprint are scarce. Many newspapers, however, have taken the lead in the use of ONP. For example, *The Los Angeles Times,* another major American user of ONP, Arthur H. Purcell reports, receives much of its recycled newsprint from the Garden State Paper Company, a model plant and portent of things to come:

> You will see newly produced, high-quality newsprint spinning off in giant twenty foot [6.06 metre] wide rolls at the rate of forty feet [12.12 metres] per second. Hundreds of metres past the steaming troughs of pulp you discover the source of the raw materials used to make the pulp that

Indent a long quotation 10 spaces and doublespace. Omit quotation marks (see RESCH 4c).

LaRose 7

An ellipsis indicates the writer has left out words from the original source (see PUNCT 6g).

Citation in parentheses comes after the end punctuation in a long, set-off quotation.

forms the newsprint. The source is 100 percent discarded newspapers. . . . (85–86).

If this is a true indication of what can be done, the outlook is good. Easterbrook shares this optimistic view, citing a Tellus Institute study that showed "recycled-paper manufacturing was five times more profitable than virgin-paper production" (*Moment* 415). "The price of newspaper in Canada dropped to $35 a tonne in 1989 from $55 a tonne in 1988" (Jensen 43). As the supply of recycled newsprint becomes more reliable and the quantity more consistent, more newspapers are likely to increase the recycled content of their papers. Federal sources reported in 1997 that "a little more than one-third of the ONP that is recovered is recycled into newsprint" (Shickage).

LaRose signals her conclusion by returning to the idea of a "throw-away society" that was introduced in the opening paragraph.

There is no denying that North America is a throw-away society, but "a throw-away society is not a sustainable society" (Hightower xv). North Americans simply cannot afford the dollars or the resources to become complacent in the assumption that someone else is taking care of the problem. Government and industry will have to work together to come up with better uses of our limited resources. One possibility that might balance the scales of opportunity would be cutting the subsidies to the logging industry or offering similar incentives to manufacturers of recycled newsprint. It might be wiser still to discontinue subsidies altogether. In a world of shrinking

LaRose 8

resources, it makes sense to recycle ONP and to save the limited supply of virgin pulp for more critical uses.

In the future, North American consumers must remain steadfast in their good habits of recycling and of purchasing recycled products. They must continue to pressure the newspaper industry to use more recycled newsprint so that paper manufacturers will continue to invest in the technology and facilities needed to recycle ONP in an environmentally safe and economically sound way.

In her conclusion, LaRose (1) answers her research question, (2) summarizes the body of her paper, (3) tells readers what they can do to help with the problem, and (4) provides closure. LaRose's conclusion shows she has assimilated her research and arrived at an informed opinion on a subject that concerns her.

LaRose 9

Notes

Information notes provide additional material or sources of interest to readers.

<sup>1</sup> For a thorough explanation of the processes involved in recycling paper, see Hagerty, Pavoni, and Heer (58–62), Pardue (54–55), and Randolph. Kent Shaw provides a complete discussion of what is meant by "recycling loop" (1, 6).

The notes appear on a separate numbered page immediately after the text and before the list of works cited (see MLA DOCU 3).

<sup>2</sup> Besides providing a potentially huge market for ONP, cellulosic insulation has extremely high insulating properties. For a complete discussion of the advantages and disadvantages of cellulosic insulation, see Purcell (157–62).

Double-space within and between note entries; leave a space but do not put a period after the superscript number.

LaRose 10

Works Cited

American Forest and Paper Association. "Old
    Newspapers." *Recycling*. 21 May 1997. http://www.
    afandapa.org/Recycling/Paper/index.html#OldNewspa
    pers (9 Sept. 1997).

Blumberg, Louis, and Robert Gottlieb. *War on Waste: Can
    America Win Its Battle with Garbage?* Washington:
    Island Press, 1998.

Brown, Elizabeth A. "Paper Recycling Catches on Slowly."
    *Christian Science Monitor* 14 Nov. 1989: 12–13.

Canada. Statistics Canada. "Consumption and Disposition
    by Packaging Type." *Environmental Perspectives
    1993*. Catalogue 11-528-E Occasional. Ottawa:
    Queen's Printer, 1993.

---. Statistics Canada. "Paper Recycling by Province 1994."
    *Households and the Environment 1994*. Catalogue
    11-526. Ottawa: Queen's Printer, 1994.

Carra, Joseph S. "Municipal Solid Waste and Sanitary
    Landfilling in the United States of America."
    *International Perspectives on Municipal Solid Wastes
    and Sanitary Landfilling*. Ed. Joseph S. Carra and
    Raffaello Cossu. San Diego: Academic, 1990. 221–34.

Easterbrook, Gregg. "Good News from Planet Earth." *USA
    Weekend* 14–16 Apr. 1995: 4–6.

---. *A Moment on the Earth: The Coming Age of
    Environmental Optimism*. New York: Viking, 1995.

Eller, Daryn. "Spare the Wrappings: Give Trees a Chance."
    *Longevity* Dec. 1990: 96.

The heading
*Works Cited* is
centred at the
top of the page.

LaRose uses
MLA style for
her list of works
cited. The list
begins on a new
page. The first
line of each
entry begins at
the left margin;
subsequent lines
are indented five
spaces. Double-
space within
entries as well as
between entries.

The correct
MLA forms for
various other
kinds of
publications are
given in MLA
DOCU 2; APA
forms are given
in OTHER DOCU 2.

LaRose 11

"Green Business Group Fears Feds May Trash Environmental Grants." *Hamilton Spectator* 10 July 1995: B5.

Grove, Noel. "Recycling." *National Geographic* July 1994: 92–115.

Hagerty, D. Joseph, Joseph L. Pavoni, and John E. Heer, Jr. *Solid Waste Management.* New York: Van Nostrand, 1973.

Hightower, Jim. Foreword. *War on Waste: Can America Win Its Battle with Garbage?* By Louis Blumberg and Robert Gottlieb. Washington: Island Press, 1989. xv–xvii.

Jensen, Holger. "The Recycling Boom: Successful Programs Have Production Gluts." *Maclean's* 19 Feb. 1998: 42–44.

Lipschutzhe, Neal. "Recycling Efforts Outpace Capacity to Use Old Papers." *Wall Street Journal* 1 Oct. 1990: B7.

McGrath, William. Personal interview. 11 Jan. 1993.

"Paper People Do Slow Burn Over Lifting Ban." *Hamilton Spectator* 10 July 1995: B5.

Pardue, Leslie. "What Goes Around Comes Around: A Look at Paper Recycling." *E Magazine* Mar.–Apr. 1990: 54–66.

Purcell, Arthur H. *The Waste Watchers: A Citizen's Handbook for Conserving Energy and Resources.* Garden City: Anchor, 1980.

Randolph, John. "Recycling of Materials." *The New Grolier Multimedia Encyclopedia.* CD-ROM. Danbury: Grolier Electronic Publishing, 1992.

Rathje, William L. "Rubbish!" *Atlantic Monthly* Dec. 1989: 99–106, 108–09.

Rushowsky, Chris. "Mine Town Split by Plan to Dump Metro Waste." [Toronto] *Sunday Star* 9 June 1995: A2.

Shaw, Kent. "Closing the Recycling Loop." *Burlington Free Press* 26 Nov. 1990, Business Monday: 1+.

Shickage, Ken. Director. Environment Canada. Personal interview, 21 Jan. 1993.

# MLA DOCU

## MLA-Style Documentation

### *Learning Objectives*

After reading this section, you should

1. know how to use MLA in-text citations in your research paper,
2. understand how to assemble a list of works cited and use the correct formats for books, periodicals, other sources, and CD-ROMs and online sources, and be familiar with the MLA style for citing electronic and Internet sources,
3. know how to include information notes in your research paper.

# MLA DOCU

## MLA-Style Documentation

$\mathbf{I}$n writing a research paper you are using the information and ideas of others. Whenever you directly quote, summarize, or paraphrase another person's thoughts and ideas, or use facts and statistics that are not commonly known, you must properly acknowledge your source.

The documentation system recommended by the **Modern Language Association (MLA)** in the *MLA Handbook for Writers of Research Papers*, 4th edition (1995) is discussed and illustrated in this section. The MLA system is used primarily, although not exclusively, in English and the humanities. We also discuss the Alliance for Computers and Writing (ACW) guidelines for citing electronic sources. The system recommended by the American Psychological Association (APA) is used in the social sciences. That system is discussed in the following section, OTHER DOCU. Other disciplines have their own style manuals; see page 394 for a listing.

# MLA DOCU **1** _____

## MLA IN-TEXT CITATIONS

In 1984 the MLA adopted the in-text system for documentation. **In-text citations** are easy to use and informative because they immediately let readers know the source of a citation without breaking the flow of the paper. If readers want to consult the source themselves, complete publication data is provided at the end of the paper in a list of works cited (see MLA DOCU 2). The student paper in RESCH 5 uses the MLA documentation system.

Most MLA-style in-text citations require only the author's last name and a page reference. The customary way to integrate this information into your text is to give an introductory signal phrase mentioning the author's name before the quoted material (see RESCH 4b) and then the page number parenthetically at the end of the borrowed material. If the author's name is not given in the signal phrase, it must appear parenthetically with the page number.

The following examples show correct MLA in-text citation form for different kinds of sources. Note that the end punctuation comes after the parenthetical citation; no *p.* for *page* is used; and there is no punctuation between the author's name and the page number.

**AUTHOR MENTIONED IN A SIGNAL PHRASE**

When the author's name is given in a signal phrase, give only the page reference in parentheses.

Blicq suggests that "the key to effective writing is good organization" (6).

**AUTHOR NOT MENTIONED IN A SIGNAL PHRASE**

If the author's name is not given in a signal phrase, it must appear with the page reference in parentheses.

One authority on technical writing suggests that "the key to effective

writing is good organization" (Blicq 6).

**TWO OR MORE WORKS BY THE SAME AUTHOR**

When you borrow material from two or more works by the same author, your citation must direct the reader to the correct publication. You can do this in one of three ways. Give the title in the signal phrase.

In *The Trail of the Stanley Cup*, Coleman claims that "the most drastic

revision in the rules of hockey had been in the introduction of blue lines

to divide the rink into zones" (1).

Give the title parenthetically at the end in an abbreviated form.

> Coleman claims that "the most drastic revision in the rules of hockey had been in the introduction of blue lines to divide the rink into zones" (*Trail* 1).

In the absence of a signal phrase, put the author's name, the title, and the page reference in parentheses.

> As far as changes to the game are concerned, "the most drastic revision in the rules of hockey had been in the introduction of blue lines to divide the rink into zones" (Coleman, *Trail* 1).

### TWO OR THREE AUTHORS
As with single-author works, you have the option of including the last names of the authors in the signal phrase or in the parentheses.

> Fedderson and Parsons agree that "the AIDA (attention-interest-desire-action) approach used for persuasive requests can be adapted to writing for sales" (105).

> Pierre Trudeau was a strong federalist, determined to show that Ottawa could promote the rights of French Canada (Winter, Cook, and Chandler 100).

### MORE THAN THREE AUTHORS
For works with more than three authors, include only the last name of the first author followed by the Latin phrase *et al.* (meaning *and others*).

> When selling goods, the primary objective of a business is to recover the contract price (Smyth et al. 384).

### AUTHORS WITH THE SAME LAST NAME
To avoid confusion, when using two or more authors with the same last name, give each author's first name and last name in all references.

> Charles Lipton believes that the trade union movement In Canada made its greatest advances during World War II (266).

> The trade union movement was, on the other hand, going through its greatest period of upheaval during the war (Wayne P. Lipton 36).

### CORPORATE AUTHOR

A corporate author is an institution, company, agency, or organization that is credited with authorship of a work. Treat the name just as you would for an individual, giving it in the signal phrase or in parentheses. The first time a corporate name is used, it must be spelled out (Canadian University Students Overseas). If it has a commonly used abbreviation (CUSO), give the abbreviation in parentheses immediately after the first reference to the organization. Thereafter, use the abbreviation.

> Canadian University Students Overseas (CUSO) offers university
>
> students an opportunity to work on humanitarian projects in various
>
> countries around the world (3–5).

### UNKNOWN AUTHOR

When the author of a work is unknown, use the complete title of the work in a signal phrase or a shortened version in the parenthetical reference.

> According to the article "It's Raining Pennies—But Not from Heaven," the
>
> penny "is under attack as a public nuisance" (31).

> The penny "is under attack as a public nuisance" ("It's Raining
>
> Pennies" 31).

### MULTIVOLUME WORK

If you use material from more than one volume of a multivolume work, include the volume number followed by a colon and then the page number in your parenthetical citation.

> In his two-volume work *The Life and Times of Wm. Lyon Mackenzie*,
>
> Charles Lindsey concludes that William Lyon Mackenzie was of a highly
>
> sensitive nature and somewhat secretive, and was never fully
>
> understood even by his most intimate friends (2: 297).

### AN ENTIRE WORK

To reference a whole book or article, give the author's name in the signal phrase or parenthetically; no page numbers are needed.

> George Woodcock, in his book *The Hudson's Bay Company*, argues that
>
> the Hudson's Bay Company represented one of the great forces that
>
> impelled Americans and Canadians alike across the plains and
>
> mountains toward the Pacific Ocean.

The Hudson's Bay Company prospers more than ever as the oldest mercantile corporation in the world (Woodcock).

**FICTION, POETRY, DRAMA, AND THE BIBLE**
Because the Bible and literary works are available in different editions, you need to include information that will help your readers locate the reference in their particular edition.

**FICTION**
When citing a passage from a work of fictional prose, give the page number of the edition you are using and then give the part or chapter number.

Mr. Digby, the teacher in W.O. Mitchell's *Who Has Seen the Wind*, is in reality talking about Canadian heroic values when he says, "The trouble with you . . . is that you're too thin skinned. . . . You've got to be tough—good and tough" (55; ch. 6).

**POETRY**
For poems, first give the part or division reference, if there is one, and then the line numbers. Use a period between.

In "Heat" by Archibald Lampman, the setting is a trance-like evocation of the Ontario landscape in summer:

From plains that reel to southward, dim,

The road runs by me white and bare;

Up the steep hill it seems to swim

Beyond, and meet into the glare. (1.1–4)

**DRAMA**
For plays, include the act, scene, and lines in your citation. Use periods without spaces to separate these items, and unless your instructor directs otherwise, use arabic instead of roman numerals.

Shakespeare's King Lear projects his own misery when he asks the Fool, "What, has his own daughters brought him to this pass? / Couldst thou save nothing? Didst thou give them all?" (3.4.61–62).

The slash (/) indicates the end of one line and the beginning of the next (see PUNCT 6h).

BIBLE

In citing the Bible, provide book, chapter, and verse. As with drama citations, use periods to separate these items. The books of the Bible may be abbreviated in the parenthetical citation but not when part of your text.

In the gospel according to St. Matthew, Christ begins his Sermon on the Mount by declaring who are the blessed (5.3–12).

Later in his sermon, Christ gives his listeners what we now know as The Lord's Prayer (Matt. 6.9–13).

WORK FROM AN ANTHOLOGY

When citing a work from an anthology, give the name of the writer of the piece you are using—not the editor of the anthology—in your signal phrase or parenthetical citation.

Tait argues that "of all the branches of Canadian literature, nineteenth century drama has received least attention for reasons that are entirely understandable" (13).

A SOURCE QUOTED IN ANOTHER SOURCE

It is always better to take your material from original sources when they are available. Sometimes only indirect sources are available. If you need to cite an author quoted in a work written by another writer, begin your parenthetical citation with *qtd. in* (for *quoted in*).

To J. Roby Kidd, "The pursuit of learning is really the pursuit of fine living" (qtd. in Colombo 302).

TWO OR MORE SOURCES IN A SINGLE CITATION

When acknowledging more than one source in a single parenthetical citation, separate the citations with a semicolon.

Historians contend that the conquest of Canada's Native peoples was primarily concerned with territorial right (Dickenson 108; Frideres 16).

INTERVIEW

To cite a personal interview, simply give the name of the person interviewed in a signal phrase or parenthetically.

Quebec premier Lucien Bouchard discussed the role of the Bank of Canada in the Canadian economy. A central bank could be free from any government intervention (Bouchard).

# MLA DOCU 2 _____
## MLA LIST OF WORKS CITED

The MLA-style list of **works cited** is a listing of the sources you cite in your paper. It is not a list of all the sources you checked, just the ones you actually cite. The list is placed on a separate page at the end of your paper. To assemble a list, follow these three simple steps.

1. Sort through your working bibliography, pulling the cards for those sources you have actually cited in your research paper (see RESCH 4a); file or discard the others.
2. Alphabetize the cited source cards by the authors' last names. If the author is unknown, alphabetize by the first word in the title, not counting *a, an,* or *the.*
3. You are now ready to prepare your list of works cited. Start the first line of each entry at the left margin and indent subsequent lines five spaces; this way authors' names stand out at the left margin, and readers can readily spot the source they are seeking. Double-space both within and between entries.

See RESCH 5 for an example of how the list of works cited should appear.

Books

**BASIC FORMAT FOR A BOOK WITH ONE AUTHOR**

Davis, Angela. *Art and Work.* Montreal: McGill-Queens, 1995.

This illustrates the basic book format: a period after both author and title, a colon between place (city) of publication and publisher, a comma between publisher and date of publication, and a period at the end. If you are underlining the title instead of using italics, the underlining is continuous (not broken). You may shorten the publisher's name (e.g., *Doubleday* for *Doubleday Canada*). Omit *Publisher, Co., Inc.,* and use *UP* for *University Press.* Give the most recent year of publication.

**TWO OR THREE AUTHORS**

Mann, Roger, and John Roberts. *The Reluctant Writer.* Markham:

Butterworths, 1993.

The name of the first author is the only one reversed; separate the names with commas.

Owen, Roger C., James Deetz, and Anthony Fisher. *The North American Indians: A Sourcebook.* Toronto: Macmillan, 1967.

**MORE THAN THREE AUTHORS**

Dreisziger, N.F., et al. *Struggle and Hope: The Hungarian-Canadian Experience.* Toronto: McClelland & Stewart, 1982.

Give the first author listed on the title page followed by the Latin phrase *et al.* (meaning *and others*).

**AUTHOR WITH AN EDITOR**

Siebel, George A. *Ontario's Niagara Parks: 100 Years.* Ed. Olive Siebel.

Niagara: Niagara Parks Commission, 1985.

Use the capitalized abbreviation *Ed.* for "edited by."

**EDITOR**

Brown, Craig, ed. *The Illustrated History of Canada.* Toronto: Lester,

1991.

If you are citing an entire edited collection and not just a work in it, use the lowercase abbreviation *ed.* for "editor" or *eds.* for "editors."

**TRANSLATION**

Yevtushenko, Yevgeny. *Don't Die Before You're Dead.* Trans. Antonia

Buis. Toronto: Key Porter, 1995.

The translator of an authored text is cited after the title; use the abbreviation *Trans.* for "translated by."

**CORPORATE AUTHOR**

Institute of Canadian Bankers. *Orientation to Banking.* 2nd ed.

Scarborough: Prentice-Hall, 1989.

Treat a corporate author—an institution, company, agency, or organization that is credited with authorship—just as you would an individual author.

**UNKNOWN AUTHOR**

*Real Life Consumer Economics.* Richmond Hill: Scholastic, 1991.

In the absence of a named author, start the entry with the title of the work. In the list of works cited, the entry is alphabetized by the first word of the title (omitting *a, an,* or *the*).

**TWO OR MORE WORKS BY THE SAME AUTHOR**

Berton, Pierre. *Hollywood's Canada: The Americanization of Our*

*National Image.* Toronto: McClelland & Stewart, 1975.

---. *My Country: The Remarkable Past.* Toronto: McClelland & Stewart,

1976.

---. *Niagara: A History of the Falls.* Toronto: McClelland & Stewart, 1992.

When you cite more than one work by the same author in your paper, list the works alphabetically by title. Give the author's name in the first entry, but in subsequent entries use three unspaced hyphens followed by a period for the name.

#### EDITION OTHER THAN FIRST

Roberts, John, Sandra Scarry, and John Scarry. *The Canadian Writer's*

    *Workplace.* 2nd Canadian ed. Toronto: Harcourt, 1998.

Give the number of the edition (1st, 2nd, 3rd) followed by *ed.* immediately after the title.

#### REPUBLISHED BOOK

Richler, Mordecai. *The Apprenticeship of Duddy Kravitz.* 1959. Intro.

    A.R. Bevan. Toronto: McClelland & Stewart, 1969.

Give the publication date for the original edition (you can find this information on the copyright page), but complete publication data only for reprint, even if the publisher is different. If the republished book includes a new introduction or other interpretive material, add that information after the original publication date.

#### WORK IN MORE THAN ONE VOLUME

Birney, Earle. *The Collected Poems of Earle Birney.* 2 vols. Toronto:

    McClelland & Stewart, 1975.

Give the number of volumes after the title, using the abbreviation *vols.* If you use only a particular volume, name it specifically before the city and publisher; although not required, the total number of volumes may be added at the end of the entry as follows:

Birney, Earle. "Way to the West." *The Collected Poems of Earle Birney.*

    Vol. 2. Toronto: McClelland & Stewart, 1975. 136. 2 vols.

#### WORK IN A SERIES

Morton, W.L. *The Critical Years: The Union of British North America*

    *1857–1873.* The Canadian Centenary Series. Toronto: McClelland &

    Stewart, 1964.

After the title of the work, give the series' name and, if available, the work's number in the series.

Fulford, Robert. "How the West Was Lost." *Canadian Content.* Eds.

Sarah Norton and Nell Waldman. Toronto: Holt, 1988. 166–174.

First give the title of the work, then the title and editor(s) of the anthology. Cite the pages on which the work appears after the publication data.

PREFACE, INTRODUCTION, FOREWORD, OR AFTERWORD

McPherson, Hugo. Introduction. *Barometer Rising.* By Hugh MacLennan.

Toronto: McClelland & Stewart, 1969. ix–xv.

When your reference is to the author of interpretive or critical material (such as a preface or an introduction) in a book by someone else, cite this author first and then the work and its author. Give the inclusive page numbers after the publication data.

ENCYCLOPEDIA OR OTHER REFERENCE WORK

Lemieux, Vincent. "Referendum." *The Canadian Encyclopedia.* 1985 ed.

Complete publication information is not needed for standard reference works, but you should include complete publication information for less well known works.

If an article is unsigned, begin with the title.

"Canadian Inflation Rate by Year." *The Canadian Global Almanac.* 1995

ed. 189.

If a reference work is not arranged alphabetically, supply the page numbers.

## Periodicals

ARTICLE IN A MONTHLY MAGAZINE

Poirier, Terry. "Second Language Learning Through Culture and Music."

*FWTAO Newsletter* Feb. 1998: 17–20.

This example illustrates the basic MLA-style format for articles in periodicals: periods follow the name of the author and title; a colon follows the date; and a period is placed at the end. With the exception of May, June, and July, abbreviate the month. If the article is numbered continuously, give the inclusive page numbers. If not, give the first page and a plus sign (+) to indicate that paging is discontinuous.

ARTICLE IN A WEEKLY MAGAZINE

Serrill, Michael S. "Ready to Go It Alone: Parizeau's Quebec." *Time* 13
    April 1992: 28–29.

Give the day, month, and year in that order without punctuation. If
an article is unsigned, start your entry with the title.

ARTICLE IN A JOURNAL PAGINATED BY VOLUME (continuous paging over a year)

Grenier-Lapierre, Madeline. "Education coup-de-fil: Ten Years of Preventive
    Work with Families." *The Social Worker* 62 (1994): 181–184.

To locate an article in a journal that continues page numbers
throughout a given year, the reader needs the volume number, the year,
and the page numbers.

ARTICLE IN A JOURNAL PAGINATED BY ISSUE (each issue begins with page 1)

Barsh, Russell, and James Henderson. "Aboriginal, Treaty and Human
    Rights." *Journal of Canadian Studies* 17.2 (Summer, 1997): 55–81.

Separate the volume number and the issue number with a period.

ARTICLE IN A DAILY NEWSPAPER

Hume, Stephen. "Hypocritical to Call Redress for Racism 'Racist.'"
    *Vancouver Sun* 18 May 1995: A9.

If there is a section letter, give it before the page number.

ARTICLE IN A WEEKLY NEWSPAPER

Daisley, Brad. "Bank Didn't Insist on Independent Advice." *The Lawyer's
    Weekly* 25 Nov. 1998: 1, 21.

EDITORIALS AND LETTERS TO THE EDITOR

"Too Many Fishermen, Too Little Salmon." Editorial. Toronto *Globe and
    Mail* 6 July 1995: A12.

Begin an unsigned editorial with the title.

Although many newspapers and magazines give titles to letters to
the editor, these titles are not part of the entry.

Maclean, Pierre. Letter. *Quill and Quire* Dec. 1997: 3.

BOOK REVIEW

Fitzgerald, Judith. "Rooke Delights, Infuriates." Rev. of *Oh! Twenty-Seven Stories* by Leon Rooke. *Toronto Star* 3 Jan. 1998: M13.

If the review has no title, simply begin with *Rev.* after the author's name.

FILM REVIEW

Johnson, Brian D. "Off-Kilter Capers." Rev. of *Search and Destroy*, dir. David Salle. *Maclean's* 19 June 1995: 61+.

## Other sources

PAMPHLET

Mohawk College of Applied Arts and Technology. *How to Conduct a Personal Job Search.* Hamilton: Mohawk, 1995.

Treat a pamphlet like a book. Italicize (or underline) the title. When no author is given, start your entry with the title of the pamphlet.

*Occupational Health: Participant Guide.* Toronto: Occupational Health and Safety Association, 1988.

GOVERNMENT PUBLICATION

Canada. Department of the Secretary of State. *The Canadian Family Tree.* Ottawa: Queen's Printer, 1967.

Give the government, the agency, and the title with a period after each. The publisher is the Queen's Printer.

LECTURE OR PUBLIC PRESENTATION

Moore, Christopher. "The Royal Highland Regiments." Scottish Studies Colloquium. University of Guelph, Guelph, Ontario, 24 Sept. 1995.

Give the name of the sponsoring organization or series, the location, and the date.

UNPUBLISHED DISSERTATION

Ostrander, Charles. "Advocates of the Aboriginal World Peace and Prayer Day for Global Healing." Diss. McMaster University, 1998.

Give the title of an unpublished dissertation in quotation marks followed by a period, two spaces, and the abbreviation *Diss.*, the name of the degree-granting university, and the year. Treat a published dissertation as you would a book with the dissertation information after the title (Diss. McMaster University, 1998).

LETTER

Proulx, E. Annie. Letter to the author. 22 Jan. 1995.

LEGAL REFERENCE

Regina v. Gardner (1995), 21 O.R. (3d) 385–401 (C.A.)

Give the name of the case (the style of cause), the date, the law report (volume, series, and page), and the court in which the opinion was delivered.

INTERVIEW

McIntyre, Dr. Keith. Personal interview. 6 July 1997.

FILM OR VIDEOTAPE

*Jesus of Montreal.* Dir. Denys Arcand. Perf. Lothaire Bluteau and
    Catherine Wilkening. Max Films, 1990.

*Between Two Worlds.* Dir. Barry Greenwald. Videocassette. 58 min.
    National Film Board of Canada, 1990.

TELEVISION OR RADIO PROGRAM

"Spirits of the West." Host Tom Jackson. *Great Canadian Ghost Stories.*
    CBC. CKVR, Barrie. 1 July 1994.

STAGE PLAY, OPERA, OR CONCERT PERFORMANCE

*The Phantom of the Opera.* By Andrew Lloyd Webber. Dir. Harold
    Prince. Pantages Theatre, Toronto. 22 July 1995.

WORK OF ART

Botticelli, Sandro. *Birth of Venus.* Uffizi Gallery, Florence.

RECORD OR TAPE

Peterson, Oscar. *Digital at Montreaux.* RCA Records, D2308224, 1980.

CARTOON

Carpenter, John. "Wild Days." Cartoon. *Western Report* 24 April 1995: 15.

MAP OR CHART

*Manitoba*. Map. Oshawa: MapArt, 1997.

ADVERTISEMENT

Imperial Oil. Advertisement. *The First Perspective* July 1995: 17.

## CD-ROM sources

When using CD-ROMS and online sources in your research, you need to know how and when to acknowledge them. For example, if you find a bibliographic reference to an article in a newspaper, magazine, or journal electronically, but you use the print version, you need only cite the print version as you would any other print resource. However, if you use the full text or an abstract provided by the electronic source, you must cite the electronic source in your Works Cited. Always remember that the electronic version of an article may differ significantly from the print version.

CD ROM UPDATED PERIODICALLY

Koch, George. "Ignorance Abroad." *Alberta Report* 8 Aug. 1994: 17+.

*Magazine Article Summaries Full Text Elite*. CD-ROM. Ebsco

Publishing. Apr. 1994–Apr. 1995, item 940928624.

Some CD-ROM databases are updated on a regular basis because they cover publications that are themselves published periodically. Your entry in the works-cited list should include the publication information for the print source followed by the title of the database (in italics or underlined), publication medium (CD-ROM), name of vendor, and the electronic publication date.

CD-ROM RELEASED IN A SINGLE EDITION

"Proactive." *The Oxford English Dictionary*. 2nd ed. CD-ROM. Oxford:

Oxford UP, 1992.

Some CD-ROM databases are not routinely updated; in fact, they are issued much as books are. Cite these electronic sources as you would a book, being careful to add the publication medium after the title and edition number.

## Online sources

Sources on the Internet that students and scholars might use in their research include scholarly projects, databases, and text from books, periodicals, and professional and personal web sites. Entries in your Works Cited for such sources should contain as many items from the list below as are relevant and available, and should be given in the order shown. Following this list are sample entries for some common kinds of Internet sources. (For an authoritative explanation of the full MLA system of online documentation, see the *MLA Handbook for Writers of Research Papers*.)

1. The name of the author, editor, compiler, or translator of the source (if available and relevant), reversed for alphabetizing and followed by an abbreviation, such as "ed.," if appropriate.
2. The title, in quotation marks, if the item is a poem, short story, article, or similar short work within a scholarly project, database, or periodical, or is a posting to a discussion list or forum. In the latter case the title is taken from the subject line and followed by the description "Online posting."
3. The title, in italics, if the item is a book.
4. The name of the editor, compiler, or translator of the text (if relevant and if not cited earlier), preceded by an appropriate abbreviation such as "Ed."
5. The publication information for any print version of the source.
6. The title, in italics, if the item is a scholarly project, database, periodical, or professional or personal web site. For a web site with no title, use a description, such as "Home page."
7. The name of the editor of the scholarly project or database (if available).
8. The version number of the source (if not part of the title) or, for a journal, the volume number, issue number, or other identifying numbers.
9. The date of electronic publication of the item, of its latest update, or of the posting.
10. For a posting to a discussion list or forum, the name of the list or forum.
11. If pages, paragraphs, or other sections are numbered, the number range or total number.
12. The name of any institution or organization sponsoring or associated with the web site.
13. The date on which you accessed the source.
14. The electronic address, or URL, of the source, in angle brackets, "< >." One function of the angle brackets is to exclude any surrounding punctuation from the URL.

**SCHOLARLY PROJECT**

*Scholarly Communications Project.* Gail McMillan, Director. 11 May 1998. Virginia

Polytechnic Institute and State University. 4 June 1998 <http://borg.lib.vt.

edu/>.

*Insect Diversity Project.* Ed. Steve Ashe et al. 9 Apr. 1998. University of Kansas, Lawrence. 4 June 1998  <http://dial.pick.uga.edu/>.

*COSMOS Project* (Congestion Management Strategies and Methods in Urban Sites). Coord. Christiane Bielefeldt. 14 Nov. 1997. Transport Sector of the Fourth Framework of the European Commission's Telematics Application Programme. 4 June 1998  <http://www.napier.ac.uk/depts/cte/projects/cosmos/cosmos.html>.

### PROFESSIONAL SITE

*The Bar Association of Erie County, Buffalo, New York.* Ed. Roger Parris. Home page. 20 May 1998. The Bar Association of Erie County, Buffalo, New York. 4 June 1998  <http://www.eriebar.org/>.

*Association of California Water Agencies Home Page.* 27 May 1998. ACWA. 4 June 1998 <http://www.acwanet.com/>.

### PERSONAL SITE

*Professor Langsam's Home Page.* Yedidyah Langsam, Ph.D. 8 May 1998. 4 June 1998  <http://eilat.sci.brooklyn.cuny.edu/>.

*Music, Melody, and Songs.* Rodney Rawlings. Home page. 21 May 1998. 4 June 1998  <http://www.druid.net/~rodney/>.

### BOOK

Richard Mitchell. *The Graves of Academe.* Site of same name. Mark Alexander. 9 Jan. 1998. 4 June 1998  <http://members.aol.com/hu4wahz/ug/index-graves.html>.

Helen P. Rogers. *Taking a Stand on Education.* 24 May 1997. The Taking a Stand Series. Wellington Publications, Carmel, CA, 1996. 4 June 1998 <http://www.wellingtonpublications.com/hpr/taso/education/>.

### POEM

Arthur Hugh Clough. "Say Not the Struggle Nought Availeth." 1849. *An Index of Poem Titles in Representative Poetry On-Line: S-U.* Ed. Professor Ian Lancashire. 13 May 1998. Dept. of English at University of Toronto. 4 June 1998  <http://library.utoronto.ca/utel/rp/poems/clough3.html>.

### ARTICLE IN A REFERENCE DATABASE

L. Berry and R. Ford. "A System to Monitor Desertification." *Natural Disaster Reference Database.* (Use gopher option to access.) 4 June 1998 <http://ltpwww.gsfc.nasa.gov/ndrd/dba.html>.

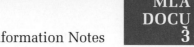

Robert Amano, Richard Black, and Marcel Kasumovich. "A Band-Aid Solution to
    Inflation Targeting." Bank of Canada Working Paper 97-11, May 1997, ISSN
    1192-5434, ISBN 0-662-25833-9. *National Library of Canada Electronic
    Collection.* The National Library of Canada. 32 pp. 21 Sept. 1996
    <http://www.nlc-bnc.ca/eppp-archive/100/200/301/bankc-wp/1997/97-
    11/index.html>.

ARTICLE IN A JOURNAL

Associated Press. "Despite Hot First Half, Mets Axe Mcilvaine." 16 July 1997.
    *Mets Online.* The Unofficial World Wide Web Site of the New York Mets. Ed.
    Bryan Hoch. 2 June 1998. 4 June 1998  <http://www.icu.com/mets/
    ARTICLES/arti0041.html>.

ARTICLE IN A MAGAZINE

Karen Reedstrom. "*Full Context* Interview with Nathaniel Branden." From
    September and October issues of *Full Context. Nathaniel Branden.* Home
    page. 4 June 1998  <http://www.nathanielbranden.net/ayn02.shtml>.

POSTING TO A DISCUSSION LIST

Keith Rawlings. "Twelve-String Guitars." Online posting. 20 Mar. 1998. *Mudcat
    Discussion Forum.* 4 June 1998  <http://www.mudcat.org/thread.cfm?
    threadid=4453&messages=33#24231>.

E-MAIL

Prentiss, Harriett. "Learning Networks." E-mail to author. 15 Jan. 1998.

For e-mail, cite the name of the sender, the subject line in quotation
marks, a description of the document as e-mail (including the recipient's
name), and the date the mail was sent.

# MLA DOCU 3 ⎯⎯⎯⎯⎯⎯⎯⎯⎯⎯
## MLA INFORMATION NOTES

**Information notes** come in two forms, content notes and bibliographic notes. Content notes allow the researcher to give readers
additional information without digressing from the point at hand. Bibliographic notes provide helpful sources for additional reading not cited

in the paper itself. Information notes are optional in a research project. They may be presented at the foot of the page on which they appear (footnotes) or on a separate page at the end of the paper (endnotes), but before the Works Cited. Indicate an information note by placing a raised (superscript) arabic numeral at the end of the sentence or passage to which the note refers. Number notes consecutively throughout the paper.

Text

> Instead of entering the recycling loop—the cycle that takes a product from the consumer to the recycling bin to a manufacturer and back again to the consumer to use[1]—most old newsprint (ONP) sits in storehouses and trailer trucks with no place to go.

Information note

> [1] For a thorough explanation of the processes involved in recycling paper, see Hagerty, Pavoni, and Heer (58–62), Pardue (54–55), and Randolph.

# OTHER DOCU

## Other Systems of Documentation

### *Learning Objectives*

After reading this section, you should

1. know how to use APA in-text citations in a research paper,
2. understand how to assemble a list of references and correctly cite books, periodicals, CD-ROMs and online sources, and other sources,
3. be familiar with the *Chicago Manual* style of documentation,
4. know what other academic style manuals are available.

# OTHER DOCU ————

## Other Systems of Documentation

$\mathbf{I}$f, when writing a research paper, you use the information and ideas of others whether by directly quoting, summarizing, or paraphrasing, or if you use facts and statistics that are not common knowledge, you must properly acknowledge your source.

# OTHER DOCU **1**

## APA IN-TEXT CITATIONS

Like the Modern Language Association (MLA) style of documentation (see MLA DOCU), the American Psychological Association (APA) style uses brief in-text citations to refer the reader to full bibliographic information in a list of references at the end of the paper. However, there are several format differences between MLA and APA. The following recommendations are based on the *Publication Manual of the American Psychological Association,* 4th edition (1994).

An APA in-text citation gives the author's last name and the year of publication. In the case of a quotation, include the page number (a page number for a paraphrase or summary is optional). Use commas to separate items in the parentheses.

### DIRECTORY OF APA IN-TEXT CITATIONS

PARAPHRASE OR SUMMARY WITH AUTHOR'S NAME IN THE TEXT
Give the year of publication in parentheses after the author's name.

Howell (1995) believes that never in the four decades of rock music

have women artists been so strong, and never have their male

counterparts seemed so weak.

PARAPHRASE OR SUMMARY WITHOUT AUTHOR'S NAME IN THE TEXT
Give the author and year of publication in parentheses at the end of
the cited material.

The 1990s have seen the rise of a new female presence in rock music,

both as solo acts and as members of female-dominated groups (Howell,

1995).

QUOTATION WITH AUTHOR'S NAME IN THE TEXT
Give the year of publication in parentheses immediately after the
author's name, and put the page number at the end of the quotation.

According to Howell (1995), "All kinds of women rockers are coming on

strong, and if you push the broader definition of rock into r'n'b, there's

equal femme firepower" (p. 10).

QUOTATION WITHOUT AUTHOR'S NAME IN THE TEXT
Give the author, year of publication, and page number in parentheses at the end of the quotation.

The times have changed since the early days of rock, when "women

were allowed to sing, but generally not to play their own instruments or

write their own material, and certainly not to arrange or produce it"

(Howell, 1995, p. 10).

A WORK WITH TWO AUTHORS
List both authors' names in the text with the year of publication immediately following, or put both names in a parenthetical citation. In
this case, note that the ampersand (&) is used instead of *and*.

The resurgence of recycling in the 1980s can be traced to the

confrontations between advocates of incineration and supporters of

landfill projects (Blumberg & Gottlieb, 1989).

**A WORK WITH THREE TO FIVE AUTHORS**

Give all authors' last names in the text or parentheses in your *first* citation only; use an ampersand (&) instead of *and* in the parenthetical citation.

Liberation begins with an awareness that we all are to some degree

prisoners of our own language (Clark, Eschholz, & Rosa, 1997).

In subsequent citations, use only the first author's name and *et al.* (Latin for *and others*).

Clark et al. (1997) maintain that language is one of humankind's greatest

achievements and most important resources.

**A WORK WITH SIX OR MORE AUTHORS**

In all citations, use the first author's name followed by *et al.*

Cognitive behaviour therapy is now recognized as an effective

intervention for disturbed body image in young women (Rosen et al.,

1989).

**AUTHOR UNKNOWN**

When the author is unknown, use the title of the work in the text, or give a shortened title in a parenthetical citation.

In *Children of the dragon: The story of Tiananmen Square* (1990) the

interconnections of the events leading up to the bloody massacre in June

1989 are presented in detail.

The interconnections of the events leading up to the bloody massacre in

China in June 1989 are presented in detail (*Children of the dragon*, 1990).

**CORPORATE AUTHOR**

For corporate authorship, give the full name of the institution, agency, or organization in the text together with an abbreviation in brackets in the first citation.

According to the Canadian National Institute for the Blind [CNIB] (1998),

seeing-eye dogs still provide an invaluable service.

In subsequent citations the abbreviation is sufficient both in the text and parenthetically.

**TWO OR MORE AUTHORS WITH THE SAME LAST NAME**
When using references by two or more authors with the same last name, include initials with all references.

A survey completed by P.J. Babin (1998) showed that sales of cellular

car phones tripled in the last five years.

**MORE THAN ONE WORK IN A PARENTHETICAL CITATION**
When acknowledging more than one source in a parenthetical citation, present the sources in the order in which they appear in your list of references (i.e., alphabetically); separate the citations with a semicolon.

Environmentalists contend that solid waste disposal will be North

America's—if not the world's—most pressing problem in the decade of

the 1990s (Blumberg & Gottlieb, 1998; Rathje, 1989).

**INTERVIEWS, LETTERS, MEMOS, E-MAIL, AND TELEPHONE CONVERSATIONS**
Bennett and Ulrich (letter, June 29, 1998) are confident that their study

on the effects of secondary smoke will be completed by the end of the

year.

Do not include these items in your list of references.

# OTHER DOCU 2 _____
## APA-STYLE REFERENCES

In APA style, the alphabetical list of works cited that appears at the end of a research paper is called *References*. The following guidelines give the basic format for APA-style references.

1. Reverse *all* authors' names within each entry, and use initials, not first names.
2. Name all authors; do not use *et al*. Use an ampersand (&) instead of *and* in naming the last of more than one author.
3. Give the date of publication in parentheses after the last author's name, followed by a period.
4. Italicize (or underline) the titles and subtitles of books and periodicals, but do not put quotation marks around titles of articles.

## DIRECTORY OF APA LIST OF REFERENCES

5.  Capitalize only the first word of book and article titles and subtitles and any proper nouns. Capitalize the titles of periodicals according to standard rules (see MECH 1i).
6.  Use the abbreviations *p.* or *pp.* for page numbers of all publications except scholarly journals.

7. Entries can be presented in one of two ways: with a paragraph indent or with a hanging indent. Ask your teacher which form to use. Either way, all the same information is included and you should double-space throughout. Here is the same entry shown both ways:

Paragraph indent: indent only the first line five spaces:

5 spaces ➜ Southwestern Region Metis Council (1997). *Catherine Annennontak: You're under my skin*. Windsor: University of Windsor.

Hanging indent: do not indent the first line; indent all subsequent lines 5 spaces:

Southwestern Region Metis Council (1997).
5 spaces ➜ *Catherine Annennontak: You're under*
5 spaces ➜ *my skin*. Windsor: University of
5 spaces ➜ Windsor.

Following are sample APA-style references for the types of sources you are most likely to encounter.

## Books

**BASIC FORMAT FOR A BOOK WITH ONE AUTHOR**

Lyons, J. (1993). *Writing fundamentals*. Scarborough: Prentice Hall.

**TWO OR MORE AUTHORS**

Metcalf, J., & Struthers, J.R. (1993). *Canadian classics*. Toronto: McGraw-Hill.

Levin, G., Lynch, G., & Rampton, D. (1989). *Prose models: Canadian, American and British essays*. Toronto: Harcourt Brace.

**CORPORATE AUTHOR**

Certified General Accountants' Association of Canada. (1989). *The accounting profession in Canada*. Toronto: CGAA.

**AUTHOR UNKNOWN**

*Children of the dragon: The story of Tiananmen Square*. (1990). New York: Collier.

**EDITOR(S)**

Innis, M.Q. (Ed.). (1966). *The clear spirit: Twenty Canadian women and their times*. Toronto: University of Toronto Press.

**WORK IN AN ANTHOLOGY**

Goddard, P. (1988). How to spot rock types. In S. Norton & N. Waldman (Eds.), *Canadian content* (pp. 113–118). Toronto: Holt, Rinehart & Winston.

**EDITION OTHER THAN FIRST**

Blicq, R.S. (1987). *Technically-write!* (3rd ed.). Scarborough, ON: Prentice-Hall.

**TRANSLATION**

Kafka, F. (1984). *The penal colony: Stories and short pieces.* (W. & E. Muir, Trans.). New York: Schocken.

**MULTIVOLUME WORK**

Daymond, D., & Monkman, L. (1985). *Literature in Canada* (Vols. 1–2). Toronto: Gage.

**TWO OR MORE WORKS BY THE SAME AUTHOR**

Mowat, F. (1952). *People of the deer.* Toronto: McClelland & Stewart.

Mowat, F. (1961). *Owls in the family.* Toronto: McClelland & Stewart.

Mowat, F. (1972). *A whale for the killing.* Toronto: McClelland & Stewart.

When listing two or more works by the same author, arrange them chronologically by year of publication. Repeat the author's name including any initials for all entries. If two or more works by the same author were published in the same year, use lowercase letters to differentiate them: (1992a), (1992b), (1992c).

## Periodicals

**ARTICLE IN A JOURNAL PAGINATED BY VOLUME**

Izraeli, D.N. (1993). They have eyes and see not: Gender politics in the Diaspora Museum. *Psychology of Women Quarterly, 17,* 515–523.

**ARTICLE IN A JOURNAL PAGINATED BY ISSUE**

Lachman, S.J. (1993). Psychology and riots. *Psychology: A Journal of Human Behavior, 30* (3/4), 16–23.

**ARTICLE IN A MONTHLY MAGAZINE**

Allick, B. (1994, January). Property standards and rent control. *Municipal World, 104,* 12–13.

**ARTICLE IN A WEEKLY MAGAZINE**

Newman, P. (1995, May 22). Will Paris decide Canada's future? *Maclean's, 108,* 48.

**ARTICLE IN A NEWSPAPER**

Aubrey, J. (1995, April 29). Program seen as key to suicide prevention. *The Ottawa Citizen,* p. 8A.

**EDITORIAL**

Praskey, S. (1995). [Editorial]. *Canadian Insurance, 100* (*7*), 5.

**LETTER TO THE EDITOR**

Malling, E. (1995). Malling vs McQuaig [Letter to the editor]. *Canadian Forum, LXXIV* (*840*), 2–3.

**BOOK REVIEW**

Walmsley, A. (1995). [Review of the book *The economy of nature*]. *Report on Business Magazine, 11* (*8*), 29–30.

## Electronic sources

When you use an electronic reference, your goal is to both credit the author and enable the reader to retrieve the source. APA recommends that you provide as much information as you can, including a specific retrieval path. For sources not covered in the following models, consult Li and Crane's (1996) *Electronic Style: A Guide to Citing Electronic Information* in the reference section of your library. Or consult Li and Crane's 1997 online version: *Electronic Sources: APA Style of Citation* (**http://www. uvm.edu/~ncrane/estyles/apa.html**).

### CD-ROM, TAPE, OR DISKETTE

Koch, G. (1994, August 8). Ignorance abroad [CD-ROM]. *Alberta Report*, p. 17. Available: Ebsco Publishing. Magazine Article Summaries Full Text Elite. April 1994–April 1995, item 9409287624.

Computer communications [CD-ROM]. (1993). *The Canadian Encyclopedia: Multimedia Version*, p. 385. Available: Toronto: McClelland & Stewart.

### ONLINE MATERIAL FROM A COMPUTER SERVICE

James, C. (1994, September 16). An army family as strong as its weakest link. *New York Times* [Online], Late Edition, Section C, p. 8. Available: NEXIS/NEWS/NYT [1995, May 17].

### INTERNET

Hamad, S. (1992). Post-Gutenberg galaxy: The fourth revolution in the means of production of knowledge. In *Directory of electronic journals, newsletters and academic discussion lists* (2nd ed.), [Online]. Available e-mail: LISTSERVE@UOTTAW Message: Get EJOURNL1DIRECTRY.

## Other sources

### GOVERNMENT PUBLICATION

Statistics Canada. (1995). Composite index tumbles. *Infomat* (Cat. 11-002E). Ottawa: Queen's Printer.

### DISSERTATION ABSTRACT

Erwin, L.K. (1990). The politics of anti-feminism: The pro-family movement in Canada (Doctoral dissertation, York University, 1990). *Dissertation Abstracts International, 51*, 3237-A.

### COMPUTER SOFTWARE

OS/2 Warp [Computer software]. (1995). Markham, ON: IBM.

### VIDEO

Symansky, A. (Producer). (1994). *Family: A loving look at CBC Radio* [Videotape]. C911054. Montreal: National Film Board.

# OTHER DOCU 3 _____

## ANNOTATED APA-STYLE STUDENT RESEARCH PAPER

Kimberly Dehate, a university student, wrote the research paper that appears on the following pages while she was enrolled in criminal justice methods class. Early on in the course, Dehate became interested in studying the relationship between physical punishment/discipline in childhood and delinquency in adolescence. Dehate reviews the research literature in her paper, presenting the key studies chronologically, summarizing the key points of each one and pointing out interconnections whenever possible.

Dehate used the APA guidelines for manuscript preparation presented in FORMAT 2. She also used the APA style of in-text citations (OTHER DOCU 1) and references (OTHER DOCU 2) to document her research paper. Dehate was required to include a title page (FORMAT 2) with her paper.

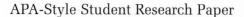

Discipline and Deviance 1

Writer's surname and the page number appear in the upper-right corner, 1 cm from the top of the page, 2.5 cm from the right-hand edge of the page.

Discipline and Deviance: Physical Punishment in

Childhood and Delinquency in Adolescence

Kimberly Dehate

Criminal Justice 4700: Introduction to Research Methods

Professor S. Eschholz

May 2, 1998

Full title of paper, writer's name, and course information are centred and double-spaced.

Discipline and Deviance    2

The physical punishment of children is a common and widely accepted practice among parents in North America. In a 1995 survey, 99% of mothers used physical punishment to correct misbehaviour (Straus, 1997). In the National Survey of Family Violence in 1985, over 90% of parents used physical punishment on children ages three to four (Straus, 1997). In a survey of community college students, 95% reported receiving some corporal punishment during their lifetime (Bryan & Freed, 1992).

Corporal punishment is commonly defined as discipline that is usually carried out in the form of slaps, spanks, and shoves, although objects such as belts and paddles may also be used. The purpose is to inflict pain so as to enforce moral behaviour. Physical punishment usually begins in the first year after birth and continues during pre-school years when the fundamental layers of the personality are thought to be formed (Straus, 1997). For about half of all children, corporal punishment continues into the teenage years. Considering the early onset and extended practice, it is not unreasonable to wonder if corporal punishment has lasting effects.

What are the consequences of corporal punishment on children? Does it influence aggressive behaviour later in life? Could it be beneficial? These are the questions I will explore in order to determine how physical punishment in childhood influences criminal behaviour in adolescence.

Discipline and Deviance     3

In 1925, Cyril Burt conducted one of the first studies exploring the relationship between corporal punishment in childhood and delinquency later in life. He examined the familial disciplinary techniques that had been used on a group of British delinquents. He found that parents of delinquents were indifferent to discipline or lax in administering it, disagreed with each other over methods, or used overly strict forms almost seven times more often than parents of non-delinquents. Burt concluded that discipline was the most important differentiating factor between the homes of delinquents and non-delinquents (McCord & McCord, 1959).

Sheldon and Eleanor Glueck (1950) followed suit with a comprehensive study of the relationship between delinquency and discipline. Over a 10-year period they examined 500 boys incarcerated in Massachusetts reform schools and 500 non-delinquent boys living in Boston's slums to identify factors which might differentiate the groups. In comparing the disciplinary approaches used within the homes, the Gluecks found a striking contrast: only 6% of the fathers of the delinquent boys were "firm but kindly" while 56% of the fathers of the non-delinquent boys were described in that way. In addition, more than twice as many fathers of delinquents than fathers of non-delinquents were erratic in their discipline, and more than three times as many were overly strict. Among the mothers of delinquents, the majority were lax in discipline and about one-third were erratic. On the other hand, 66%

Signal phrase gives authors' names followed by date in parentheses.

Writer is careful to put borrowed description in quotation marks.

of the mothers of non-delinquents were "firm but kindly." These findings indicated a strong relationship between delinquency and erratic or overly strict paternal discipline and a strong relationship between delinquency and erratic or lax maternal discipline. The Gluecks concluded that the consistency of punishment is more important than the actual type of punishment in determining delinquency.

In 1959 William and Joan McCord examined data on disciplinary practices in 250 families that was gathered over a period of two years for the Cambridge-Somerville study. Their findings supported the Gluecks' conclusions that erratic or lax discipline involving physical punishment was the strongest predictor of criminal behaviour. Children who had been disciplined consistently had the lowest rate of criminality. In fact, the McCords discovered that the children who had been severely but consistently punished had the lowest rate of crime. They concluded that the consistency of discipline was more important than the type of punishment in determining criminality.

In another study, Gelles and Straus (1979) compared spouse-hitting with being hit for punishment as a child. They found that individuals who had been hit infrequently (less than six times a year) as children hit their spouses less (16%) than those who had never been hit as children (38%). Those who had been hit frequently as children hit their spouses most. Gelles and Straus's findings indicate that physical punishment is associated with violence later in life depending upon the frequency of such punishment

---

*Sidebar annotations:*

Writer presents clear statement of authors' conclusions.

The word *and* is used between the authors' names in the signal phrase.

The writer points out that the findings of this study support those of one discussed earlier.

The writer highlights a surprising conclusion.

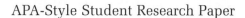

Discipline and Deviance    5

in childhood. In addition, their findings suggest that physical punishment can be beneficial if used moderately by competent, nurturing parents.

Larzelere (1986) explored the effects of moderate physical punishment on children (spanking). When he compared frequency of spanking with aggression toward parents, he found that any frequency of spanking makes children aggressive toward their parents. Larzelere, however, was not willing to accept this conclusion for its face value. Rather, it seemed more plausible that the *intensity* of spankings—rather than the frequency— negatively affects children. For example, Larzelere notes that permissive parents, the most anti-spanking group, were more likely to use infrequent, but severe, physical punishment. Permissive parents were prone to "explosive attacks of rage in which they inflicted more pain or injury upon the child than they intended" (Larzelere, p. 33).

In 1964, the McCords found evidence supporting the connection between parenting style and subsequent aggression. They discovered that frequent, harsh physical punishment temporarily coerces children into obedience, but once the threat of punishment is removed, children who were emotionally deprived lack inner restraints, a moral conscience, to inhibit delinquent behaviour. The McCords concluded that the more severe the parental rejection, the more likely the child will lack the capacity for remorse or guilt, leading to aggressive, delinquent behaviour (Rathus & Nevid, 1991).

When using direct quotations, give a page number preceded by "p."

The McCords' results have been summarized by Rathus and Nevid.

**OTHER
DOCU
3**

APA-Style Student Research Paper

Discipline and Deviance    6

Bryan and Freed (1992) tested the connection between physical punishment in childhood and later aggression from the viewpoint of working class youth in a survey sample of 170 community college students. Eighty-four percent of the students were between the ages of 18 and 23, and the median annual family income was reported to be $30,000. It was 95% of these students who reported receiving corporal punishment as children. Students were asked to rate the intensity and frequency of physical punishment they received in childhood and were then placed into one of three groups: the High Corporal Punishment group (intense and frequent), the Medium Corporal Punishment group (intense and infrequent and/or not intense but frequent), or the Low Corporal Punishment group (not intense and infrequent). The High CP group contained the largest number of males and had the lowest median family income ($24,000) of the three groups. Students in the High CP group were also most likely to describe their grades as "below average," yet a cross-check of the students' actual college transcripts revealed no differences in grades among the groups. The High CP group reported significantly more negative social interactions, such as aggression, lack of friends, and delinquency, and significantly more negative psychological states, such as depression and anxiety. Although not statistically significant, the High CP group reported greater problems with addictions, learning disabilities,

The writer highlights this study because it is the only one that examines the responses of children rather than parents.

hyperactivity, lack of motivation, dependency, and identity diffusion. The High CP group also tended to rate themselves as "below average" in both mental and physical health.

It is important to note that the 95% figure reported by students in Bryan and Freed's study is higher than the figures reported by parents in other studies and national surveys of parental use of physical punishment at some point in their child's life. Perhaps parents are more reluctant to admit that they administered the punishment than the students were to admit that they had received it (Bryan & Freed, 1992). For this reason it is important to continue to collect data from youth as well as from parents.

After reviewing his own research and that of others, Murray Straus (1997) constructed a broad theory to explain the relationship between corporal punishment and delinquency. His "Cultural Spillover Theory" holds that "violence in one sphere of life tends to engender violence in other spheres, and that this carry-over process transcends the bounds between legitimate and criminal use of force" (p. 137). Crime, then, according to Straus (1997), is the result of an inappropriate coping skill learned from within the family. Because physical punishment is used by authority figures to enforce moral behaviour, it teaches that violence can and should be used to handle difficult situations and difficult people. Ironically, the process used to produce morally and socially

Writer returns to studies mentioned in opening paragraph as she begins to conclude her review of the literature.

Writer introduces broad theory that explains results from foregoing studies.

OTHER
DOCU
3

APA-Style Student Research Paper

conforming behaviour instead produces criminal behaviour.

On the basis of her review, writer calls for new research.

More research, particularly like that of Bryan and Freed, needs to be done on the adverse effects of corporal punishment on children. Researchers should focus on the degree of severity and the frequency of corporal punishment during childhood and how these factors influence the degree of violence and the frequency of delinquency in adolescence. If important links are established, perhaps the conservative definition of family violence that discourages research on physical punishment as a vital element of family violence will crumble, thus stimulating more research on the adverse effects of corporal punishment on children. Criminologists may then begin to view physical punishment as an important factor in the development of criminal behaviour (Straus, 1997).

Writer concludes with statement about the importance of research on the effects of corporal punishment on children.

The primary importance of such research lies in its tremendous potential to prevent criminal violence. If a significant relationship is found between physical punishment and later violence, important implications could emerge for both individual parents and national policy. For individual parents, the results may suggest that parents who do not use physical punishment will have better-behaved children. National policy could discourage or even prohibit the use of corporal punishment on children in order to reduce crime in our society.

Discipline and Deviance    9

## References

Bryan, J., & Freed, F. (1992). Corporal punishment: Normative data and sociological and psychological correlates in a community college population. *Journal of Youth and Adolescence, 11,* 77–87.

Gelles, R., & Straus, M. (1979). Determinants of violence in the family: Towards a theoretical integration. In W. Burr, R. Hill, F. Nye, & I. Reiss (Eds.), *Contemporary theories about the family,* Vol. 1. (pp. 549–581). New York: Free Press.

Glueck, S., & Glueck, E. (1950). *Unraveling juvenile delinquency.* New York: Commonwealth Fund.

Larzelere, R. (1986). Moderate spanking: Model or deterrent of children's aggression in the family? *Journal of Family Violence, 1,* 27–36.

McCord, W., & McCord, J. (1959). *Origins of crime.* New York: Columbia University Press.

Rathus, S., & Nevid, J. (1991). *Abnormal psychology.* New Jersey: Prentice-Hall.

Straus, M. (1997). Discipline and deviance: Physical punishment of children and violence and other crimes in adulthood. *Social Problems, 38* (2), 133–151.

The heading *References* is centred at the top of the page.

Writer follows APA guidelines for list of references.

The list begins on a new page, and all entries are given in alphabetical order by authors' last names.

The first line of each entry is indented 5 spaces; subsequent lines begin at the left margin.

Doublespace within entries as well as between entries.

The correct forms for various other kinds of publications are given in OTHER DOCU 2.

# OTHER DOCU 4 _____

## *CHICAGO MANUAL* DOCUMENTATION STYLE

The *Chicago Manual of Style* recommends the use of endnotes and accepts footnotes as an alternative. Endnotes are presented together at the "end" of the paper, whereas footnotes are found at the bottom (the "foot") of the page on which the citations occur. A raised arabic numeral is placed immediately after the item being acknowledged. Endnotes or footnotes are numbered consecutively throughout the paper.

The first time you cite a source, provide complete publication data including the page number for the material you are quoting, paraphrasing, or summarizing. For subsequent references, you can use a shortened version of the citation (see OTHER DOCU 4b).

For endnotes, indent the first line five spaces and bring all subsequent lines flush-left to the margin. Single-space within each endnote and double-space between notes.

To compile your list of references, called the *Bibliography*, start each entry flush-left and indent subsequent lines five spaces (see OTHER DOCU 4a). Single-space within each entry and double-space between entries. Provide complete publication data including inclusive page numbers for articles in the bibliography entry.

Traditional text citation

> People must strike a delicate balance between the right to dispose of their estate as they wish and their duty to provide for their family. To serve these needs, "the estates and trusts business is a rapidly growing area in legal and accounting offices."[1]

Footnote or endnote (same form for both)

1. Jim Kershaw, "You Can't Take It with You." *BC Business* Jan. 1995: 24.

## OTHER DOCU 4a   *Chicago Manual* endnotes (or footnotes) and bibliography entries

The following are model citations for the most commonly used research sources. For each source the endnote and the bibliography entries appear together for easy access.

### DIRECTORY OF *CHICAGO MANUAL* NOTE AND BIBLIOGRAPHY MODELS

## Books

### ONE AUTHOR

1. Constance Rooke, *The Clear Path: A Guide to Writing English Essays* (Toronto: Nelson, 1995), 101.

Rooke, Constance. *The Clear Path: A Guide to Writing English Essays.* Toronto: Nelson, 1995.

### TWO OR THREE AUTHORS

2. M. Garret Bauman and Clifford Werier, *Ideas and Details: A Guide to Writing for Canadians* (Toronto: Harcourt, 1996), 11.

Bauman, M. Garret, and Clifford Werier. *Ideas and Details: A Guide to Writing for Canadians.* Toronto: Harcourt, 1996.

### FOUR OR MORE AUTHORS

3. Harold Bloom and others, *Deconstruction and Criticism* (New York: Seabury Press, 1979), 133.

Bloom, Harold, P. De Man, G.H. Hartman, and J.H. Miller. *Deconstruction and Criticism.* New York: Seabury Press, 1979.

### AUTHOR WITH AN EDITOR

4. George Bowering, *Poems 1961–1992*, ed. Roy Miki (Toronto: McClelland & Stewart, 1993), 201.

Bowering, George. *Poems 1961–1992.* Edited by Roy Miki. Toronto: McClelland & Stewart, 1993.

### EDITOR

5. John Lennox, ed., *Margaret Laurence–Al Purdy: A Friendship in Letters* (Toronto: McClelland & Stewart, 1994), 354.

Lennox, John, ed. *Margaret Laurence–Al Purdy: A Friendship in Letters.* Toronto: McClelland & Stewart, 1994.

### UNKNOWN AUTHOR

6. *The Canadian World Almanac and Book of Facts* (Toronto: Global, 1998), 259–261.

*The Canadian World Almanac and Book of Facts*. Toronto: Global,
    1998.

EDITION OTHER THAN FIRST

7. John Roberts et al., *The Canadian Writer's Workplace*, 3rd ed.
(Toronto: Harcourt, 1998), 592.

Roberts, John, Sandra Scarry, and Richard Scarry. *The Canadian Writer's
    Workplace*. 3rd ed. Toronto: Harcourt, 1998.

WORK IN MORE THAN ONE VOLUME

8. L.B. Pearson, *The Memoirs of the Rt. Hon. Lester B. Pearson*, Vol. 1
(Toronto: University of Toronto Press, 1973), 119.

Pearson, L.B. *The Memoirs of the Rt. Hon. Lester B. Pearson*. Vol. 1.
    Toronto: University of Toronto Press, 1973.

WORK FROM AN ANTHOLOGY

9. Alfred LeBlanc, "The Reel Thing," in *Reader's Choice*, eds. Kim
Flachmann, Michael Flachmann, Alexandra MacLennan, and Sharon
Winstanley (Toronto: Prentice Hall, 1997), 145.

LeBlanc, Alfred. "The Reel Thing." In *Reader's Choice*. Eds. Kim
    Flachmann, Michael Flachmann, Alexandra MacLennan, and
    Sharon Winstanley. Toronto: Prentice Hall, 1997.

## Periodicals

ARTICLE IN A JOURNAL PAGINATED BY VOLUME

10. Harold Fromm, "My Science Wars," *Hudson Review* 49 (1987): 601.

Fromm, Harold. "My Science Wars." *Hudson Review* 49 (1997):
    599–609.

ARTICLE IN A JOURNAL PAGINATED BY ISSUE

11. Michael Lobel, "Warhol's Closet," *Art Journal* 55, no. 4 (1996): 47.

Lobel, Michael. "Warhol's Closet." *Art Journal* 55, no. 4 (1996):
    42–50.

ARTICLE IN A MAGAZINE

12. Laura Pratt, "Blueprint for Success," *CA Magazine*, January/ February 1998, 28.

Pratt, Laura. "Blueprint for Success." *CA Magazine*, January/February 1998, 25–29.

UNSIGNED ARTICLE

13. "Decline of the Blue Collar Worker," *Canada and the World*, April 1995, 4.

"Decline of the Blue Collar Worker." *Canada and the World*, April 1995, 4.

ARTICLE IN A NEWSPAPER

14. Mark Lawson, "What Is English Coming To?" [Toronto] *Sunday Star*, 9 July 1997, F4.

Lawson, Mark. "What Is English Coming To?" [Toronto] *Sunday Star*, 9 July 1997, F4.

## Electronic sources

SOURCES ON CD-ROM

15. Caryn James, "An Army Family as Strong as Its Weakest Link," *New York Times*, 16 September 1994, C8, *New York Times Ondisc* [CD-ROM], UMI-ProQuest, October 1997.

James, Caryn. "An Army Family as Strong as Its Weakest Link." *New York Times*, 16 September 1994, C8. *New York Times Ondisc* [CD-ROM], UMI-ProQuest, October 1997.

ONLINE SOURCE

16. Catherine Yoes, "The Science Fiction Web Project: Adventures in Teaching with Storyspace," *Computers, Writing, Rhetoric and Literature* [electronic journal], accessed 1 October 1997: available from http://www.cwrl.utexas.edu/~cwrl/v2n1/yoes.html

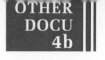

Yoes, Catherine. "The Science Fiction Web Project: Adventures in
Teaching with Storyspace." *Computers, Writing, Rhetoric and
Literature* [electronic journal]. Accessed 1 October 1997. Available
from http://www.cwrl.utexas.edu/~cwrl/v2n1/yoes.html

## Other sources

**GOVERNMENT PUBLICATION**

17. Canada, Statistics Canada, *Households and the Environment*,
Catalogue 11-526 Occasional (Ottawa: Queen's Printer, 1998), 8.

Canada. Statistics Canada. *Households and the Environment.* Catalogue
11-526 Occasional. Ottawa: Queen's Printer, 1998.

**INTERVIEW, LETTER, OR E-MAIL**

18. Carol Hosford, telephone interview by author, 7 April 1998.

Hosford, Carol. Telephone interview by author, 7 April 1998.

19. E. Annie Proulx, letter to author, 22 January 1998.

Proulx, E. Annie. Letter to author, 22 January 1998.

20. Harriett Prentiss, e-mail to J. Roberts, 17 February 1998.

Prentiss, Harriett. E-mail to J. Roberts, 17 February 1998.

**FILM OR VIDEOTAPE**

21. *Saskatchewan*, dir. Raoul Walsh, with Alan Ladd and Shelley
Winters, 1 hr. 45 min., Universal-International, 1954, videocassette.

*Saskatchewan*. Directed by Raoul Walsh with Alan Ladd and Shelley
Winters. 1 hr. 45 min., Universal-International, 1954. Videocassette.

# OTHER DOCU 4b   Subsequent reference

After you cite a source for the first time in a paper and fully document it, all subsequent references to that source are shortened. For most
notes give the author's last name followed by a comma, and the page
number. If no author is given use a shortened title.

22. Roberts, 502.

23. *Canadian Almanac*, 225.

If you cite two or more works by the same author or works by authors with identical last names, include a shortened title.

24. Roberts, *Writer's Workplace*, 13.

25. Roberts, *Troubleshooting*, 213.

The abbreviation *ibid.* (Latin for "in the same place") can be used to refer to the work cited in the previous note. When citing the same page, use *ibid.* alone. When citing from a different page include the page number.

26. Ibid.

27. Ibid., 217.

# OTHER DOCU 5 _____
## OTHER DOCUMENTATION STYLES

Many academic disciplines publish a style manual for their particular system of documentation. These manuals may be found in the reference section of the library.

American Chemical Society. *American Chemical Society Style Guide: A Manual for Authors and Editors.* 2nd ed. Washington, DC: American Chemical Society Publishing, 1986.

American Psychological Association. *Publication Manual of the American Psychological Association.* 4th ed. Washington: American Psychological Association, 1994.

Associated Press Staff. *Associated Press Stylebook and Libel Manual.* Reading: Addison, 1994.

Bates, Robert L., Rex Buchann, and Marla Adkins-Heljeson, eds. *Geowriting: A Guide to Writing, Editing, and Printing in Earth Science.* 5th ed. Alexandria, VA: American Geological Institute, 1992.

Canada. Department of the Secretary of State. *The Canadian Style.* Toronto: Dundurn Press, 1985.

The Canadian Press. *Canadian Press Stylebook: A Guide for Writers and Editors.* Toronto: 1995.

CBE Style Manual Committee. *Scientific Style and Format: The CBE Manual for Authors, Editors, and Publishers.* 6th ed. New York: Cambridge University Press, 1994.

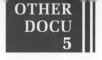

Chicago Editorial Staff. *The Chicago Manual of Style.* 14th ed. Chicago: U of Chicago P, 1993.

Corder, J.W., and S. Ruszkiewicz. *Handbook of Current English.* Toronto: HarperCollins, 1988.

Dodds, Jack, and Judi Jewinski. *The Ready Reference Handbook.* Canadian ed. Scarborough: Allyn and Bacon Canada, 1998.

Gibaldi, Joseph. *MLA Handbook for Writers of Research Papers.* 4th ed. New York: MLA, 1995.

*The Globe and Mail Style Book.* Ed. J.A. McFarlane and Warren Clements. Toronto: Penguin, 1996.

Holoman, D. Kern, ed. *Writing About Music: A Style Sheet from the Editors of 19th-Century Music.* Berkeley: U of California P, 1988.

Linguistics Society of America. "LSA Style Sheet." Published yearly in the December issue of the *LSA Bulletin.*

Messenger, William E., and Jan de Bruyn. *The Canadian Writer's Handbook.* 3rd ed. Scarborough: Prentice-Hall, 1995.

Scherf, Kathleen. *A Brief Canadian Handbook for Writers.* Toronto: Harcourt Brace, 1995.

Shaw, Harry. *McGraw-Hill Handbook of English.* 4th ed. Whitby, ON: McGraw-Hill, 1986.

Turabian, Kate L. *A Manual for Writers of Term Papers, Theses, and Dissertations.* 6th ed. Chicago: U of Chicago P, 1996.

Yogis, John A., I.M. Christie, and M.J. Iosipescu. *Legal Writing and Research Manual.* Markham: Butterworths, 1994.

# INDEX

# CORRECTION SYMBOLS _____

| | |
|---|---|
| | faulty abbreviation MECH **2** |
| | improper use of adjective EDIT **4** |
| | improper use of adverb EDIT **4** |
| | faulty agreement EDIT **1, 3** |
| r | inappropriate word WORD **2** |
| k | awkward |
| s | biased language WORD **3** |
| | capital letter MECH **1** |
| | error in case EDIT **3c** |
| | error in citation MLA DOCU **1–2**, OTHER DOCU **1–2** |
| | replace cliché WORD **1f** |
| | coherence PARA **3** |
| rd | faulty coordination SENT **5** |
| | comma splice EDIT **6** |
| | add details PARA **2a** |
| ion | inappropriate diction WORD **1–7** |
| | inadequate development PARA **2** |
| | dangling construction SENT **2b** |
| t | inexact word/language WORD **1** |
| | sentence fragment SENT **5** |
| | fused sentence EDIT **6** |
| | ESL basics ESL **1–7** |
| s | See Glossary of Usage WORD **7** |
| | error in grammar GRAM **1–5**, EDIT **1–6** |
| h | error in hyphen MECH **5** |
| m | nonidiomatic WORD **1d** |
| | italics MECH **4** |
| | jargon WORD **2d** |
| | use lowercase letter MECH **1** |
| | error in logic PARA **3a**, SENT **4** |
| ed | mixed construction SENT **4b** |
| | misplaced modifier SENT **2a** |
| d | error in mood EDIT **2e** |
| | error in manuscript form FORMAT **1–2** |

| | |
|---|---|
| **no ¶** | no new paragraph PARA **1** |
| **num** | error in use of numbers MECH **3** |
| **om** | omitted word ESL **5a** |
| **p** | error in punctuation PUNCT **1–6** |
| **. ? !** | period, question mark, exclamation point PUNCT **6** |
| **,** | comma PUNCT **1** |
| **no ,** | no comma PUNCT **1m** |
| **;** | semicolon PUNCT **2** |
| **:** | colon PUNCT **3** |
| **'** | apostrophe PUNCT **4** |
| **" "** | quotation marks PUNCT **5** |
| **—** | dash PUNCT **6d** |
| **( )** | parentheses PUNCT **6e** |
| **. . .** | ellipsis PUNCT **6g** |
| **/** | slash PUNCT **6h** |
| **par, ¶** | new paragraph PARA **1** |
| **pass** | ineffective passive voice ESL **1d**, SENT **3d**, EDIT **2f** |
| **ref** | error in pronoun reference EDIT **3b** |
| **rep** | unnecessary repetition WORD **4a** |
| **sexist** | sexist language WORD **3**, EDIT **3a** |
| **shift** | distracting shifts SENT **3** |
| **sl** | slang WORD **2b** |
| **sp** | misspelling MECH **6** |
| **sub** | error in subordination SENT **5** |
| **t** | error in verb tense EDIT **2c** |
| **trans** | add transition PARA **3b** |
| **vag** | use specific words WORD **1c** |
| **vb** | error in verb form EDIT **2a, b** |
| **wdy** | wordy WORD **4** |
| **ww** | wrong word WORD **1** |
| ⌒ | close up space |
| ℓ | delete |
| ∾ | transpose letters or words (teh) |
| ∧ | insert |